Philosophy After Nature

Philosophy After Nature

Edited by
Rosi Braidotti and Rick Dolphijn

ROWMAN &
LITTLEFIELD
──────INTERNATIONAL
London • New York

Published by Rowman & Littlefield International Ltd
Unit A, Whitacre Mews, 26-34 Stannary Street, London SE11 4AB
www.rowmaninternational.com

Rowman & Littlefield International Ltd.is an affiliate of Rowman & Littlefield
4501 Forbes Boulevard, Suite 200, Lanham, Maryland 20706, USA
With additional offices in Boulder, New York, Toronto (Canada), and Plymouth (UK)
www.rowman.com

Selection and editorial matter © 2017 by Rosi Braidotti and Rick Dolphijn
Copyright in individual chapters is held by the respective chapter authors.

All rights reserved. No part of this book may be reproduced in any form or by any electronic or mechanical means, including information storage and retrieval systems, without written permission from the publisher, except by a reviewer who may quote passages in a review.

British Library Cataloguing in Publication Data
A catalogue record for this book is available from the British Library

ISBN: HB 978-1-7866-0385-2
   PB 978-1-7866-0386-9

Library of Congress Cataloging-in-Publication Data

Names: Braidotti, Rosi, editor.
Title: Philosophy after nature / edited by Rosi Braidotti and Rick Dolphijn.
Description: Lanham : Rowman & Littlefield, 2017. |
   Includes bibliographical references and index.
Identifiers: LCCN 2017013912 (print) | LCCN 2017017902 (ebook) |
   ISBN 9781786603876 (Electronic) | ISBN 9781786603852 (cloth : alk. paper) |
   ISBN 9781786603869 (pbk. : alk. paper)
Subjects: LCSH: Philosophy—History—21st century.
Classification: LCC B805 (ebook) | LCC B805 .P44 2017 (print) |
   DDC 190—dc23 LC record available at https://lccn.loc.gov/2017013912

∞™ The paper used in this publication meets the minimum requirements of American National Standard for Information Sciences—Permanence of Paper for Printed Library Materials, ANSI/NISO Z39.48-1992.

Printed in the United States of America

Contents

1 Introduction: After Nature   1
Rosi Braidotti and Rick Dolphijn

PART I: AFTER MATTER   11

2 Information and Thinking   13
Michel Serres

3 *'Die Natur ist nur einmal da'* [Nature Is There Only Once]   21
Françoise Balibar

4 Generic Mediality: On the Role of Ciphers and Vicarious Symbols in an Extended Sense of Code-based 'Alphabeticity'   31
Vera Bühlmann

5 The Resonance of Disparates: Spinoza, Damasio, Deleuze and the Ecology of Form   55
Rick Dolphijn

PART II: AFTER MACHINES   71

6 Media Entangled Phenomenology   73
Mark B. N. Hansen

7 On Reason and Spectral Machines: Robert Brandom and Bounded Posthumanism   99
David Roden

8 Circuits of Desire: Cybernetics and the Post-natural According to Lyotard and Stiegler   121
Ashley Woodward

of a nature–culture continuum. The categorical separation between the non-human habitat and human deeds has been challenged by a combination of elements: the climate change on the one hand and the limitations of economic globalization on the other. We can safely state that all the contributors to this volume foreground the impact of capitalism as one of the main factors in the current crisis, which has been ironically called the 'Capitalocene' (Jason W. Moore), the 'Chthulucene' and the 'Plantationocene' (Donna Haraway) and the 'Anthrobscene' (Jussi Parikka).[3]

This volume adopts a materialist approach, which assumes that the *actual* motor of the historical development of modernity, with its emphasis on progress through science and technology (and resting on the Enlightenment ethos of emancipation *through* reason), is capitalism itself. The logic of advanced capitalism that we want to defend in this volume is drawn from Deleuze and Guattari's pertinent analyses of capitalism as schizophrenia. Extremely simple at some level, this system can be defined as a never-ending search for ever-growing profit. This axiom is so evident that its loyal believers assimilate it to human nature, thereby elevating greed and self-interest to the height of an evolutionary human trait. We follow the critical Spinozism of Deleuze and Guattari in two parallel ways: We question the possessive individualism hypothesis and its aggressive view of evolution and then propose to replace it with a monistic ontology that supports a cooperative vision of human relationality and its evolutionary capacity.

The profit motive is the unquestionable axiom of capitalism. Traversing the territorial order that stratified the earth in affiliative circles, in fixed hierarchical regimes, the capitalist motor has deterritorialized these patterns for more than two centuries now – decoded them rigorously. It did so not according to a rational monetary logic based on trade and commodities but according to the irrational flows of capital as a desiring machine.

In order to secure the flows of capital (i.e. in order to minimalize the resistance against these flows), the project of modernity makes use of the simplest dualisms, often absolutizing ancient presuppositions and hierarchies. This dualistic device opposes male to female, white to black and the West to the rest. It is important to note that in the end, *for capitalism*, it is *not* the actual content of the terms that matters as much as their sustained opposition. Capitalism is the negative of society, of culture, of any kind of social formation. Or as Deleuze put it in one of his lectures:

> Capitalism is constituted on the failure of all the pre-existent codes and social territorialities. If we admit this, what does this represent: the capitalist machine, it is literally demented. A social machine that functions on the basis of decoded, deterritorialized flows, once again, it is not that societies did not have any idea of this; they had the idea in the form of panic, they acted to prevent this – it was the overturning of all the social codes known up to that point.[4]

In other words, capitalism is not interested in any one specific, let alone 'dominant', code; it only works by decoding, which means that it does not come with any specific *form* of knowledge. Rather, it practices a serial dis/re-organization of information in order to secure the flows of capital. The multiple racisms and the sexisms and all other dualisms find their basis in what we can call a 'culturalism', an organization of the world that more and more alienates itself from nature, which it constructs as its extreme limit. This social constructivist method, however, begs the question of grasping the shifting relationship between nature and culture, which is currently reshaped by the flows of deterritorialization of advanced capitalism. The transcendent force needed for the capitalist machine to keep on producing *rests* on the systemic *undoing* of the ties that bind the clever animal – Anthropos – to nature. This disconnection allows for the undoing of the territorial, planetary as well as social ties that have enabled life in the first place.

This 'undoing' of the bonds between human life and nature postulated rational consciousness as the flight into transcendence, projecting the burden of physical materiality – and consequently the natural world order – unto the bodies of the 'others' of the European subjects. These sexualized, racialized and non-human 'others' have paid a heavy price, in both material and symbolic terms, for their supposed association with the natural order. The closer to nature, the further from social and legal rights, from the cultural and social entitlements and from the future that 'the clever animal' had in mind. And this is actually what Nietzsche himself was noticing when he discussed 'the problem of the actor' (in *The Gay Science*)[5]: He mentions Jews and women (which were, along with 'natives', the 'others' of the nineteenth-century discourse) in particular, as people *obliged to act*, to play a social role, to adapt themselves to a 'truth' that was never theirs.

Even the great emancipatory projects that emerge from the interstices of modernity postulate human freedom as the emancipation from our collective dependence upon a natural order. Long before Nietzsche, in the eighteenth century and in the aftermath of the French revolution, both Wollstonecraft and Toussaint Louverture embraced the Enlightenment project as the possibility of a general human liberation from servitude, oppression and dependency. They severely critiqued the orders that build upon a dismissal of nature (moving away from the allegedly inferior nature of women towards the abstract technicities of culture). This uniformizing ideal of progress, as it moved the western world away from nature, blinded us to the immanence of life. It also alienated us from the different futures that were not in line with the Enlightenment ideals. It is these alternative future scenarios that are becoming more feasible and necessary in the era of the Anthropocene, and which are emerging as new paths of becoming.

With capitalism as its motor and nature as its extreme limit, modernity has introduced a highly segregated non-cohesive and schizoid society that acts according to the flows of capital. Modernity has by now realized much of the future it had anticipated, including a massive ecological crisis that may have revealed itself only recently but is definitely here to stay. The financial inequalities of globalization since 2008, notably the crisis that hit Wall Street (and the rest of the world), also increase the disenchantment with the project of modernity as does the necro-political governmentality of our terror-infested times. When Félix Guattari published his *Three Ecologies* in 1989, he foresaw integrated world capitalism, the post-media age, the decline of social cohesion and companionship. He argued forcefully that such a situation demanded a rethinking of what he called *ecosophy*: an ethico-aesthetico-politico challenge to Enlightenment philosophy as a whole. Guattari encourages us to rethink modernism as a whole in order to understand the many crisis that had been announcing themselves for so long.[6] With similar visionary claims as Nietzsche, Guattari foresees the interweaving of the convulsive social and political crises that, by now, have made Donald Trump the forty-fifth president of the United States:

> More than ever today, nature has become inseparable from culture; and if we are to understand the interactions between ecosystems, the mechanosphere, and the social and individual universes of reference, we have to learn to think 'transversally'. As the waters of Venice are invaded by monstrous, mutant algae, so our television screens are peopled and saturated by 'degenerate' images and utterances. In the realm of social ecology, Donald Trump and his ilk – another form of algae – are permitted to proliferate unchecked. In the name of renovation, Trump takes over whole districts of New York or Atlantic City, raises rents, and squeezes out tens of thousands of poor families. Those who Trump condemns to homelessness are the social equivalent of the dead fish of environmental ecology.[7]

As stated above: Traversing the territorial order that stratified the earth in affiliative circles, in fixed hierarchical regimes, the capitalist motor has deterritorialized these patterns for more than two centuries now – decoded them rigorously. It did so *not* according to money and commodities but according to *the flows of capital*.

BEYOND DUALISM

At a deeper conceptual level, therefore, 'we' come after nature in understanding the limitations of dualism as both a principle of political economy and as a system of thought that for centuries has dichotomized the relationship between mind and body, nature and culture, human life (bios) and non-human life (*zoe*).

As the careful readers of the history of philosophy know, however, the awareness – both cognitive and moral – of the continuity between the poles of these false dichotomies has been emphasized before. Insights and explicit warnings about the nature–culture continuum can be found back at the dawn of western modernity, in another year of turbulent transition. They are best represented in the impressive corpus of Frederich Nietzsche. Nietzsche's writings brilliantly bring together the timely and the untimely when it comes to the relation that we have with the earth. Contrary to the dominant philosophers in Western tradition (like René Descartes and Immanuel Kant), Nietzsche never considered knowledge to be *our* ability to understand everything that surrounds us. Nietzsche did not think in terms of mind versus matter, nor did he subscribe to any of the dualisms that define modernity up until today. But he did see how the 'modernist' humanism, implicit in the opposition of mind versus matter, not only dominated our thinking (especially since the early nineteenth century), but actively gave form to our world, realizing its own gospels by alienating our ideas from the world that surrounds us.

For Nietzsche, then, knowledge is about the organization of information, and this is by all means a territorial organization that organizes the face of the earth and the people along with it. For Nietzsche, knowledge equals administration, and it is something very different from thinking and wisdom. Knowledge is about building up of consensus and, as such, it mendaciously distorts the way we think about otherness, about the earth and, in the end, about 'life'. Nietzsche's doubled reading of 'knowledge' is spot on. It proves that even at the turn of the last century, at a time marked by the greatest successes of the modernist project and its technological apparatus, a time in which the dark sides of progress did not yet show its devastating effects on geology, one did not *have* to be blind to the consequences of our reckless belief in this progress.

Nietzsche shows us that it was possible to see, from the very beginning, that the speeding-up of the capitalist machines will alienate us from the earth and lock us up in our territories far away from the soils to which we, in the end, always have to return. This is the project which today, in many ways, urgently needs rethinking. Now, more than ever, we need a philosophy that is *after* nature, after how we have been struggling with this concept in the history of thought, how we need to rethink it now that we have come to realize that our previous philosophies of nature so blatantly failed. We need a philosophy that is able to read the undercurrents in thought, in the earth, giving rise to another earth – the earth on the other side of thought.

Rereading the general critique on humanity (human knowledge) that Nietzsche expresses, and keeping in mind that he claimed to write for a new earth and a future people, it is tempting to read his ideas as if directed at the peoples living in our days. As if we – living on an earth that has been suffering more than enough from these mendacious ideas more than a century later – would have understood the devastating consequences of dualist thinking by now. The very serious warnings that Nietzsche gives the reader are still poorly understood by the master narratives of our time. Perhaps the situation is even far more serious than that; perhaps the many crises that rule the world today (ecological, financial, and political) proves that we have grown blind to the consequences that these dualisms had, for us, for our thinking, for technology and for the earth.

The pertinent question is, then, this: How is this 'knowledge' that we have called modernity capable of continuously realizing itself? How come its rigid dualisms keep disturbing the earth and all of the relations in which we have to live our lives? The answer to this question is as simple as it is haunting: It is because of capitalism.

Nietzsche's tragic joy in both asserting the flaws of western modernity and pointing to brand new paths in thinking resonates with the contributions in this volume. First and foremost among them is the work of Michel Serres, who stresses that it is time we start accepting this new truth – that we exist *after* nature and that this condition, far from being a crisis, opens up new perspectives for critical thinking. We need to ask ourselves, 'How did we *inevitably* end up here?' Serres brilliantly summarizes this as follows:

> From reading a thousand history books, we also naively believe that the past behavior of the Roman people continuously clamoring for *panem et circenses*, bread and games, was the *result* of their decadence – or at least its manifestation. Not at all: it was the *cause*. To believe that a society can solely live on bread and games, the economy, spectacles, consumption, banks and television, as we do today, is such a fundamental misunderstanding of any collectivity's real functioning, that this exclusive and erroneous choice will simply hurl it to its demise, as we saw in Rome.[8]

Being so caught up in the systems of consumption, and thus unable to see the vast desertification induced by the capitalist machineries for the last two centuries, one wonders whether this clever animal has not vacated the stage for some time. Maybe the exacerbated sense of subjectivity and worldliness that capitalism continues to sell is just like one of those bright stars that we see glittering in the sky but that in reality had ceased to exist long ago.

> the bond that connects us to the world, the one that binds the time passing and flowing to the weather outside, the bond that relates the social sciences to the sciences of the universe, history to geography, law to nature, politics to physics, the bond that allows our language to communicate with mute, passive, obscure things – things that, because of our excesses, are recovering voice, presence, activity, light. We can no longer neglect this bond.[9]

How to open our eyes to the relations that incorporate us in the world, that connect everything but were simply left out of the equation by capitalism? Again, Serres in the quote above comes up with a practical program that not only connects the different ecologies to one another but also shows that in order to take up responsibility for the crisis of today, academia, as well, has to get rid of the modernist–capitalist oppositions that have *splintered* the university into completely separated faculties, departments, research groups and chairs that increasingly seem to have little to do with one another. Or to phrase it very cynically, the only thing that unifies the university these days has nothing to do with shared social values or any other form of united content; what unites them is the search for financial funding. Indeed, within the university, as anywhere else, the capitalist machinery has had deep and devastating consequences.

AND AFTER?

It is also the case, however, in a reversal that may appear paradoxical, that we are going after nature in many different ways: first, in taking seriously our ethical responsibilities towards the Anthropocene; second, in applying rigorously a materialist, vital, monistic process ontology as the philosophical point of reference and third, in rethinking the process of naturalization. An ecosophical, monistic position implies a different, that is to say, non-unitary, vision of the knowing subject – an autopoietic understanding of matter and the inclusion of technological apparatus within this monistic system ('machinic autopiesis').

This is what Guattari was writing about all along when he emphasized that any ecology had to be written by taking into account the 'post-media age', as he coined it. As early as 1985, in lectures in Tokyo and Paris (January 1986), Guattari foresaw how philosophy after nature has to experiment with what technology can do. In a later publication, Guattari explains:

> The emergence of these new practices of subjectification of a post-media era will be greatly facilitated by a concerted reappropriation of information and communication technologies in so far as they will increasingly authorize: (1) the promotion of innovative forms of consultation and collective action, and in the long run, a reinvention of democracy; (2) the miniaturization and personalization of apparatuses, a resingularization of mediatized means of expression. One may assume, in this respect, that it is the extension into a network of databanks that will have the biggest surprises in store for us; (3) the multiplication to infinity of 'existential shifters' permitting access to creative mutant Universes.[10]

This new era, in which the hegemonic power of the media so powerful in fascist, communist and capitalist propaganda is behind us, offers many new possibilities to *perform* anti-capitalist and (therefore) ecosophical resistance *with* technology and *after* nature.

Last but not least, we are going after nature in following the lead of what some call the contemporary 'neo-naturalistic' turn, not only in the life sciences but also in philosophy and critical theory. Methodologically, this translates in a switch from a social constructivist method, which relies on the dualistic oppositions mentioned above, to the intensive methodology of vital materialism. The latter privileges cartographies of power – in its dual inception as both negative (*potestas*) and positive (*potentia*) – and the actualization of virtual alternatives. Expressionism, rather than constructivism, is the approach that best captures the vital flow of differential becoming, which is the core of a monistic understanding of matter as intelligent and self-organizing. Contemporary genomics and algorithmic cultures are also going 'after' nature in their pursuit of the complexity and self-organizing capacity of living matter and in trying to account for it in adequate theoretical terms.

In many different ways, this volume aims to open our eyes to the many relations that have been structural components of our world for a long time but those which critical theory in the humanities failed to see. They are bonds between natures and cultures, or 'naturecultures' as Haraway calls them, which today have become 'medianatures'.[11] Thus, the authors in this book aim to rewrite the ties between different times and different traditions in philosophy (between continental and analytic thinking, for instance) and also in academia as a whole (between physics and media studies, for instance). They do so, as philosophers and critical thinkers, by rereading the concepts developed by major thinkers in the past, revealing the radical (monistic) *ontographies* that are of relevance today. Dualism itself has to be rethought radically after nature, especially the dualisms that support the mental, social and environmental realities of our subjectivity. They have been structured according to the powers of modernity and the interest of the capitalist machinery.

This volume argues passionately that the most elementary of all dualisms, the opposition between culture and nature, needs our full attention today. Practicing the media–nature–culture continuum, doing philosophies of nature across ages and traditions, the different contributions to this book express materialist thinking at its finest. What needs to be done in times of severe crisis is to affirmatively search for a new earth and people to come, a missing 'we' which can be collaboratively brought about – actualized – in thinking together against the grain and speaking truth to the powers of our times.

NOTES

1. Friedrich Nietzsche, 'Truth and Lies in an Extra-moral Sense'. In *On Truth and Untruth: Selected Writings*. Trans. Taylor Carman, New York: Harper Collins, 2010: 15.
2. Paul Crutzen and Eugene Stoermer. 'The "Anthropocene"'. *Global Change Newsletter*, 41 (May 2000): 41–42.
3. See Jason W. Moore (Ed.), *Anthropocene or Capitalocene? Nature, History, and the Crisis of Capitalism*, PM Press, 2016; Donna Haraway, 'Anthropocene, Capitalocene, Plantationocene, Chthulucene: Making Kin', *Environmental Humanities*, 6 (2015): 159–165, Duke University Press; Jussi Parikka, *The Anthrobscene*, Minnesota University Press, 2015.

For a full overview, see: R. Braidotti and Maria Hlavajova (Eds.), *The Posthuman Glossary*. London: Bloomsbury Academic, forthcoming 2017.

4. Gilles Deleuze, 'Capitalism, Flows, the Decoding of Flows, Capitalism and Schizophrenia, Psychoanalysis, Spinoza'. *Lecture, Cours de Vincennes*, 16 November 1971.
5. Friedrich Nietzsche, *The Gay Science: With a Prelude in Rhymes and an Appendix of Songs*. Trans. Walter Kaufmann. New York: Vintage Books, 1974.
6. Félix Guattari, *The Three Ecologies*, 1989. Trans. Ian Pindar and Paul Sutton, Athlone Press, 2000.
7. Guattari, *The Three Ecologies*: 135.
8. Michel Serres, *The Natural Contract*, 1990. Trans. Elizabeth MacArthur and William Paulson, University of Michigan Press, 1995.
9. Serres, *The Natural Contract*: 48.
10. Guattari, *Schizoanalytic Cartographies*. Trans. Andrew Goffey. London: Bloomsbury, 2013: 42.
11. Parikka, *A Geology of Media*. Minneapolis: University of Minnesota Press, 2015: 13.

BIBLIOGRAPHY

Crutzen, Paul, and Euegene Stoermer. 'The "Anthropocene"'. *Global Change Newsletter*, 41 (May 2000): 41–42, www.igbp.net/.

Deleuze, Gilles. 'Capitalism, Flows, the Decoding of Flows, Capitalism and Schizophrenia, Psychoanalysis, Spinoza'. Lecture, Cours de Vincennes, 16 November 1971. Transcript accessed at *Void Manufacturing*, 9 September 2008. Wordpress, https://voidmanufacturing.wordpress.com/2008/09/09/the-indomitable-deleuze/#more-441.

Guattari, Félix. *The Three Ecologies*. 1989. Translated by Ian Pindar and Paul Sutton, Athlone Press, 2000.

———. *Schizoanalytic Cartographies*. Translated by Andrew Goffey. London: Bloomsbury, 2013.

Haraway, Donna. 'Anthropocene, Capitalocene, Plantationocene, Chthulucene: Making Kin'. *Environmental Humanities*, 6 (2015): 159–165. Duke University Press, doi: 10.1215/22011919-3615934.

Moore, Jason W. (Ed.). *Anthropocene or Capitalocene? Nature, History, and the Crisis of Capitalism*. PM Press, 2016.

Nietzsche, Friedrich. 'Truth and Lie in a Nonmoral Sense'. In *On Truth and Untruth: Selected Writings*. Translated by Taylor Carman, New York: Harper Collins, 2010, 15–50.

———. *The Gay Science: With a Prelude in Rhymes and an Appendix of Songs*. Translated by Walter Kaufmann. New York: Vintage Books, 1974.

Parikka, Jussi. *The Anthrobscene*. Minneapolis: University of Minnesota Press, 2015.

———. *A Geology of Media*. Minneapolis: University of Minnesota Press, 2015.

Serres, Michel. *The Natural Contract*. 1990. Translated by Elizabeth MacArthur and William Paulson, University of Michigan Press, 1995.

Part I

AFTER MATTER

Better yet, if thinking means inventing, what is left to say? Emitting information that becomes increasingly rare, increasingly controlled during the emission, increasingly independent from the reception, storage and process, increasingly removed from its balance. So dive into bifurcations, branches, yes, real inventions that emerge in the 'grand narrative'[3] of the Universe or the Evolution of life.

By the way, what is a computer? A machine that emits, receives, stores and processes information, a strange machine with four universal rules – a universal machine, which functions as a thing of the world or as you and me.

INFORMATION, SOMETHING NEW

Common to everything that has had the chance to exist, information has nothing in common with what we call by that name; media channels overwhelm us every day with it. It is often reduced to dreary repetitions, ad nauseam, to announcements of corpses and disasters of power and death, while war and violence are ranked at the bottom of global causes of human deaths. The information that I am speaking of, instead, is closer to a rarity. Léon Brillouin defines it as the opposite of entropy, which is the characteristic of high energies. He even terms it 'negentropy'.[4] At the same time that the Industrial Revolution, based on thermodynamic science, comes to an end, a concept from that same science, but contradicting entropy, takes the relay. Just as entropy, in fact, reigns the 'hard', so is information equivalent to what I call the 'soft'.

By soft age, I would willingly comprehend a time in which we finally understand that the four rules that I have set forth govern, and they always have governed, and they without doubt forever will govern all that, being contingent, has the rare chance to exist. This information circulates in the world of things and between living things as well as between us – humans – and it constitutes the bedrock of thinking.

Information, in its everyday sense, contradicts that sense several times: the repetitions are opposed to its rarity, as the identical is opposed to the new and death to life. In the sense of information theory, the information of the media thus provides mostly no information. Inversely, thinking means inventing: getting hold of rarity, discovering the secret of that which has the huge and contingent chance to exist or to be born tomorrow – *natura*, nature, means that which will be born.[5] Such a secret allows us to understand that inventing or discovering requires the same effort for a similar result since everything that exists, contingently, has a given quantity of rarity, that is to say, something new.

ANCIENT NETWORKS

Where does this information circulate? Basically, in networks. For a long time, I've been surprised by this recent form of circulation that is nonetheless quite ancient. The Roman roads already made one such information network, and a sizeable one, all around the Mediterranean, from Iran to Scotland, from the Danube to the Nile and to the Atlas Mountains. I would not be surprised if one day a specialist discovered the vague traces of comings and goings of our hunter-gatherer ancestors, depending on the seasons, fruits and game, before the agrarian settlement of the Neolithic period. For their part, ethnologists recognize the traces of various tribes in the Amazon rainforest whose marks reflect immemorial gaps, tied with ephemeral housings, through a forest allegedly known as 'virgin', though these identifiable passages reveal it to have been 'cultivated' and thus 'cultural' for a long time. From those distant moments and through ever-expanding spaces, we have continued to cover our landscapes and the portolans of the Silk Routes, of the Incas or of spices – of land, maritime, rail or air ways. We still decorate the planet with a web of hertz – an electronic web – with a thousand and one names, repeating, thereby, a hominid practice that is at least a thousand years and at most a million years old.

Even better, every life constructs itself from admirable networks whose number of paths and connections defies the combinatorial explosion and whose delicacy surprises us. Earth physics, or even chemistry, extracts refined details from it. These tangles bridge the hard sciences and the soft sciences, and the long duration of their form still distances them, a billion years from us. Nothing truly new under the sun, under the 'yellow dwarf'[6] lost in the giant network of singularities known by astrophysicists.

MATTER AND INFORMATION

Information circulates through the inert, living and human world, where everything and everyone emits it, receives it, exchanges it, conserves it and processes it. Interactions are thus not only material, or hard, but they are also informational, or soft: interactions, for sure, of causes, forces and energies – but also interferences, interpretations and intersections of signs, codes, images, co-possibilities and filters.

Something powerfully new has emerged in our vision of the world: the universe is made up of matter and information, paired and without doubt inseparable. This means that all things express, in some way, other things and the world; all things conspire and consent to it. All things, in some way, perceive – see, write, read – just like us.

No, we are not so exceptional; we are not the only ones endowed with the capability to see, read or write: the wind traces its musical partition over the waves of the sea and the dunes of the desert; running water weaves rich branches of river-like arborescence; dust engraves cliffs that are already sculpted or drawn by erosion; by their distinctive style, earthquakes, fractures, hot spots, the low plate tectonics define the higher relief. The living leave their remains, be it only bones. Magnetism marks itself and remains etched on soft rock on its way to crystallization, indicating the time of its hardening; radioactivity counts time; the climate leaves traces in dust buried in the deep ice of the poles and the ice sheets; evolution deploys itself on organisms, more disparate than systemic. We are not the only ones endowed with the capability to count or remember; the trees calculate their years, crowned in their wood. Nor are we the only ones endowed with the capability to code; everything ultimately gets spelled out in the language of mathematics. I have already said that we think like the world; now I am saying that the world thinks like us.

The world, so here it is.

THE CAVE STREAMED WITH LIGHT

Dazzled with the light after so long a darkness ... [the two heroes] thought at first they were the prey of some ecstatic illusion, so splendid and unexpected was the sight that greeted their eyes. They were in the center of an immense grotto. The ground was covered with fine sand bespangled with gold. The vault was as high as that of a Gothic cathedral, and stretched away out of sight into the distant darkness. The walls were covered with stalactites of varied hue and wondrous richness, and from them the light of the torches was reflected, flashing back with all the colors of the rainbow, with the glow of a furnace fire and the wealth of the aurora. Colors of the most dazzling, shapes the most extraordinary, dimensions the most unexpected, distinguished these innumerable crystals. They were not, as in most grottoes, pendants, monotonously similar to each other, but nature had given free scope to fancy, and seemed to have exhausted every combination of tint and effect to which the marvelous brilliancy of the rocks could lend itself.

Blocks of amethyst, walls of sardonyx, masses of rubies, needles of emeralds, colonnades of sapphires deep and slender as forest pines, bergs of aquamarine, whorls of turquoise, mirrors of opal, masses of rose gypsum, and gold-veined lapis lazuli all that the crystal kingdom could offer that was precious and rare and bright and dazzling had served as the materials for this astonishing specimen of architecture; and, further, every form, even of the vegetable kingdom, seemed to have been laid under contribution in the wondrous work. Carpets of mineral mosses soft and velvety as the finest gauze, crystalline trees loaded with flowers and fruits of jewels recalling the fairy gardens of Japanese art, lakes of diamonds, palaces of chalcedony, turrets and minarets of beryl and topaz, rose pile upon pile, and heaped together so many splendors that the eye refused to grasp them. The decomposition of the luminous rays by the thousands of prisms, the showers of brilliancy that flashed and flowed from every side, produced the most astonishing combination of light and color that had ever dazzled the eyes of man.

—Jules Verne, *The Star of the South*[7]

Jules Verne's cave reverses the Platonic one.[8] The latter sings the glory of one sun, discovered in the daylight, as one emerges from the shadow, while the former is an invitation to penetrate under a vault that is so deep that one's gaze is as lost as if it stared at a starry sky: Here, in this cave, a thousand lights dazzle the thinker.

SWEET NIGHT

Philosophy loves light and has turned it into the model of excellent knowledge, especially the splash of daytime sunshine. Sparkling with truth, light is supposed to chase away the darkness of obscurantism. That is an absurd and rather counter-intuitive idea, as we all know that any candle, as weakly as it may shine, immediately pushes back the shadow of the night, while no one has ever seen darkness overcome any source of light. This ideology is terrifying because if we turn the day into the champion of knowledge, we are left with only one unique and totalitarian truth, as hard and unsubtle as the sun at high noon, the star that astrophysics has eventually confined to the minor rank of the yellow dwarf. I say no to this tyranny, no to the yellow dwarfs.

Thus the day makes us believe in the unicity of truth. In fact, thinking is much less like the day than like the night, where every star shines like a diamond, where every galaxy flows like a river of pearls, where every planet, like a mirror, reflects the light it receives. Thus authentic knowledge overflows with results and intuitions; it sets up multiple reference points grouped into constellations with forms that are as disparate as those of scholarly disciplines. Thus knowledge finds temporary truths, whose luxuriously coloured sparkle flickers and changes with the duration of the Great Story. The only lights that do not tremble emanate from planets without an original brilliance and that, as I said, behave like mirrors. Magnificent, but modest enough to be reduced to the punctual – punctuated, however, by the blue supergiants, Vega or Rigel, and the heads of the ogre in the manner of Antares. Great in size but wavering in doubt and questioning, those truth-stars stand out against the enormous black

NOTES

In the original title 'L'information et la pensée', the word 'la pensée' plays with thought as a doctrine and thought as a faculty. By translating 'la pensée' as 'thinking', the English title focuses upon thought as a creative, active and endless process.

1. Emitting, receiving, storing and processing information traditionally only applies to our memory or the functioning of computers.

2. In psychoanalysis, this temporal chasm prevents us from genuinely engaging with events from the past.

3. Michel Serres rehabilitates a historiographic discourse by playing with Jean-François Lyotard's acclaimed notion of the end of the 'grand narratives'.

4. In Léon Brillioun's information theory, the term 'entropy' is applied to uncertainty and the term 'negentropy' (negative entropy) is used for information. In this definition, entropy and negentropy should ceaselessly collaborate in order to decrease uncertainty.

5. The word *natura* is the future tense of the verb *nascor* and can, indeed, be translated as 'what is to be born'.

6. 'The Yellow Dwarf' ('*La nain jaune*') is a fairy tale by Marie-Catherine Le Jumel de Barneville (Baroness d'Aulnoy) and was published in 1698. The story stages a jealous and vile yellow dwarf who constantly manipulates the course of fate. The similarly called 'Game of the Yellow Dwarf' is a traditional and popular French card game where one has to frustrate one's opponents by starting sequences of cards that are not yet formed. Apart from the fairy tale and the card game, a G-type main-sequence star is also called a 'yellow dwarf'.

7. Jules Verne, *The Star of the South*. Trans. and Ed. by Charles F. Horne (New York: Vincent Parke, 1911), 276–77.

8. Plato's metaphor of the cave is also an exposition of his theory of Ideas. These transcendent Ideas represent a more fundamental, true and accurate reality.

9. Michel Serres linguistically alludes to the absolutism of the 'Roi-Soleil' by using the word 'Moi-Soleil' as a critique of the philosophy of Kant.

10. Michel Serres uses the French expression '*bataille picrocholine*' alluding to the obscure war between Picrochole against Grandgousier in Rabelais's novel *Gargantua* (1534). The French expression is used to designate a silly conflict between nations or individuals that has no significant cause.

11. Democritus, a Greek atomist philosopher, and Lucretius, a Roman materialist philosopher, both considered the world, nature and man as an accidental clashing of atoms. Serres, in his book *La naissance de la physique dans le texte de Lucrèce* (Minuit: 1977. Translated as *The Birth of Physics*, Clinamen Press: 2001), revalues and revitalizes these atomist thoughts.

BIBLIOGRAPHY

Verne, Jules. *The Star of the South*. Trans. and Ed. Charles F. Horne. New York: Vincent Parke, 1911: 276–77.

Chapter Three

'Die Natur ist nur einmal da' [Nature Is There Only Once]

Françoise Balibar

The title of this chapter, '*Die Natur ist nur einmal da*', came to mind as a free association induced by the title of this book, *Philosophy After Nature*. While I was unconsciously wondering (was it in French or in English? Probably in no definite language) whether the word 'after' should be understood as following in time or in space, before I could even formulate the choice in these terms, another use of the French word *après* flashed in my head, along with the reminiscence of an old popular song from back in the twenties: '*Je cherche après Titine/ Titine, oh ma Titine/ Je cherche après Titine/ Titine n'est pas là*'.[12] '*Je cherche* après *Titine*'. This is a rather rare instance of *après*: Added to '*Je cherche*', it denotes a kind of anxiety – an emphasis that is often to be found in popular spoken French, in contradiction with strict grammatical correctness – and a *distinction* that favours plain style and prohibits 'unnecessary' emphasis. From this popular '*Je cherche après Titine*', I went to what I thought was its most adequate transcription into English, namely 'Desperately Looking after Susan', before I even realized that the title of the film I had in mind was in fact *Desperately Seeking Susan*.[13] A famous quotation from the German physicist Ernst Mach emerged, which nicely united all this brooding, search and anxiety for Nature: '*Die Natur ist nur einmal da*'.

The phrase comes in Mach's text[14] as an illustration of the complete deterministic character (*eindeutige Bestimmtheit*) of natural sciences, as a justification for the introduction of single-valued analytic functions in physical theories. Nevertheless, as soon as I read this phrase for the first time, I became aware of the anxiety that emanates from it: *nur einmal*, that is, nevermore – as if Nature were a kind of lonely animal, a lonely wanderer that never returns to the same place (*da*), just like Titine in the song '*Titine n'est pas là*' – so that, when searching for it (maybe 'her' would be more appropriate), if by chance you come across her, you'd better seize her right away, since she won't come again (at least, not before long).

Such a way of desperately seeking Nature in order to catch it has a name: hunting. This comes as no surprise, since in the European tradition, hunting and Nature are closely related, as evidenced by the name given to one of the most intriguing museums in Paris, the Musée de la Chasse et de la Nature. Evoking animal hunting in relation with Mach's phrase '*Die Natur ist nur einmal da*' sounds farfetched – or at least excessive. But is it really? Just think of the metaphors used in relating the Higgs boson discovery, not by tabloids but most officially by serious and respectable institutions such as *Le Courrier du CNRS* ('*La chasse au boson de Higgs*') or at the London Science Museum ('Are you ready to have a go at hunting for the Higgs particle? ... then Go!').

I am not going to elaborate on that matter. I mentioned it because, along with Michel Serres, I believe that thinking is (or should be) a soft, mild process ('*doux*' is the French word Serres uses to qualify it) – not because 'soft' is more feminine than 'hard' (claims to the contrary could be advocated), but because, in Serres's terms ('*le doux régit ce qui a la chance rare d'exister*'[15]), existence is rare and therefore fragile, so that which exists (i.e. Nature) should be 'handled with care'. This is a sophisticated statement that should not be confused with the widespread instruction to the effect that you ought to be in communion with Nature. This moral, not to say religious, commandment wrongly passes among people who write about the situation of man in Nature, as the opposite of the previously sketched 'hunter stance'. Donna Haraway has convincing statements on the matter of 'communion', which she defines as 'an erotic fusion in form of action', an action that may include death, as is well known. She then adds, 'Feminists have not paid sufficient attention to love in specular domination's construction of Nature'.[16] In other words, as far as the question of 'man in relation to Nature' is concerned, love (and all that stuff of communion, symbiosis, immersion, etc.) does not fundamentally differ from what I just called the hunter stance; they are both instances of domination. Below I therefore turn to Mach's '*Die Natur ist nur einmal da*'. I will try to analyse it in a way that avoids both the 'hunter stance' and the lethal trick of erotic fusion.

EINDEUTIG, EINDEUTIGKEIT, AND SO ON

As already hinted at, the phrase '*Die Natur ist nur einmal da*' is generally, and correctly, associated with a philosophical trend, now completely forgotten, that used to be popular among physicists, especially German 'philosopher-physicists', in the last decade of the nineteenth century and the first three decades of the twentieth. This trend is known by the name of its main concept: *'Eindeutigkeit'*. The word itself, apart from its suffix *'-keit'* denoting an abstract quality, comes from an expression quite usual in mathematics, more precisely in the theory of functions, that of *'eindeutige Funktion'* ('single valued function' in English and *'fonction univoque'* in French). Thus, *Ein-deutig-keit* refers to that quality of being uniquely (*ein*) or unambiguously (*eindeutig*) determined, *eindeutig bestimmt*. Since, according to a then common view, 'the concept of function constitutes the general schema and model according to which the modern *concept of nature* has been moulded in its progressive historical development',[17] it is no surprise that *Eindeutigkeit*, that mathematically characterizes those functions that are easier to handle (and therefore most usual and useful), be viewed first as a property of the specific type of knowledge epitomized by modern mathematical physics and then by extension from knowledge of the thing – its modes of determination (Riemann, in his famous 1854 *Habilitationsvortrag*, calls them *Bestimmungsweisen*) – to the thing itself, that is, Nature. In this context, *'Die Natur ist nur einmal da'* is to be understood as asserting that *Eindeutigkeit* is a property of the world itself. *Eindeutigkeit*, it would seem, has migrated from characterizing some mathematical objects (functions of a certain type) to denoting a property of Nature itself. In other words, the reason for the prevalence of *eindeutigen Funktionen* in the field of mathematical physics is now attributed to Nature itself: Nature is *eindeutig*.[18]

A HUNDRED AND TWENTY YEARS LATER

A hundred and twenty years later, all this sounds crazy. Physicists have come to realize that mathematics is not restricted to (univocal) functions; these form a class of mathematical objects, a very limited one for that matter, associated to the notions of number and quantity. As Boole noted as early as in 1854, 'It is not of the essence of mathematics to be conversant with numbers and quantities'.[19] In other words, mathematics exists as such independently of physics and should not to be reduced to its application to physics. For those who take seriously the Galilean idea that the *Book of Nature* is written in mathematical characters, this implies that the range of mathematical objects which are said to be adequate to the description of Nature could (and ought to) be enlarged, extending outside the domain of univocal functions. This, in turn, ruins the idea that Nature is *eindeutig bestimmt*.

From the end of the nineteenth century onwards, physics did evolve in that direction, enlarging its mathematical 'toolbox' to vectors, quaternions, tensors, matrices, numbers of all kinds, geometrical objects, n-dimensional spaces and so on, for which unique determination is not the rule, as is made obvious by consideration of vectors, a very elementary mathematical object. Vectors, we are taught at school, are defined 'up to a spatial translation', therefore they are not univocally determined. Still, they are fundamental in the description of Nature; just think of the physical concepts of 'force' and 'velocity'. Unique determination, *eindeutige Bestimmung,* is not the rule but just a special case of determination. In this respect, the philosophical trend that has come to be known by the name of *Eindeutigkeit* appears as a rearguard action against what was to come (and did come): *Mehrdeutigkeit,* multiple determination.

DETERMINATIO AND *BESTIMMUNG*

Although it would be pure nonsense to argue that the change that occurred in mathematics during the nineteenth century was 'anticipated' by Leibniz (the teleological category of 'precursor' has no meaning in history, especially in history of science), it must be kept in mind that Leibniz in his times had advocated a similarly enlarged conception of mathematics. When speaking of Leibniz's influence on physicists and mathematicians of the late nineteenth century almost two hundred years after his death, I think the most suitable metaphor is one of a geographic nature, that of 'resurgence': a river might at one point disappear in the ground and reappear (resurge) miles away from where it vanished, having travelled underground and therefore unnoticed all the way through. Similarly, Leibniz's remarks on mathematical concepts, although they had been apparently ineffective for two hundred years, were on the minds of most of the mathematicians during the eighteenth and nineteenth centuries, ready to emerge in case of a suitable opportunity. It is as if Leibnizian philosophy of mathematics and natural sciences had always been there, 'underground', while the history of mathematics was evolving at the surface.

At this point, Leibniz's ideas concerning mathematics, quantity and quality should be made more explicit. For Leibniz, mathematics (which he sees as 'the Logic of Imagination') should not be concerned only with quantities but should include among its objects, next to quantities or magnitudes, what he calls 'qualities', or 'forms'.[20] Leibniz sketched a new theory of 'relations' in which the range of applications of the word 'relation', far from being restricted to quantities (such as relations of equality, proportionality and inequality, to which mathematics of his times was limited), is extended to all types of relations,[21] including relations between forms (or qualities) – such as identity, congruence, coincidence, similarity (he calls it *'similitude'* in French) and 'determination'.[22] Leibniz clearly distinguishes two types of determination, one related to the category of *'l'Unique'* (*Unico* in Latin, which corresponds to the German *'eindeutig'*) and the other one an equivocal (*mehrdeutig*) determination. Couturat[23] names this second type a 'semi-determination'.[24]

Rightly so, for the important point here is that, contrary to a determination of the first type (*eindeutig*) that cannot be combined with any other determination, a determination of the *mehrdeutig* type – precisely because it is incomplete – may be combined with another *mehrdeutig* one, resulting in a more restrictive (less *mehrdeutig*, more complete) determination. There are degrees in determination (as suggested by Cournot's formula, semi-determination); repeating that same procedure as often as possible improves the determination and may even result in complete determination, when possible. This is illustrated by Leibniz himself in a simple geometric example: defining a point as 'equally distant from two others' is a semi-determination; it can be completed by combining it with another semi-determination, requiring, for instance, that the point 'be on the same line as the two given points'.

As a matter of fact, determination (*determinatio* in Leibniz's works and words) can be understood in two ways. First as an effort towards *more numerical precision*, aiming at a situation in which the *determinatum* is so well determined that it cannot be subject to controversy (*eindeutig bestimmt*) and can be measured and therefore characterized by a number. But the Leibnizian *determinatio* can also be viewed as a process of *progressive refinement*, as evidenced by the above geometrical example. This progressive refinement can be rendered in German by *Bestimmung* (the suffix *-ung* added to a verb denotes an action; in this case, that of refining). The quality of what is *bestimmt* is *Bestimmtheit* (the suffix *-heit* added to an adjective points to the corresponding abstract quality, here being determined). Leibniz remarks that, contrary to the common idea that qualities cannot be made numerical, some qualities, such as *Bestimmtheit*, can be numerically characterized by the degree of their fulfilment. There are degrees in *Bestimmtheit*, as they are in *Wahrheit* (truth) or *Dunkelheit* (obscurity).

It is worth noting that this second meaning of the Leibnizian *determinatio* is similar in its objectives to classification as a specific procedure for naming things in Linné's natural history. Both *determinatio* and classification aim at *reducing the difference* between things[25] by other means than numbering. Both procedures are progressive in the sense that they proceed by building classes through dichotomy, each class being divided in successive sub-classes by introducing more and more requirements to the definition of the considered object until a complete determination, that is, no more differences, is to be met, *if possible*.

DIGRESSION

I suspect that the difference in meaning between the German words *Bestimmung* and *Bestimmtheit* – a difference that can be described from the Latin point of view as a homonymy of the word *determinatio* – is responsible for the gross misinterpretation, on the part of French philosophers (whose maternal language is of Latin origin), of the meaning of quantum mechanics, and more specifically, that of 'Heisenberg relations'. These mark the limits of adequateness of classical concepts – such as, among others, location and momentum as defined in classical mechanics – in the so-called quantum domain (roughly speaking, objects of the order of less than a micron). This inadequacy can be compared to a lack of focus in optics, resulting in a blurred 'picture' on the photographic plate or film and similarly in the quantum domain in a non-univocal determination of the concepts through measure.

'*Unbestimmtheitrelationen*' is the name given by Heisenberg in 1927 to inequalities characterizing this new state of affairs. It was translated into French as '*relations d'indétermination*', without taking into account (or ignoring?) that 'détermination' (along with *indétermination*, its antonym) translates as both *Bestimmtheit* (a state of affairs) and *Bestimmung* (an action dedicated to improving the state of affairs).[26] Since physicists, who 'naturally' tend to adopt an operational point of view on their own discipline, identify it with measurement, '*indétermination*' was understood in French laboratories as *horresco referens*, the impossibility of measurement (the univocity of which was considered as a synonym of precision) – in other words, the end of physics.[27] It took some years until it was eventually realized that multiple results in measuring do not put an end to the investigation of Nature. To the contrary.

DAS GESETZ DER EINDEUTIGKEIT AND EINSTEIN

It might seem like I have gone far from '*Die Natur ist nur einmal da*', but this is not quite true. I hope to have convinced the reader that the idea of *eindeutig* which is expressed in that phrase (*nur, einmal, da*) applies to *Bestimmung* and not to the Leibnizian *determinatio*, which is open to ambiguity and multivocity and aims at treating qualities on the same footing as quantities.

Retrospectively, the late-nineteenth-century debate around *Eindeutigkeit* appears as a rearguard action. Emphasizing the property of *Eindeutigkeit*, which up to then had gone without saying, became a necessity precisely at the moment one came to realize that it does not go without saying, ambiguity and multivocity being more and more frequently encountered. As an example, I can mention the ubiquity attached to the concept of 'field' (usually attributed to Faraday around 1850): clearly, asking for the location of a field could not be given a unique (or univocal; *eindeutig*) answer. In this context, being able to oppose a mathematical argument to the effect that Nature itself (and not only the way it is represented) is univocal became a necessity for the tenants of the univocal character of knowledge.

The so-called principle of least action, an ancient 'metaphysical' principle dating back to Fermat and the seventeenth century, then appeared as the sought-for justification. In very rough terms, this principle, first elaborated as a mathematical principle governing classical mechanics by Maupertuis, states that the path of a particle when going from point A to point B can be mathematically defined as the one which renders minimum a certain function called 'action' (in this case, a combination of kinetic and potential energies).[28] The minimum of a function being unique (almost by definition), the principle of least action thus appeared as 'explaining' univocity or, at least, giving a mathematical 'reason' for it. A latecomer in the history of physics (in the eighteenth century), the principle of least action very rapidly emerged as *the* principle that rules Nature itself, when it became clear that new theories, such as Maxwell's electromagnetism and the theory of light, did conform to that principle and it was even essential to their elaboration. From then on, a common view among physicists was that non-univocity (significantly named 'ambiguity') was not to be met in physics and that there was no way to escape the conclusion: *Nature is 'nur einmal da', eindeutig bestimmt*. This was to the effect that checking theoretical results for *Eindeutigkeit* became a common heuristic practice, that one of Mach's followers, Joseph Petzoldt, did not hesitate to baptize '*das Gesetz der Eindeutigkeit*',[29] as if it were on the same epistemic level as laws such as the energy principle or any conservation law.

That Einstein himself, years later, considered *Eindeutigkeit* as a *sine qua non* requirement gives to this notion a status more interesting than that of a relic from a past and outgone era. While working on the theory of general relativity in 1913, Einstein presented to himself an objection (known as the hole argument) to his own theory, then still in progress. He imagined a distribution of 'material events' (meaning matter or energy) with a 'hole' in it, meaning a place of limited extension devoid of material events. Considering the corresponding field equations he had arrived at in 1912, on the basis of the so-called general covariance (a mathematical expression of the principle of general relativity), he realized that he could easily build two *different* solutions corresponding to *the same* 'reality' (i.e. the same distribution of matter). This, he thought, was intolerable; the reason being that the gravitational field should be completely and therefore uniquely determined by means of the field equations, which do not comply with *eindeutige Bestimmung*. The strength of the argument was such that Einstein even contemplated the idea of giving up general covariance, in other words the relativity principle itself, just for the benefit of complying with what looks very much like Petzoldt's *Gesetz der Eindeutigkeit* (even if Einstein does not hint at it as such).

This happened in 1913. Einstein eventually got out of trouble in December 1915, when he realized that general covariance, far from being in contradiction with 'the uniqueness of events' (*Eindeutigkeit des*

Geschehens), is precisely what makes the realization of two simultaneous *different* solutions impossible. More precisely, the two solutions he had previously built that he thought to be different were not; as solutions of generally covariant equations, they were equivalent (and could not count for two). In two weeks' time, he then completed the theory of general relativity.

This happy end does not mean that Einstein had rejected the so-called *Eindeutigkeit* principle. Looking more closely, one comes to realize that the same epistemology lies behind both the hole argument and the solution to the contradiction it entails. In 1913, Einstein had rejected generally covariant field equations on the basis of their failure to satisfy the *Eindeutigkeit* requirement (two solutions for one distribution of matter). The reason why the same field equations became acceptable in 1915 is that he had, by then, come to realize that the two solutions were in fact only one.

AS A CONCLUSION: EQUIVALENCE, SAMENESS AND DIFFERENCE

So, it would seem, for Einstein too, Nature is *nur einmal da*. This is not quite so and the analysis needs to be complicated – since equivalence is not a straightforward notion. I am not going to enter into considerations of similarity, equivalence, equality, sameness and so on. Just to give a hint at the complexity of the notion of equivalence, let me just consider the German term '*gleich*' and its translation in French (the same would hold for any other language related to Latin). '*Gleich*' in French could be '*égal*', as in '*Alle Menschen sind gleich*' ('*tous les hommes sont égaux*'), but it could be '*le (la) même*' as in '*Ich habe die gleiche Jaquette wie Du*'. These are instances taken out of ordinary language. One can simply imagine how complicated and intricate things might become in the case of scientific parlance; it is not sure that bringing mathematics in makes things any clearer. In any case, it goes beyond the scope of this chapter. Maybe another time, in another life.

NOTES

1. This 'rengaine', that is, more precisely, the tune without the lyrics, has become worldwide famous when Charles Chaplin introduced it in his film *Modern Times* (1936).

2. *Desperately Seeking Susan*, a 1985 film directed by Susan Seidelman, starring Rosanna Arquette and Madonna.

3. Ernst Mach, *Die Mechanik in ihrer Entwicklung* (Leipzig: F.A. Brockhaus, 1897), 474.

4. 'That which by (rare) chance does exist is ruled by softness' (unauthorized and unsatisfying translation; 'softness' imperfectly renders 'le doux').

5. Donna Haraway, *Primate Visions: Gender, Race and Nature in the World of Modern Science* (New York: Routledge, 1989), 385.

6. Ernst Cassirer, *Substanzbegriff und Funktionsbegriff. Untersuchungen über die Grundfragen der Erkenntniskritik* (Berlin, 1910), 27. Cited in D. Howard, 'Einstein and Eindeutigkeit: A Neglected Theme in the Philosophical Background to General Relativity', *Studies in the History of General Relativity*, Ed. by J. Eisenstaedt and A.J. Kox, Einstein Studies, 3 (Boston, Basel and Berlin: Birkhäuser, 1992), 154–243.

7. An instance, among many, of finalist arguments concerning Nature. Similar to that other one, attributed to Bernardin de Saint Pierre (1737–1814): Nature divided melons in apparent parts, so that they can be eaten *en famille* – to the effect that family order is natural, just as univocal functions are.

8. George Boole, *Collected Logical Works*, 2 (Chicago and London, 1916), 13. Cited in Nicolas Bourbaki, *Éléments d'histoire des mathématiques* (Paris: Hermann, 1969), 32.

9. Gottfried Wilhelm Leibniz, *Elementa Nova Mathescos Universalis*: 'Imaginatio generaliter circa duo versatur: Qualitatem et Quantitatem, sive magnitudinem et formam', In Louis Couturat, *La logique de Leibniz d'après des documents inédits* (Paris: Alcan, 1901), 290–291. Leibniz's text is available on the Internet at gallica.bnf.fr.

10. See Louis Couturat, *La logique de Leibniz*, 290–291 and 313–314.

11. Leibniz, 'Determinatum enim est, cui aliquid, iisdem positis conditionibus, coïncidere debet', *De Calculo Situm, Mathematische Schriften* (Berlin and Halle: C.I. Gerhardt, 1849–1863); V, 311, note 3, in Couturat, *La logique de Leibniz*.

12. Louis Couturat (1868–1914) is a French philosopher, well-trained in mathematics. A great admirer of Leibniz, he contributed to the rediscovery of the latter's importance for the development of mathematics.

13. Univocal relation and equivocal relation correspond to application and correspondence in modern mathematical terms.

14. Michel Foucault, 'Là où le langage demandait la similitude des impressions, la classification demande le principe de la plus petite différence possible entre les choses'. *Les mots et les choses* (Paris: Gallimard, 2001 [1966]), 173. English translation: 'Where language required the similarity of impressions, classification requires the principle of the smaller difference' (Foucault, *The Order of Things*, London: Tavistock/Routledge, 1970, 174).

15. '*Unbestimmung*' does not exist in German: there is no antonym for *Bestimmung*.

16. English-speaking physicists were immunized against such a panic attack since *Bestimmtheit* and *Bestimmung* can be translated by two different words: determinacy and determination.

17. See R.P. Feynman, 'A Special Lecture, Almost Verbatim', *Lectures in Physics*, 3, 1964. Available at http://www.feynmanlectures.caltech.edu/.

18. J. Petzoldt, 'Das Gesetz der Eindeutigkeit', *Vierteljahrsschrift für wissenschaftliche Philosophie und Soziologie* 19 (1895): 146–203. For more information on Petzoldt, see D. Howard, 'Einstein and Eindeutigkeit: A Neglected Theme in the Philosophical Background to General Relativity', *Studies in the History of General Relativity*, Ed. by J. Eisenstaedt and A.J. Kox, Einstein Studies, 3 (Boston, Basel and Berlin: Birkhäuser, 1992).

BIBLIOGRAPHY

Bourbaki, Nicolas. *Éléments d'histoire des mathématiques.* Paris: Hermann, 1969.
Couturat, Louis. *La logique de Leibniz.* Paris: Alcan, 1901.
Feynman, R.P. 'A Special Lecture, Almost Verbatim'. *Lectures in Physics,* vol. 3 (1964). http://www.feynmanlectures.caltech.edu/.
Foucault, Michel. *Les mots et les choses.* Paris: Gallimard, 2001 [1966].
Haraway, Donna. *Primate Visions: Gender, Race and Nature in the World of Modern Science.* New York: Routledge, 1989.
Howard, D. 'Einstein and Eindeutigkeit: A Neglected Theme in the Philosophical Background to General Relativity'. In *Studies in the History of General Relativity*. Edited by J. Eisenstaedt and A.J. Kox, 154–244. Boston, Basel and Berlin: Birkhäuser, 1992.
Leibniz, Gottfried Wilhelm. 'Determinatum enim est, cui aliquid, iisdem positis conditionibus, coïncidere debet', *De Calculo Situm, Mathematische Schriften.* Berlin and Halle: C.I. Gerhardt, 1849–1963.
Mach, Ernst. *Die Mechanik in ihrer Entwicklung.* Leipzig: F.A. Brockhaus, 1897.
Petzoldt, J. 'Das Gesetz der Eindeutigkeit'. *Vierteljahrsschrift für wissenschaftliche Philosophie und Soziologie* 19 (1895): 146–203.

Chapter Four

Generic Mediality

On the Role of Ciphers and Vicarious Symbols in an Extended Sense of Code-based 'Alphabeticity'

Vera Bühlmann

Algebra is the art of subsuming givens under a rule.

—Immanuel Kant

HORS-LÀ

Guy de Maupassant invented a character called Horla, which the protagonist in his short story keeps encountering in a peculiar kind of shadow. Horla is a phantom that is transparent (passive, lets shine through) but not without an irreducible lucidity of its own. It sits in front of the mirror and catches the images the mirror is about to reflect, before the mirror can actually do so. Michel Serres, the polymath writer who has been pursuing, for more than five decades, the project of a natural philosophy of communication, writes about this peculiar character:

> What a strange shadow: it is and is not, present and absent, here and elsewhere, the middle which ought to be excluded but cannot, hence contradictory. This is why he [Maupassant] calls him Horla.[1]

Horla is, to Michel Serres, the character of a kind of spectrality that actively sums up all projections that could possibly be reflected in a kind of summation whose total is indefinite and, because of that, determinable. What is at stake with this proposal by Serres?

Let us approach this indirectly. There are phenomena that are to be considered as *genuinely simulacral but nevertheless real*, as said by Mark Hansen in a recent talk.[2] The question he raised thereby is of generic interest to media theory at large: How to *address* philosophically the particular kind of 'spectrality' at work in communication media, and how to address the *rendering of appearances* that technical spectra afford in quantum physics-based science, chemistry, for example, or electro engineering? The predominant question with regard to quantum physics is that of location and the point of view of the observer. But in order to address the active role of those spectra, their rendering of appearances, we will have to complement that question with one that asks how to think of the temporality involved in such observations. For they are, in a strict sense of the term, *mediagenic:* They are engendered by mediation, by resorting to a middle ground 'that ought to be excluded but cannot'.[3] Posthumanist scholars like Karen Barad have begun to address the temporal dimension of the phenomena such observations refer to in terms of an *agential realism*, or in the case of Bruno Latour, it is being approached through an impersonal kind of agency within networks. Mark Hansen, as well, maintains that considering 'phenomena that are genuinely simulacral but nevertheless real' need not be a capitulating gesture for philosophy but can be one of intellectual reclamation: If phenomena are considered as mediagenic, that is, if it is mediate intervention, the augmentation of some givens through technical lucidity in terms of which such phenomena are reasoned,[4] then they must have to be approachable within the tentative framework of what he would like to think of as 'speculative phenomenology'.

While there clearly is an emerging common sense with regard to the importance of attending to the temporality dimension at work in quantum-physical 'positivity', the 'eventfulness' of probability spaces, the 'massive activity' in particle physics (radioactivity) and in chemistry (molecular bondages), there are many proposals of how to do so. Serres's interest in Maupassant's character Horla lies in that it impersonates *cryptographically* the source of a peculiar kind of originality. It is an originality that affords tracing back lineages and hence gives birth to continuity, but the afforded tracing is not one that heads for a beginning that would reside in some transcendent beyond. It affords a kind of tracing within a space that opens up from and co-extends with just such tracing. It is a kind of originality, hence, of which we might feel inclined to call *vicious*, because by all apparent evidence it appears to be circular (just consider the vocabulary of quantum physics: radiating activity, returning frequencies, extension in phases, etc.). We must also consider that the agency at work in this self-referentiality is indeed attributed, by Maupassant and also by Serres, 'character'. We seem to have good reason, hence, for rejecting to even consider such a space (one that springs from circular tracings and that is to co-extend with the lineages that are thereby being traced) *as* a space; both notions, that of 'character' as well as that of 'vice' (in 'vicious') are words with primarily moral connotations.[5] Surely, the positivity at stake in quantum-physical phenomena cannot be grounded, ultimately, in moral categories;

this would indeed force philosophy to sacrifice its own knowledge of how to articulate and maintain space for hesitation, by demanding accounts that are considerate and capable of withstanding scrutiny – accounts which demand intersubjective, methodical evaluation and argument rather than subjection to absolute authority. Is Serres, with his proposal to conceive a space that were capable of accommodating this fabulous character, Horla, with this peculiar, paradoxical 'transparent lucidity', indeed suggesting that philosophy make this sacrifice?

HOW TO ADDRESS THE SPECTRAL SPACE OF MASSIVE CONDUCTIVITY?

The notion of the *vicious circle in reasoning* was given the general sense of 'a situation in which action and reaction intensify one another', according to the etymological dictionary, by 1839.[6] An agency that was caught up within such a space of vicious circularity would inevitably be a dangerous agency, a corrupting one, a pretentious one, one that mocks any idea of perfection – from which all moral notions of justness, righteousness, balanced valency and so on are inevitably being derived. Let's pause and remember our starting point: How can phenomena that are genuinely simulacral but nevertheless real possibly be approached by philosophy in a gesture of reclamation rather than capitulation? And how can Serres's proposal of a space called *hors-là* (out, there) possibly be of service to this?

The space which is at stake here is mediated by *Horla, the fabulous phantom*. By attributing this character to technical spectra, Serres indeed affirms that the quantum space of a physics of light is a space where intensification is triggered, where interferences show up and cannot be entirely reduced, where the directed beams of reflection are thwarted and go in all directions, diffractively. It is a noisy, querulous space, but it is also a rational space (quantum physics supports a certain kind of mathematics). Yet it is that of a rationality within which no one particular order can be purified (quantum physics involves probabilistics and complex numbers, numbers whose rationality is constituted by imaginary units). A particular order, in this space of abundant 'orderality', can only be exposed before the noisy background of all of this exposed order's 'others', all those other possible orders with which the one exposed has originally been mixed up and from which it has set itself apart. And it is exactly this crystallizing kind of separation process from within an entropic orderality of mingled bodies that Serres's proposal of a space called hors-là serves to address. How? By rendering these mingled bodies *measurable*, in maps drawn by ciphered graphisms (cryptography and topology).[7] Like this, what appears within moralist terms as the space of *vicious circularity* thereby turns into the space of *objective vicariousness*: Horla, as well as the source of self-referential originality Maupassant's fabulous character impersonates for Serres, is *vicarious* in the literal sense of 'taking the place of another',[8] from the Latin *vicarious*, 'that supplies a place; substituted, delegated' and from *vicis*, 'a change, exchange, interchange; succession, alternation, substitution'.[9] But this taking of a place, in the quantum-physical space of light's radiating activity, is not the taking away of a place that had been occupied by something else; it is the place-making exposition of a temporal order, as a contract among pre-specific orders (an active 'frequenting'). This exposed temporal order is set apart from its own originality, namely the noisy background of all of its possible others, which querulously keep manifesting what the contracted order originates in, and from which it is cast off. It can be rendered apparent only by a spectrum that acts as the 'filter' (made of code) and that enables such separation of negentropic order relative to an entropic background.

Such exposed orders, and this will be the interest in my text, can be addressed as pre-specific orders through thinking of them as channels. The contract among pre-specific orders can be stabilized by these channels, but the contract itself cannot be reduced to their geometric and arithmetic formality alone because this formality is spectral (it keeps together in that it affords percolation). Serres's vicarious space of *hors-là* thereby can be considered as a space of conductivity. It is the space that affords measurement in a physics where matter is not only thought of as active (quantum physics), but where this material activity can be addressed no longer within the ideal framework of a restoration (or exploitative optimization) of an order of originally well-balanced values. It must be approached within a mathematical and yet realist scope of a querulous panchrony, pantopy, panglossy – an entropic noise from which negentropic order can set itself apart through a price-oriented 'import–export economy of information'.[10] The activity of matter is *massive*, and Serres's philosophy of communication crucially depends upon integrating a purely quantitative notion of mass into philosophy, one that does not qualify energy and/or information in any one particular sense. The unit of such a notion of mass is, for Serres, provided by the *binary digit* in mathematical information theory. Note that this doesn't mean that a philosophical and quantitative notion of 'mass' would postulate that mass were in an ontological sense 'discrete' (or, indeed, 'digital' as, for example, Stephen Wolfram maintains with his Cellular Automata Universe in *A New Kind of Science* [2002]).[11] But it also discredits the complementary view, which wants to see an ontological reality of matter as analogue and continuous, as do those views which refuse to address the format of electricity for energy in any of its own rights and instead keep referring electricity (and quantum physics!) back to a classical physics of forces that dates even anterior to the thermodynamic physics of heat.[12] The unit in terms of information theory is the BIT, the binary digit. In its unit-icity, mathematics is inextricably mixed up with physics: it is code and energy. Insofar as information theory is a *mathematical* theory, the BIT can count as little (or for some metaphysicists, as much!) as an ultimate and immediate ontological reality as natural, rational, irrational or imaginary numbers, or any of the formats in terms of which we measure empirically in physics (meter, kilogram, mole, etc.), can. In the vicarious space of *hors-là*, we can think of the BIT as a cryptographical unit of translation between formats, as a unit within and relative to, in each case, a particular cipher.

In the empirical measurements in physics, the unit-icity applied is rooted in so-called natural constants that feature as coefficients of transformations in the mathematical equations that render physics a rigorous science. The constancy at stake is thereby formulated, for the first time by Emmy Noether in 1918, in terms of *formal laws of conservation* (not predicative 'laws' of determination, like the Newtonian laws of classical physics or Laplacean stochastic determinism). The most intuitive example of grasping the difference between laws of conservation and predicative laws is that of how energy is treated in thermodynamics: The sole assumption made is that there is an *invariant amount* of energy in the universe, invariant in that it can neither be increased nor decreased. This assumed amount does not need to be determined with a positive value (number), nor does energy need to be further qualified in any metaphysical sense. All that the thermodynamic theory of heat provides for is to study *transformations* of energy, bare of assumptions about energy as a qualified 'substance'.

Here we come to Serres's starting point: Mathematical information theory can provide a philosophical notion of mass *because it gives us just such a coefficient of transformation* – not between one form of energy into another, as thermodynamics does, but between energy and information.[13] This is indeed the background before which Serres dares to begin speaking of a *physics* of communication. A philosophy that accommodates a purely quantitative notion of mass counts to him as a natural philosophy of such a physics because this vicarious space about which we have been talking, that which Serres names *hors-là*, is not only a spectral space but also a nascent space: Transformations can be learnt to understand and control on more and more levels of complexity. It is a space that is natural insofar as it is born from how the originality of its unit-icity can be traced, by encoding this originality in terms of ever vaster 'genericity' (the genericness of mass). It extends in code, it is vicarious, it is where the diffractive massivity of quantum-physical nature can be indexed and channelled in the transformations this physics affords to check and control. And these controllable transformations are no longer restricted to that domain which nineteenth-century physics called the electromagnetic domain. It includes all the augmentations afforded by the communication, engineering ways of digitally encoding those channels, where a single frequency can host literally myriads of coexisting separate channels that allow for 'inframaterial' transformations that can be realized manifestly through 'printing' – this diffracts the classical idea of 'imprint' into manifold layers of relative 'exprimation' and 'imprintation'.[14]

TECHNICITY RATHER THAN LOGISTICS: THE VICARIOUS SPACE OF AN ELECTRIC CIRCUITRY

The space indexed by Horla need no longer be regarded as the corrupt space of a vicious circularity; it can be addressed critically as a vicarious space of an electric circuitry. Indexical as it is, code-based rather than number- or distance-based, this space provides conductivity rather than localization. From a point of view within that space, number and distance are inverse to each other, while code is an abstraction of distance (linearity), at the cost of inverting the real numbers by thinking of them as a circularity (rather than as a number line continuum).

Originality in terms of such a space, *hors-là*, provides for an *in* that 'indexes' an *out* without making positive statements, epistemological or ontological, about this *in* or this *out*. This space itself, the space of a physics of communication, is neither *out* nor *in*, neither *here* nor *beyond*, neither *past* nor *future*, neither *physical* (in the classical, pre-quantum sense) nor *metaphysical* (in the classical or the modern sense): It is the *vicarious* space that is, continually but diffractively and intermittently, *being sourced through indexing* an out in an in. *Hors, là. Out there, here.* The positivity of quantum physics can only be addressed in a vicarious domain of a representation where the reference relation is indefinitely intermitted by substitutes – substitutes that supply places by indexing what has not been indexed before. The space of this vicarious domain co-extends with the tracings of its own point zero, its own mathematical, metrical 'originality'.

Of just such strange 'nature' is the quasi-physical domain that communication channels have been establishing for real and for nearly a century now. Channels are literally technical spectra: They render apparent a certain generic order which can be observed only before a 'plentiful background' of noise (entropy), rather than one of an empty tabula rasa. Serres illustrates this idea of a plentiful background with the colour spectrum, where white light stands for such a 'plenty' because it expresses any colour at all, and this in a material, physical manner: 'white light' is, ultimately, radiating nuclear activity of quantum-physical mass. Within such 'materiality', channels are established for 'surfing' on top of the singled-out frequencies, but nevertheless *amidst* the massive agitation of what is technically called *Brownian motion*.

The space of such generic and entropic materiality must be considered as having as many formats of coordination as it has channels: a communicational web, a 'pancentric' (rather than centralized or decentralized) network. This is what Serres proposes to address as hors-là, a space of conductivity sourced from indexing. It is a *vicarious* space of substitutional operators, a space hence bare of signification and sense and undetermined with regard to meaning. Not because it would be empty in the sense of 'lack' as a substantive, but in that of 'lacking' as a kind of frequentative preposition: the zero neutrality of white light *lacks* in that it *leaks*, in the same sense as spectra *lack* in that they *leak,* and such leaking is accessible only through measuring its *frequent happening* (a frequency). The formality in this vicarious space is spectral; it lacks in that it leaks. White light is percolating not because it lacks colour but because it is 'abundantly full' of colour. This vicarious space is a space where points are indexes that *point actively*, points that are literally *pointers*. And yet, because their expressiveness is code-based, they are as indifferent to *what* it might be that they, essentially, link up as algebraic symbols used within formulae are indifferent to what, in essence, were to occupy the place they hold, as substitutes. Algebraic symbols are substitutional operators, entirely indifferent to how they are being rendered 'substantial' whenever such a formulation is considered, in empirical experiments, as a description, a simulation or a technical graph of something. They are indifferent, and yet their neutrality has 'character': because symbols themselves cannot have exponents, only numbers can. The exponent is a self-reference of a number, and the different kinds of numbers transport us into different numerical spaces (natural, rational, real, complex or those of particular numerical corpora that are being specified in category theory).[15] Symbols used in equations have to be seen as indexes, speculative points that must (somehow, this is the inventive part of mathematics in a vicarious, spectral space) be capable of spanning up adequate spaces of reflection. It is clear that the kind of physics science is capable of transforms with the introduction of novel number spaces: Classical modern mechanics would be unthinkable without the extension of numbers to the negative and the involvement of zero as a number in the domain of integers, just as Newtonian and Leibnizian dynamics would be unthinkable without the extension of numbers to a domain that involves infinitesimal incrementality. The same goes for all the creative inventions in number theory since the nineteenth century.

Let us come back now to our initial concern, namely that of raising the question of temporality for phenomena that are genuinely simulacral, rendered through technical spectra, but that which must, nevertheless, count as real. We can now see how channels, within such a vicarious, indexical space of electromagnetic conductivity that is being endowed, augmentatively, with 'exprimacy' provided by digital code, must be considered as countering both: the reversible time of classical physics as well as the irreversible passing of time in thermodynamics (and in dialectical history). Communicational channels provide for passage that 'goes upstream' and establishes spaces of relative and locally sustainable reversibility as particular temporary 'niveaus' or 'plateaus'.[16]

The remainder of this chapter will focus on the peculiar role that technical *channels* play in the kind of instrumentally augmented perception of phenomena that I have suggested to call 'mediagenic'. While the perspective from which I am writing here draws from Serres's proposal of considering a vicarious, indexically sourced space of conductivity as the metrical reference for thinking both the locality and the temporality for a physics of communication, I will not discuss much (beyond the preliminary introduction above) the philosophical novelty and relevance of Serres's proposal. Instead I will restrict myself here to highlighting the importance of the role of codes, symbols and ciphers as an extended sense of code-based 'alphabeticity' for grasping theoretically a 'mediagenic real'.[17] I will do this from the practice-based point of view of electro engineering, by translating core techniques from this field to contemporary discussions in media theory, new (and not so new) materialisms (e.g. media archaeology), object-oriented philosophy and the like.

ASSESSING THE POTENTIALITY OF WHAT-HAS-NOT-HAPPENED

As a guard rail to hold on to when trying to orientate within such a set-up as this, abstract and scarcely familiar outside of strictly disciplinary communities of experts, let us consider two exemplary positions: one that seeks to tie back the media-theoretic discussion of the role of digitally coded channels to electromagnetism as a kind of physical 'medium of the real' and another one that departs from this first position but seeks to address the speculativity of digital coding with the help of the first position. Let us attend to Wolfgang Ernst's theory of what proposes as 'time-criticality' immanent to a kind of horizontal-basedness that he calls '*Gleichursprünglichkeit*' (equality in originality) (first position) and Mark Hansen's phenomenological take on this by bringing in an active role of embodiment with regard to a power of speculation, a notion of embodiment that processes what he calls 'micro-temporal events' (second position). Before the background of the above, I will profile the first position (Ernst) as the orthodoxy of a *physicalist's theory on the communicative activity of media*, while I will discuss the second position (Hansen) as one that seeks a kind of *physics of mediated communication* that in many ways is quite close to Serres's physics of communication. An evaluative discussion of this postulate is out of the scope of this chapter. But in Serres, too, it is an embodiment which plays a crucial role in how philosophy can integrate a quantitative notion of mass along with those of space and time.[18]

Mark Hansen's interest is, as shown above, in how to address phenomena that must count as genuinely simulacral but nevertheless real. In my understanding, Hansen's genuinely simulacral phenomena are phenomena in which something is at work similar to what Deleuze has called *dark precursors*.[19] Hansen's phenomena depend upon speculation; what appears in them is neither predicative nor directly anticipative, but the phenomena are also not quite premonitions because it is not a message whose content is sinister that these phenomena have to deliver and neither are they, despite their simulacral nature, apparitions that merely pretend to be what they in reality cannot display and effectuate. Mediagenic phenomena are to be accredited a reality that is genuinely natural, and hence they can be approached in the registers of physics because they correspond to real magnitudes that manifest in nothing else but the discretable and registerable (physical) actuality of their apparent appearance – that is, their *mode* of appearing. I call their reality 'genuine' because these phenomena are not in need to be legitimated and authorized as 'substantial' by way of testing and determining what may have in *fact*, that is, in a linearly preceding *past*, caused them. All the abundant reasons that conflue and cause the effects they display are to be looked for 'entirely within the present', as Hansen insists.[20] It is not *despite* but rather *because* of a peculiar kind of non-signifying autonomy – we could say their impredicativity – that Hansen attributes to these phenomena by treating them within the quantitative registers of physics that simulacral phenomena – like global warming in his example – can help us to *prehend that of which we know not (yet) how to assess, how to measure and relate it*. Such phenomena are like speculative integrals, meant to embody rational, calculable links between the global and the local, between the predicative and the predicated, in our case between climate and weather. Hence the reality Hansen claims for his simulacral phenomena, and the magnitudes in which they manifest themselves, is not a representational one but a performative or, rather, an operative one. There is a Real whose *potentiality is referent beyond the manifestation of it as a particular fact*, as Hansen put it.[21]

In order to gain knowledge from such an operative reality, Hansen suggests, one needs to look for a *physical* approach. By following Wolfgang Ernst's approach of theorizing media in their operative dimension,[22] which Ernst calls *media's time-basedness* and their *time-criticality*, Hansen sympathizes with locating this 'physics' in the electromagnetic domain that comprehends all the radiation of physical particles in wave form. But Hansen's own approach seems to distinguish itself from that of Wolfgang Ernst in an important manner. Hansen's interest with a speculative phenomenology seems less interested in demarcating *a horizon of 'simultaneous origination'* (Gleichursprünglichkeit), as is Ernst's declared interest for his media-archaeology.[23] Hansen's own focus is less on such a horizon or, as I would call it, such a master integral that would comprehensively and objectively register the past, and the potential future, and that which can be 'recorded only by media themselves', by their 'superior wisdom', as Hansen quotes from Ernst.[24] Instead it is the bodily agency that is dispersed and active in media communication – involving both poles, senders and receivers – that Hansen seems to be interested in with his outlook on a speculative phenomenology. With that, his project seems to be the development of a veritable *physics of mediated communication*, rather than a *physicalist's theory on the communicative activity of media*. A physics of mediated communication includes a phenomenological notion of embodiment into its account. At the risk of overdrawing it a little, let me further dramatize the implications of this difference: One way of expressing this distinction, it seems to me, would be to say that the Ernst view wishes to see Hansen's *Real whose potentiality is referent beyond the historical manifestation of it as a particular fact* as a *white spectrum*, in which the embodiment of media, that is from a phenomenological perspective always singular, be purified and normalized into the mathematical ideality of a transcendent order. What Ernst refers to, when he speaks of 'technomathematics', seems to be exactly this. For Hansen, on the other hand, such a Real figures as a *dark spectrum*, whose knowledge resides in the essential darkness of the manifest embodiment of things themselves and shimmers through only in speculative renderings of an integral of which all we can specify, speculatively, is that it is to comprehend actual links between a *now and here of the manifest body or fact* and the belonging of this *'now and here'* to *an insisting anywhere and anytime.*

In other words, Hansen's phenomenological view seems to suggest that we should think of this Real, which takes the electromagnetic domain as a dark spectrum, as an active state of latently vibrant radiation, more probable than factual, a Real that insists in embodied things. By profiling the two positions before the background of Serres's vicarious space of indexical sourcing, I would like to make a suggestion of how this laid-out programme of a speculative phenomenology could perhaps be complemented by a further aspect: namely a distinction between what I call *functional technology* and *equational technics*, respectively manifesting as *dispositional apparatuses* and as *encrypted applications*. The crucial difference is that one is dependent upon a stable framework of coordination, whereas the other encrypts manners of coordination symbolically – a distinction that somehow escapes Ernst's important identification and exposition of electronic media's time-criticality altogether. In relation to this distinction, it will be necessary to reconsider 'alphabeticity' and to question an assumption that arguably holds a near-foundational status for media studies at large: namely that our age be a post-alphabetical age (e.g. McLuhan, Kittler, Ernst, Rotman, to name just a few of the 'classics').

SPECTRA, DEPICTING MAGNITUDES THAT ARE GENUINELY SIMULACRAL

First I would like to try disentangling some of the implications involved in assuming such an initial state of activeness (that captured by spectra of electromagnetic waves and the therein depicted radioactivity of white light) before going on with a more technical part which discusses the importance, and at the same time the philosophical insufficiency, of time-criticality for the inception of a 'physics' of mediated communication that considers the Real as a dark spectrum. There are seven strings I would like to distinguish and expose, so that they can resonate through the more technical discussions that will follow:

(1) We begin with the assumption of a Real as an active state that is virtually 'pregnant' in an indefinite manner, such that it allows for *the speculative interplay between discerning/discreting* (*Ermessen*) *and prehending* (*Vorwegnehmen*). This interplay can be seen as a kind of technical criticality that applies to simulacral phenomena whose magnitudes are real despite being simulacral, real in a sense that is purely operational.

(2) This assumed activeness, if it is to be approached speculatively and physically, that is, non-hermeneutically, requires that fluctuating ratios (*fluktuierende quantitative Verhältnisse*) are considered to make up a peculiar relationality that affords measurement, *a kind of rational fabric or texture* that constitutes this activeness's latently vibrant radiation. Now, because the kind of measurement at stake is to be a *speculative* interplay between discerning/discreting and prehending, this rational fabric must precede and provide *abundant rather than sufficient reason* for whatever mensural order of being or having one might come to characterize of this activeness's appearances. In other words, we could say that this kind of measurement must look *for a common factor* rather than for a common denominator.

(3) These ratios are to be dealt with as analytic points rather than as representations of geometric points. This distinguishes *operativity* from *functionality*.

(4) We can call dealings with ratios-as-analytical points *computations*. Computations are themselves purely rational, but they are so in a reckoning, numbering, calculating manner that does not respond to strict,

arithmetically predicative necessities. There are strategic and tactic levels involved which place computations in an agoratic setup – not unlike the one Lyotard has characterized for 'the state of knowledge in computerized societies'[25] – rather than in a historically dialectical one. Such an activeness never yields neutral recording; its recording always elects according to a direction that is, within certain constraints, arbitrarily imposed (*Operation als Ausrichtung*).

(5) From the point of view of a speculative phenomenology of media's microtemporal operations, the computations these operations perform do not at all legitimate and autonomize thought in a disembodied, noncorporeal manner; quite inversely, so understood, computations place considerable weight on the role of our bodies in whatever it may be that we call 'thinking'. Possible abstractions proliferate and abound, and hence 'rigorously thought-up' (German: *erdachte*) abstractions amount to nothing much of value if there are no lived experiences that correspond to them.[26] But this same point of view also seems to insist that it is only with the employment of abstractions that the body's affectivity is capable of opening up *a mediate Real* that in principle does and forever will continue to be elusive with regard to how we can pinpoint facts by words that name, concepts that comprehend and delimit, forms that manifest regularities or numbers that count predicatively.

(6) Such a stance of *abstractions that must be lived* 'phenomenalizes' the very quantities that are being processed in technical instrumentality.

(7) These phenomenalized quantities are speculated to characterize *real* magnitudes that are, so to speak, *genuinely simulacral magnitudes* – like Hansen's example of global warming. Because there is an operator that induces phenomena at work (something like Deleuzian dark precursors) within the system that provides mensurability, these simulacral phenomena can help us to *prehend that which we know not (yet) how to assess, how to measure and relate*.

SPECULATIVE (SPECTRAL) PHENOMENOLOGY, PHYSICS OF MEDIATED COMMUNICATION

Hansen's speculation of where-off and how the simulacral phenomena of such a physics of mediated communication might be decrypted follows Wolfgang Ernst and the latter's distinction of 'measuring media' from 'mass media'. We must perhaps specify that 'media' here is related to 'technical media' in the sense of communications engineering more narrowly.[27] Within these restrictions, *mass media* figure in the *time domain* of waves propagating in space and *measuring media* figure in the *time-critical domain*, which is the frequency spectrum of *how* waves propagate in space. That is why 'mass media' are called time-based, whereas 'measuring media' are called time-critical. Both are operating within the electromagnetic continuum. The frequency domain regards it *analytically* and represents it via a spectrum mask, a technical image, whereas the time domain regards the electromagnetic continuum that is analytically captured by a spectrum mask as *mechanical* and hence pictures it as a field. Now, what Ernst calls a *time-critical event* features as an analytical point in the electromagnetic field depicted as a spectrum. Let us bear in mind that an analytical point, unlike a geometrical one, is a *split* point, a *ratio,* the *encapsulation of a quantitative relation* (a 'difference'). This is important because it demarcates where Ernst's time-criticality remains silent about the aspect of digital computation, which is perhaps the most powerful of all its aspects: that analytical points need to be integrated, and that this can be done in myriads of ways by encryption.

If we consider this aspect of how the electromagnetic continuum needs to be encrypted before it can be taken into account, then we can more clearly characterize three distinct levels that are involved in what Ernst calls 'measuring media': (1) a *geometric and mechanical level* of a wave propagating in the electromagnetic continuum, the physical substrate of telecommunications; (2) a *dynamical and analytical level* where a propagating wave is singled out of the field and where it is attributed a particular frequency number, as a kind of identity tag within the larger spectrum. Through this singling out, a particular wave is being dynamized, that is, it is identified as a particular *temporality* that can be differentiated and integrated and (3) a *level of encrypting manners of how to integrate and differentiate* this temporality, what we can call its *sequencing*. This third level is the level of coding. It is *mechanical* again, yet algebraically so: it subsumes the ratios, the analytic points, under an encrypted, symbolic form. I will come back to what we can understand by such a 'symbolic form'. What is important now is that this third level is mechanical, like the first, but on a different level of abstraction than the wave level – it is only here that we might be in the realm of *quantizing dynamical systems* through *encryptive probabilistic procedures* and where we might face what in quantum mechanics is called the measurement problem. Hansen is interested in media's time-criticality on this third level, as I understand him, because it is here that a notion of media's embodiment, insofar as it is not normalized and idealized, can be seen to play a role at all.

So, how far can Ernst's distinction between 'mass media' and 'measuring media' carry us with regard to this third level of algebraic mechanics, or quantum mechanics? Technically speaking, each frequency itself can be treated as a field for other frequencies. A masked field of fields of waves is called a spectrum, a *technical image*. It is by way of manipulating this technical image and rendering its manipulations back into the physical continuum that Ernst can speak of media's measuring time-criticality. In this indirect manner, the amplitudes of waves are encoded in terms of distinguished phases. As a consequence of this, where we have one mass-media channel per frequency that can broadcast the programme from one particular source, we can have n, that is, an indefinite amount of 'discreted' channels (distinct articulations of one and the same) per frequency in measuring media. With them, it is not one source that broadcasts but distributed populations of sources that send messages in parallel. The time-based manner of broadcasting is now being coded, in the strict sense of the term – it is being encrypted according to probabilistic alphabets – and like this, it can serve to host not simply one channel but myriads of channels. In such probabilistic set-ups, we have, in its most extreme form of peer-to-peer file sharing, one channel for each 'message' sent. Many channels can be encoded onto one and the same physical carrier (a wave). Let us picture the level of artistry and sophistication we are talking about: In this modulatory manner, one telecom cable, for example, the one which supplies our household in Zürich with phone and Internet connections, is capable of maintaining more than ten million distinct channels 'within' or rather 'with the carrier of' one single frequency. This is of course an extraordinarily large number because we are talking about a cable, and a cable allows waves to propagate with fewest disturbances (as opposed to air, light or water, for example), but *in principle* this explosion of sustainable channels applies also to services without manifest cables, like mobile cellular services or Bluetooth. Now this encryption, which relies on probabilistic procedures, may well be working 'mechanically' (algorithmically) – but that does not mean that it does not involve incredible diligence and sophistication on the side of the engineers! The mechanical work they perform is algebraic before it is functional; it has to make different protocols compatible. We will see in a moment why this is important politically. It is why I think that the emphasis on 'measuring media' for what is actually an entire compound of both symbolic encryption and performed time-criticality is somewhat obscure. On this technical level of telecommunication that Ernst addresses, it seems more productive to speak of *generic mediality* rather than of reified *'measuring media'*.[28]

CHANNELS, KEYS AND CIPHERS (CODE SYSTEMS AS MANNERS OF DISCERNING NO-THING-AT-ALL)

Let me try to illustrate what is actually happening in such encryptive coding, using an example that is perhaps easier to grasp. Gian Battista Alberti, the Italian architect and polymath in Renaissance-era Florence, famous of his legendary ten books on architecture, wrote a book entitled *De Componendis Cifris*. It is a 'code of practice' for how to encrypt texts in a manner that is augmented by a mechanical device, the so-called cipher disk (which he is said to have invented). Such a disk consists of two concentric circular plates mounted one on top of the other. The larger plate is called the 'stationary' and the smaller one, the 'moveable' since the smaller one could move on top of the 'stationary'. The first incarnation of the disk had plates made of copper and featured the alphabet, in order, inscribed on the outer edge of each disk and coordinated in cells that are split evenly along the circumference of the circle. This enabled the two alphabets to move relative to each other and thus to create an easy-to-use key – one could give orders like 'shift one unit to the right after every fifth turn of the movable disk' in order to reconstruct the right letters of the text message in the right sequence.

Communication engineers today are not dealing with cipher disks anymore when they organize for the coexistence of ten million distinct channels within one frequency, of course. But they are still providing channels for communication through just such an encryption. The frequency would be the 'static plate', and each modulation of its amplitude in phases would be a 'mobile' plate. Obviously, such plates can be stacked and set relative to one another in an indefinite amount of manners. With digital channels, every channel is one such key, crafted for every single message that is to be transmitted. Alberti's cipher disk is still the best illustration of the peculiarly *rational, yet not reasonable, 'laws'* which technical telecommunication media obey when they enframe how messages can be *stored, processed and transmitted*. It is algebraic *laws of equations* that enframe in particular notations (code systems) a particular calculus of variations. In encrypted mediation, that which circulates remains invariant in the algebraic sense of the word – algebraic because we are on the level of *equations*, not their derivatives, which would be that of *functions*.[29]

TWO KINDS OF TECHNICS: CONCENTRATING ON NO-THING (EQUATIONAL) AND BEING CONCERNED WITH SOME-THING (FUNCTIONAL)

This is important to realize: every act of coding spells out a code system, which is in fact *a measured nothingness* – a system of rationality entirely decoupled from any reasonable ground. That's why it can be a system (unlike Saussure's semiology, for example): precisely because it introduces a notion of zero, upon which it operates.[30] Zero was indeed the name attributed to the cipher's character, once it was introduced from Indian and Arabic mathematics to Europe. A cipher (and there can be indefinitely many ciphers!), as far rather cryptogrammatical and analytical ones), Hansen's impatience with idealist transcendentalism gains, on the one hand, in support; yet at the same time, thought cannot adequately be conceived as the other to bodiliness, given that such measurement nevertheless involves a kind of conceptualization that affords and demands diligence, sophistication and intellectual mastership. It is the complication of this relation, I suggested, that might be addressed in such a speculative phenomenology, as 'lived' or, perhaps better, as 'quick and prolonging' rather than 'short-cutting' abstractions. Information and communication technology, then, do not place us in a post-alphabetical age where the Real would be immediately 'recorded', 'sensed' and 'expressed'; rather, such recording operates relative to the probabilistic alphabets of code it uses. In code, an alphabetical order and a numerical one are mutually implicative – no linear ordering of the finite elements of an alphabet from first to last without applying a symbolization of how to operate by numerals within an element of the infinite (an algebra), and no notational symbolization of how to operate in an element of the infinite by numerals (an algebra) without indexing with an alphabet's place system a sequential or tabular order of how givens (data points, indexes) can be organized such that they may be subsumed under the rule of this symbolization.[34] *Code is alphanumerical.* The two are orthogonal, and they mutually transverse or 'co-evoke' one another. As far as the measurement of quantum phenomena is concerned, the alphabetical as well as the numerical are derived from the *ciphers that operate technically and thoughtfully in code* – even if the measurements themselves can be said to remain 'unthinkable', as long as 'thinkable' is restricted to mean 'critical' within a representationalist paradigm. The question, then, for such a speculative phenomenology that articulates the unthinkable (and hence is never critical without being inventive, but that may, on the other hand, very well be inventive without being critical), is this: 'Who' is thinking in such objective thoughtfulness that operates in technically manipulable code? On this level, the proposed sobriety and libidinous-less-ness that go along with keeping a distinction between equational technics and functional technology prevent us from identifying (with) such an agency in an uncritical manner – be it as Truth, Beauty, History, Nature, God, People or Science.

NOTES

1. Michel Serres, *Atlas* (Berlin: Merve, 2005 [1994]), 59.

2. This text is based on the response I was invited to give to Mark Hanson's keynote lecture 'Entangled in Media, Towards a Speculative Phenomenology of Microtemporal Operations' at the 'Philosophy After Nature' conference in Utrecht, September 2014.

legendary ten books on architecture, wrote a book entitled *De Componendis Cifris*. It is a 'code of practice' for how to encrypt texts in a manner that is augmented by a mechanical device, the so-called cipher disk (which he is said to have invented). Such a disk consists of two concentric circular plates mounted one on top of the other. The larger plate is called the 'stationary' and the smaller one, the 'moveable' since the smaller one could move on top of the 'stationary'. The first incarnation of the disk had plates made of copper and featured the alphabet, in order, inscribed on the outer edge of each disk and coordinated in cells that are split evenly along the circumference of the circle. This enabled the two alphabets to move relative to each other and thus to create an easy-to-use key – one could give orders like 'shift one unit to the right after every fifth turn of the movable disk' in order to reconstruct the right letters of the text message in the right sequence.

Communication engineers today are not dealing with cipher disks anymore when they organize for the coexistence of ten million distinct channels within one frequency, of course. But they are still providing channels for communication through just such an encryption. The frequency would be the 'static plate', and each modulation of its amplitude in phases would be a 'mobile' plate. Obviously, such plates can be stacked and set relative to one another in an indefinite amount of manners. With digital channels, every channel is one such key, crafted for every single message that is to be transmitted. Alberti's cipher disk is still the best illustration of the peculiarly *rational, yet not reasonable, 'laws'* which technical telecommunication media obey when they enframe how messages can be *stored, processed and transmitted*. It is algebraic *laws of equations* that enframe in particular notations (code systems) a particular calculus of variations. In encrypted mediation, that which circulates remains invariant in the algebraic sense of the word – algebraic because we are on the level of *equations*, not their derivatives, which would be that of *functions*.[29]

TWO KINDS OF TECHNICS: CONCENTRATING ON NO-THING (EQUATIONAL) AND BEING CONCERNED WITH SOME-THING (FUNCTIONAL)

This is important to realize: every act of coding spells out a code system, which is in fact *a measured nothingness* – a system of rationality entirely decoupled from any reasonable ground. That's why it can be a system (unlike Saussure's semiology, for example): precisely because it introduces a notion of zero, upon which it operates.[30] Zero was indeed the name attributed to the cipher's character, once it was introduced from Indian and Arabic mathematics to Europe. A cipher (and there can be indefinitely many ciphers!), as far as algebra and operability are concerned, is genuinely *neutral and vacuous*, neither positive nor negative. *Empty*, as Kant and especially Hegel insisted. *Gleichursprünglich*, as Ernst says today. Coding, because it is algebraic, operates outside of historical time. That is why a quantum-logical approach to information and data seems so promising. The set-up of a code system is formulaic, equational. It literally represents nothing, or in other words, it constitutes a cipher: A notational body of reciprocal transformability that is transcendent to the distinction between positive and negative. Programming languages are algebraic, and they are heterogeneous with respect to each other.[31] It is the epistemological concerns that, within the programme of providing logical foundations for knowledge, try to systematize them in one globally consistent symbolic order. Within the mathematical domain itself, to determine the solvability of an equation, all the terms on both sides of the equation sign must be arranged such that *they cancel each other out* and sum up to zero. Thus, they literally and actually do *describe nothing*. In literally describing nothing, they can conserve what is contained in the givens (the data). This is different from a function. A function is derivative to an equation, and it *doesn't concentrate on nothing*, like the formula it is derived from. Unlike an equation, it *is concerned with something*: namely, with determining *that one variation of the invariant conforms to another variation of it*. A function is always directed, while an equation rests in itself – although it never really 'rests'. I would like to suggest that the character of a function may be considered as *dynamic* and that of an equation, as *active*. Or in other words, functional technology comes in the form of apparatus (with strictly controlled dispositions that are fixed, such that they allow to support variations of a same behaviour) while equational technics come in the form of *applications*. The latter live from the opposite of centrally controlled dispositions: they open up their own zones of exchange through encrypting the domains in which they operate.[32] On the basis of this idea *that equations, while resting in themselves, do actively nothing, rather than represent and stand in for something, we can modulate and actualize their proper 'domains of activity' by endowing it with particular dispositions*. This may sound farfetched and hard to picture, but it describes, for example, how solar cells work. In the case of *photovoltaics*, a semiconductor is dispositioned such that it is capable of capturing photons from the light to which it is exposed. With solar cells, this disposition is a certain balance between the atomic weights of bohrium and phosphor. Once exposed to sunlight, the electrons begin to jump in order to keep the balance of the initial saturation and eventually spill over the framework of the cell, hence producing electric current garnered from sunlight. Their character cannot be captured in terms of functions (dynamics); it is equational (active). Solar cells don't need an overall framework; they tap into streaming radiation of light and encapsulate some of its energy by 'imposing' their own 'rationality' upon it (by capturing photons in a particularly coded – encrypted – receptivity). This is what 'measuring media' do, too: they engender the domains in which they operate through partitioning. We can regard not only Internet apps as instances of such equational technics, but also any kind of computer simulations. Their activity is operational and hence strictly technical: *they produce what they are set up to produce*. If you set up a simulation that computes global warming, you will get values that indicate global warming. If you set up a simulation that computes the limits to population growth, you will get values that indicate limits to population growth. I don't mean to ridicule these simulations, and the seriousness and urgency of the themes they address, but if we would set up a simulation that computes the end of the world, we would also get a result that must be considered valid within the constraints embodied by the parametric model – by the equation – on which the simulation runs. Equational technics are strictly rational, and yet they are entirely decoupled from logic and reason – which is indeed why they can support speculative reasoning so well.

ABSTRACTIONS THAT PROLONG RATHER THAN CUT SHORT: ARTICULATING WHAT IS UNTHINKABLE

Hansen's interest with his programme for a speculative phenomenology is to affirm what he calls the absolute inaccessibility of quantum events to thinking.[33] Quantum phenomena are produced by the operation of measurement, he insists, but it is a kind of operationality that comes with its own duration that lasts on, rather than cutting through or intervening, as an act. One cannot find orientation about the phenomenon of climate change from single acts of measurement. It is measuring itself that produces the phenomenon, and hence Hansen suggests calling them 'originary phenomena' – phenomena that are themselves actively real, instead of an appearance or manifestation of some underlying and hidden reality. Phenomena so conceived, he maintains, cannot be *thought*, only *sensed* (measured). By suggesting to complement his programme with a distinction between functional technology and equational technics, respectively manifesting as dispositional apparatuses and as encrypted applications, my own discussion aims at mobilizing and somewhat displacing what appears for Hansen to be an exclusionary relation between thinking and bodily entanglement (affect and sense). By looking at the probabilistic procedures with which the measurement of quantum phenomena is actually carried out in practice by information scientists and electro engineers, and by exposing how they are working with non-representationalist concepts as well (they are working with cryptological or rather cryptogrammatical and analytical ones), Hansen's impatience with idealist transcendentalism gains, on the one hand, in support; yet at the same time, thought cannot adequately be conceived as the other to bodiliness, given that such measurement nevertheless involves a kind of conceptualization that affords and demands diligence, sophistication and intellectual mastership. It is the complication of this relation, I suggested, that might be addressed in such a speculative phenomenology, as 'lived' or, perhaps better, as 'quick and prolonging' rather than 'short-cutting' abstractions. Information and communication technology, then, do not place us in a post-alphabetical age where the Real would be immediately 'recorded', 'sensed' and 'expressed'; rather, such recording operates relative to the probabilistic alphabets of code it uses. In code, an alphabetical order and a numerical one are mutually implicative – no linear ordering of the finite elements of an alphabet from first to last without applying a symbolization of how to operate by numerals within an element of the infinite (an algebra), and no notational symbolization of how to operate in an element of the infinite by numerals (an algebra) without indexing with an alphabet's place system a sequential or tabular order of how givens (data points, indexes) can be organized such that they may be subsumed under the rule of this symbolization.[34] *Code is alphanumerical.* The two are orthogonal, and they mutually transverse or 'co-evoke' one another. As far as the measurement of quantum phenomena is concerned, the alphabetical as well as the numerical are derived from the *ciphers that operate technically and thoughtfully in code* – even if the measurements themselves can be said to remain 'unthinkable', as long as 'thinkable' is restricted to mean 'critical' within a representationalist paradigm. The question, then, for such a speculative phenomenology that articulates the unthinkable (and hence is never critical without being inventive, but that may, on the other hand, very well be inventive without being critical), is this: 'Who' is thinking in such objective thoughtfulness that operates in technically manipulable code? On this level, the proposed sobriety and libidinous-less-ness that go along with keeping a distinction between equational technics and functional technology prevent us from identifying (with) such an agency in an uncritical manner – be it as Truth, Beauty, History, Nature, God, People or Science.

NOTES

1. Michel Serres, *Atlas* (Berlin: Merve, 2005 [1994]), 59.
2. This text is based on the response I was invited to give to Mark Hanson's keynote lecture 'Entangled in Media, Towards a Speculative Phenomenology of Microtemporal Operations' at the 'Philosophy After Nature' conference in Utrecht, September 2014.

3. Serres, *Atlas*, 59.

4. cf. Mark Hansen, *Bodies in Code: Interfaces with Digital Media* (London: Routledge, 2006).

5. According to etymonline.com, 'vicious' means 'unwholesome, impure, of the nature of vice, wicked, corrupting, pernicious, harmful', when applied to a text 'erroneous, corrupt', from Anglo-French *vicious*, Old French *vicios* 'wicked, cunning, underhand; defective, illegal', Latin *vitiosus* (Medieval Latin vicious) 'faulty, full of faults, defective, corrupt; wicked, depraved' and *vitium* 'fault'.

6. www.etymonline.com

7. This is really the overall theme of Serres's book *Atlas* – he discusses how we can exercise a kind of map-making for the globalizing world, where maps do not depict territorial order but communicative order. Such map-making combines 'prophecy with geometry': it demands that calculations based on stochastic integrals, statistical mappings and probabilistic predictions be graphed out and treated in geometric and constructive terms as well, no longer exclusively in analytical and deductive manners.

8. This is the core theme of Serres's book *Le Parasite* (1980), where he discredits the idea of a restoration of a balance as the ideal successfulness of communication and instead begins to theorize a natural economic order that is genuinely communicative, where the sun must count as the ultimate capital. Capital, then, can no longer be thought of as the exploitative accumulation and concentration of resources. It must be addressed as the primary source of all kinds of banks of energy information that nature organizes in. It is a very early view of a world naturally globalized through communication, an idea Serres picks up, in its ethical implications, in *Le Contrat Naturel* (1990).

9. www.etymonline.com

10. This is not merely a metaphorical way of speaking. The unsettling insight that drove the development of information theory since its mathematical formulation is that the acquisition of information, like that of energy in systems that maintain themselves over a certain time in thermodynamics (organisms, ecology), is not gratuitous but comes as a price: energy is treated as a kind of disorder that is a plenty of possibility (entropy), while information is treated as the order that provides stability through warding off of entropy; hence, its order is called negatively entropic (negentropy). This means that novel amounts of information (always 'novel' in relative sense to the order at stake) must be acquired at the price of sacrificing some of the settledness of this order, by 'importing' and 'banking' more of entropy (energy, possibility) than is necessary to maintain itself. The key theoretician of this aspect is the quantum physicist Léon Brillouin, who began to foreground for the first time the particular role of code in information science in *Science and Information Theory* (New York: Academic Press, 1956). Among Serres's texts, the following are the key ones where he discussed this: 'Mathématisation de l'empirisme' in *Interférence, Hermes II* (Paris: Minuit, 1972), 195–200; and 'Vie, Information, Deuxième Principe' in *La Traduction, Hermes III* (Paris: Minuit, 1974), 43–72. For an introductory overview cf. my glossary entries 'Negentropy', 'Maxwell's Demon (Non-Anthropocentric Cognition)' and 'Invariance' in *The Posthuman Glossary,* Rosi Braidotti et al. (Edinburgh: Edinburgh University Press, 2017).

11. Stephen Wolfram, *A New Kind of Science* (Champaign: Wolfram Media, 2002).

12. This was at stake already in the forceful disputes around Dialectical Materialism and the Empirico-critical Materialism in the Vienna School around the turn of the twentieth century. Lenin criticized Mach for a corruption of an absolute notion of time just as much as Mach rejected Boltzmann's theory of the atom for just that same reason. Today's struggles around New and 'classical' Materialism seem to revolve around those same old issues, and they begin to crystallize in the question of how a certain 'materiality' can and must be attributed to code and the role it plays in knowledge. For an introduction to the New Materialism approach cf. *New Materialism: Interviews and Cartographies*, Eds. Rick Dolphijn, Iris van der Tuin (Ann Arbor: Open Humanities Press, 2012).

13. Denis Gabor, MIT lectures, 1951: 'We cannot get anything for nothing, not even an observation'; here cited in Léon Brillouin, *Science and Information Theory* (Dover: New York, 1956), position 3800 in the Kindle edition. What Brillouin, following Gabor, calls 'the price of information' can be quantified precisely, even with a number (10^{-16} in Brillouin's 1957 book, a number which by today's state-of-the-art particle physics has reached to 10^{-32}, as my theoretical-physicist friend Elias Zafiris tells me [in a private conversation]). The rising value of this coefficient refers to the increasingly small scale on which nuclear science empirically observes particle behaviour. In the case of 10^{-32}, it is the coefficient allowing the famous Higgs boson to be traced in the CERN Accelerator. It is a central topos throughout Serres's oeuvre. Some key texts in which he discusses its relevance are 'Mathématisation de l'empirisme' (cf. fn. 10) and 'Vie, Information, Deuxième Principe' (cf. fn. 10).

14. cf. Vera Bühlmann, Ludger Hovestadt (Eds.). *Printed Physics, Metalithikum I* (Vienna: Springer, 2013), here especially Ludger Hovestadt, 'A Fantastic Genealogy of the Printable' (17–70).

15. cf. Fernando Zalamea, *Synthetic Philosophy of Contemporary Mathematics* (London: Urbanomic, 2012); and Giuseppe Longo, 'Synthetic Philosophy of Mathematics and Natural Sciences: Conceptual Analyses From a Grothendieckian Perspective, Reflections on 'Synthetic Philosophy of Contemporary Mathematics' by Fernando Zalamea', available on Longo's institutional website: http://www.di.ens.fr/users/longo/files/PhilosophyAndCognition/Review-Zalamea-Grothendieck.pdf.

16. This is, very generally, the theme in Serres's *L'Incandescent* (Paris: Le Pommier, 2003), where he introduces the concept of 'Exodarwinism' to refer to such temporality.

17. The sense in which I refer to the alphabetical might raise the expectation that the following arguments will resonate with Brian Rotman's increasingly well-received work on ciphers and on the alphabet, but this would be somewhat misleading. In his study *Signifying Nothing: The Semiotics of Zero* (New York: St. Martin's Press, 1987), the rise of algebra in Renaissance-era Italy is described as the beginning of an ongoing reign of a meta-order that begins to relativize 'an alphabetical' order. This tendency is seen as completing itself in what he calls, for example in 'The Alphabetic Body' (*Parallax* 8.1 (2002): 92–104), the end of the alphabetical. In this, my own stance differs: My interest is to examine how long before an explicit sign for the symbolization of zero had been invented have ciphers been at work in symbolizing nothingness (albeit not in signifying it). My focus is on the mutually implicative

relation between the alphabetical and the numerical in code – as it is constitutive for information science today, and as it can also be studied in the early rise of algebra. Thereby, I want to address the strangely neglected status in today's philosophical approaches to communication and media of the diverse, and yet peculiarly so 'void', character of symbols that operate in algebra as pure placeholders and substitutes. We are dealing with many 'nothingnesses', to put it a bit dramatically. Recognizing this affords to gain a technical understanding of communication channels through the encryption and decipherment of cryptograms – an aspect not at all thematized by Rotman's linguistically semiotic perspective.

18. The main references of this aspect are Serres's *The Five Senses: A Philosophy of Mingled Bodies* (Manchester: Continuum, 2008 [1985]), as well as *Variations sur le corps* (Paris: Le Pommier, 1999).

19. In *Difference and Repetition* (New York: Columbia University Press, 1994 [1968]), Gilles Deleuze introduces the concept of the dark precursor as something that affords communication within an element of what he calls 'the disparse'. The dark precursor is called the 'in-itself of difference', a 'differenciator', the 'the self-different which relates different to different by itself' (119) and it is meant to afford communication between heterogeneous series. The characterization on which I rely most with this proposed analogy to Hansen's mediagenic phenomena, of which he says they originate in a kind of speculation that is driven by microtemporal operations of media, is this: Dark precursors 'induce phenomena within a system' in which it itself 'has no place other than that from which it is "missing"' and 'no identity other than that which it lacks' (120).

20. Here we encounter a divergence from the suggested analogy to Deleuzian dark precursors: Deleuze does not subject his concept to a temporalization that would be external to the concept's own operability as a differentiator; rather, much suggests that dark precursors describe for him the substitute position of algebraic symbols in a mathematical structure, for example, when he holds that the dark precursor 'is precisely the object $= x$, the one which "is lacking in its place" as it lacks its own identity' (*Difference and Repetition,* 120). I am referring with my citation to Hansen's lecture, which is accessible online: https://lecturenet.uu.nl/Site1/Play/126f9811aad94d12bed e84e7da2efe4a1d?catalog=6aa828db-767a-487c-8ba1-d635a20245e6.

21. In his original paper delivered at the 'Philosophy After Nature' conference in Utrecht, Hansen formulated, 'The prehension of this scheme is one more example that actual fact includes in its own constitution real potentiality *which is referent beyond itself*.

22. Wolfgang Ernst, 'Experimenting with Media Temporality: Pythagoras, Hertz, Turing', in *Digital Memory and the Archive*, Ed. by Jussi Parikka (Minneapolis: University of Minnesota Press, 2013), 184–192.

23. Wolfgang Ernst, *Gleichursprünglichkeit. Zeitwesen und Zeitgegebenheit technischer Medien* (Berlin: Kadmos, 2012).

24. See Hansen, 'Media Entangled Phenomenology', in this volume.

25. Jean-Francois Lyotard, *La condition postmoderne: rapport sur le savoir* (Paris: Minuit, 1979).

26. Michel Serres has elaborated on this extensively in his book on Leibniz's philosophical system (*Le Système de Leibniz et ses modèles mathématiques,* 1968); cf. also his first three chapters in *Hermes II, Interférence.*

52   Chapter Four

27. My following and very brief discussions of the physics of communication engineering build upon basic knowledge in this field. For an elaborated and detailed account cf. for example Leon W. Couch, *Digital and Analog Communication Systems*, 8th edition (New York: Pearson, 2013).
28. cf. Vera Bühlmann, *Die Nachricht, ein Medium. Generische Medialität, städtische Architektonik* (Vienna: Ambra, 2014), especially the 'Coda: Ein generischer Begriff von Medialität', 266–271.
29. It is important to realize that the invariant quantity whose fractions are circulating in the transformability space which an equation constitutes features neither as variable nor as constant (coefficient) within the equation. A Calculus of Variation is today referred to as obeying The Laws of Conservation. They find their perhaps most important application in physics, where energy is treated as the invariant quantity (its total amount in the universe can neither be expanded nor diminished) on the basis of which we can modulate its 'partitioning' or even, to put it a bit drastically, its 'communication' (German: *Mitteilung*) by the electrons which 'commute' or jump between particles. This is for example how a photovoltaic cell is working: It is a material disposition rendered such that it captures photons from the light to which it is exposed, thereby moving electrons to jump and 'spill over' the bounds of the chemical saturation of the cell, thus producing electric power. Such technics, like photovoltaic cells, I suggest to call equational technics. cf. regarding applications of such physics John W. Orton, *The Story of Semiconductors* (London: Oxford University Press, 2008); for an introduction to invariance theory, see Dwight E. Neuenschwander's *Emmy Noether's Wonderful Theorem* (London: The John Hopkins University Press, 2010).

This aspect, that 'content' is treated as that which can be conserved throughout transformations within a reciprocal space constituted by signal horizons – in short, probabilistic encryption – seems to me the main characteristic distinguishing digital media categorically from analogue media. A further context which can help us to better comprehend this aspect is this: In a simplificatory manner, we can think of analogicity as the idea where the words that can be articulated by the alphabet are taken to make up, all together, an inventory which names all things existing, in other words, a kind of Adamitic or Original Language which represents a (or rather, *the*) conceptual order. We can easily find this idea at work in our intuitive but naive idea of the measurement system with all its normalizations based on prototypical material artifacts – the Original Meter in Paris, for example, or the Original Kilo in France, and so on. Now, just as language is being studied from a structural and systematical point of view since the end of the nineteenth century, the International System of Units also began to rid itself of these material prototypical artifacts. The units are defined today within a structural system of conversion – an idea already propagated by Maxwell in the nineteenth century – where all the units must cohere, that is, exact values must be formalizable for some base units, and all the other units must be derivative from these base units. In the form that is authoritative today, all the definitions of the base units are precise algebraic formulations of possible conversions that can be applied to the base unit as an invariant (metre for length, ampere for electric current, kelvin for thermodynamic temperature, second for time, mole for the amount of substance, candela for luminous intensity [light]) – except for the kilogram. It too is a base unit, but its definition is still a prototypical artifact. Thus, it is the declared goal of recent meetings in 2007 and 2010 to eventually set up a New International System of Units, where the structure of the system is to shift from giving explicit, precise definitions for the base units themselves to giving explicit, precise definitions for the natural constants involved, like the speed of light. Like this, so is the ambition, it will be possible to do away with the kilogram as well and find a formulaic definition for it. In order to come up with such a coherent system, it is necessary to assume 'natural constants' – as of today, this is the speed of light, the elementary charge of atoms et cetera. I owe my thanks to Nathan Brown for drawing my attention to this in his talk 'Hegel's Kilogram', given at the conference 'Quantity and Quality, the Problem of Measurement in Philosophy and Science' which he organized in April 2014 at UC Davis, California, USA. For further information, the Wikipedia entry on The International System of Units provides a valid starting point.

30. Every equation, in order to yield a solution, must literally be set equal to zero. Algebra is the art of moving around the terms of the equation from one side of the balance to the other, such that they cancel each other out.

31. cf. the manuscript to my talk at the 'Universal-Specific, from Analysis to Intervention' conference at ETH Zurich in November 2013, 'The Question of "Signature" and the Computational Notion of Genericness', available at www.academia.edu/5117590/The_question_of_signature_and_the_computational_notion_of_genericness.

32. A distinction between what I suggest here to call *apparatus* and *application* is at work in the partitioning of communication systems into different abstraction layers, and it is the main conceptual set up of the Open Systems Interconnection Model (OSI Model) behind the international and national standards for how to organize communication networks, developed since the 1980s by the Institute of Electrical and Electronics Engineers IEEE. cf. the Wikipedia entry for an introductory overview.

33. I am referring with my citation to Hansen's lecture, accessible online at https://lecturenet.uu.nl/Site1/Play/126f9811aad94d12bede84e7da2efe4a1d?catalog=6aa828db-767a-487c-8ba1-d635a20245e6.

34. The best study on the philosophical implications of algebra I know of is Jules Vuillemin, *La Philosophie d'Algèbre* (Paris: PUF, 1962).

BIBLIOGRAPHY

Braidotti, Rosi (Ed.). *The Posthuman Glossary.* Edinburgh: Edinburgh University Press, 2016.
Brillouin, Léon. *Science and Information Theory.* Dover: New York, 1956.
Bühlmann, Vera. *Die Nachricht, ein Medium. Generische Medialität, städtische Architektonik.* Vienna: Ambra, 2014.
———. 'The Question of "Signature" and the Computational Notion of Genericness', n.d. www.academia.edu/5117590/The_question_of_signature_and_the_computational_notion_of_genericness.

Bühlmann, Vera and Ludger Hovestadt (Eds.). *Printed Physics, Metalithikum I.* Vienna: Springer, 2013.
Couch, Leon W. *Digital and Analog Communication Systems.* 8th edition. New York: Pearson, 2013.
Deleuze, Gilles. *Difference and Repetition.* Translated by Paul Patton. New York: Columbia University Press, 1994 [1968].
Dolphijn, Rick and Iris van der Tuin (Eds.). *New Materialism: Interviews and Cartographies.* Ann Arbor: Open Humanities Press, 2012.
Hansen, Mark B.N. *Bodies in Code: Interfaces with Digital Media.* London: Routledge, 2006.
Hovestedt, Ludger. 'A Fantastic Genealogy of the Printable'. In *Printed Physics, Metalithikum I.* Edited by Vera Bühlmann and Ludger Hovestadt, 17–70. Vienna: Springer, 2013.
Longo, Giuseppe. 'Synthetic Philosophy of Mathematics and Natural Sciences: Conceptual Analyses from a Grothendieckian Perspective, Reflections on "Synthetic Philosophy of Contemporary Mathematics" by Fernando Zalamea'. Translated by Fabio Gironi, 2015. http://www.di.ens.fr/users/longo/files/PhilosophyAndCognition/Review-Zalamea-Grothendieck.pdf.
Lyotard, Jean-François. *La condition postmoderne: rapport sur le savoir.* Paris: Minuit, 1979.
Neuenschwander, Dwight E. *Emmy Noether's Wonderful Theorem.* London: The Johns Hopkins University Press, 2010.
Orton, John W. *The Story of Semiconductors.* London: Oxford University Press, 2008.
Rotman, Brian. 'The Alphabetic Body', *Parallax,* 8.1 (2002): 92–104.
———. *Signifying Nothing: The Semiotics of Zero.* New York: St. Martin's Press, 1987.
Serres, Michel. *Atlas.* Berlin: Merve, 2005 [1994].
———. *Le Contrat Naturel.* Paris: Flammarion, 1990.
———. *Leibniz et ses modèles mathématiques.* Paris: PUF, 1968.
———. *Le Parasite.* Paris: Grasset, 1980
———. *L'Incandescent.* Paris: Le Pommier, 2003.
———. 'Mathématisation de l'empirisme'. In *Interference, Hermes II,* 195–200. Paris: Minuit, 1972.
———. *The Five Senses: A Philosophy of Mingled Bodies.* Translated by Margaret Sankey and Peter Cowley. Manchester: Continuum, 2008 [1985].
———. *Variations sur le corps.* Paris: Le Pommier, 1999.
———. 'Vie, Information, Deuxième Principe'. In *La Traduction, Hermes III,* 43–72. Paris: Minuit, 1974.
Vuillemin, Jules. *La Philosophie d'Algèbre.* Paris: PUF, 1962.
Wolfram, Stephen. *A New Kind of Science.* Champaign: Wolfram Media, 2002.
Zalamea, Fernando. *Synthetic Philosophy of Contemporary Mathematics.* London: Urbanomic, 2012.

Chapter Five

The Resonance of Disparates

Spinoza, Damasio, Deleuze and the Ecology of Form

Rick Dolphijn

Everything happens through the resonance of disparates.

—Gilles Deleuze

THE BUILDING (BRAIN), OR 'THAT WHICH FEELS AS ONE'

It is a sphere composed of a few hundred stones cemented together, with a large circular hole at the bottom. The top of its dome bears seven or eight sturdy spikes, each a cairn of stones, larger ones at the base, the smallest at the tip creating a sharp point. The most distinctive architectural detail, the one that gives the name to the species that builds it, is the collar to the circular aperture. It is a pleated coronet constructed from particles too small to be distinguishable from the cement that binds them. The diameter of this whole dwelling, for that is what it is, is about one hundred and fifty thousandths of a millimeter (i.e. micrometres, written μm). Smaller than the full stop at the end of this sentence, it is the portable home of the *Difflugia coronata,* a species of amoeba.[1]

    The *D. coronata* is not an animal. It is a single-cell creature that feeds and reproduces but has no nervous system (thus no brain). Academics interested in animal architecture, like the quoted Mike Hansell, have difficulty explaining how such a simple organism is capable of creating or 'inventing' such a complex form. Hansell's analysis raises a series of questions. A crucial one concerns the necessity of 'having a brain' when it comes to realizing material complexity. Hansell (and many others in this field) have long wondered how relatively small-brained animals like weaver birds are able to create complex patterns and how honey bees make perfect hexagons. Every time, behaviour and interaction with 'outside materials' are considered to be a consequence of a thought, or caused by the brain, however small this brain might be.[2]

Not only those interested in animal architecture have problems with complex yet brainless cytoplasm. Neurophysiology, of course, also has difficulty accepting this, as a recent uproar in *Nature* shows us (12 May 2005 issue). I am referring now to the discussions (between Rüdiger Wehner and Dan-E. Nilsson et al.) on the Cubozoa, also called box jellyfish or sea wasp (though these creatures are family of neither the jellyfish nor the wasp). Cubozoas move most elegantly and rapidly and react with great refinement on their environment (they are fierce hunters). They have an elaborate sensory apparatus most remarkable for the complex eyes that include highly sophisticated camera lenses that come very close to our own. In other words, 'Making good lenses seems to be a demanding task, because only a few animal phyla have accomplished it'.[3] But having complex eyes is not what struck neuroscientists/biologists like Wehner in the first place: As with the *D. coronata*, it strikes them that these complex senses are not mirrored by a brain.

Or at least, that's what, for instance, evolutionary paleobiologist Simon Conway Morris claims: The Cubozoa has a most intricate sensory apparatus but no brain. He adds to this that his definition of the brain excludes four cardiac pacemakers laced up in the nerve net organizing its body plan. Referring to a conversation with Nick Strausfeld, Conway Morris holds the belief that the brain has always been a device to 'assess the asymmetries in the sensory surround and to compensate for these by appropriate motor efferent reply',[4] which has of course little to do with what pacemakers do. Nilsson et al.[5] disagree and instead keep faith in the necessity of the brain, claiming that these pacemakers are in fact brain-like organs. Nilsson holds the idea that there *has* to be a brain responsible for this complex behaviour, necessary for interpreting the information these complex eyes produce. Thus, they revive the idea that these four very small central or peripheral nervous systems (galgia) should function as the control centre of the animal, according to which it lives. But how does one keep faith in the brain when it comes down to the life of plants and the way they anticipate and sense their environment? Think of the chlamydomonas, flagellate green algae that actively 'look for' optimal photosynthetic growth. Chlamydomonas do not have eyes with sophisticated camera lenses, but they definitely make use of eye-like ways of sensing. Of course, they do this without 'interpreting' the data received in a brain.

In a recent online lecture entitled 'How Does the Mind Connect with the Body, Neurologically?',[6] neurobiologist Antonio Damasio (implicitly) commented on the issues raised above very elegantly by stating,

We have a brain for a very interesting reason. We have a brain because with a brain we can run the economy of the body in a better way. Throughout evolution you have organisms that are bodies without brains – and they do a pretty good job of running their economy and running their life.

Similar to contemporary thinkers like Shaun Gallagher,[7] Damasio's 'life' starts with the *actuality of the body* and not with the *necessity of a brain*. This new and exciting rise of a new science theory that Braidotti would call a 'matter-realism'[8] has enormous consequences for the nineteenth-century humanisms that dominate academia up to this day. This becomes clear especially when we turn Damasio's idea upside down. For by telling us that we humans have a brain since it benefits the economy of *our* bodies, he also tells us that other forms of (organic) life might function better without having a brain, without a central nervous system, even, that would control or unify the body. Life is capable of creating a brain, and thus it is also capable of not accomplishing those things of which it is capable. Starting from such a principle of contingency, thus, by no means ends up in instability but rather allows us to rethink, in this case the actuality of the body, from a much more liberal perspective. If we refuse to think of nature according to the Laws of Nature, which have been thought of by us human beings, and which keep stressing that complex structures – for instance – cannot be built (or 'thought of') by brainless cytoplasm, a radically different philosophy of life (also of human life) is bound to occur.

Damasio's actuality of the body finds its unity by means of feelings, affects and fears. They are bodily awarenesses that time and again cause the *contraction* which is the body, whether this concerns the human body, the body of the Cubozoa or of the chlamydomonas. To no surprise, Damasio thus refuses Cartesian dualist thinking as it has been so influential in fields like neurobiology and animal architecture, plainly referring to the mind–body problem as a mistake (see for instance Damasio, 2003). Turning to Descartes's contemporary Spinoza instead, for whom the mind is nothing but an idea of the body, Damasio allows us to think of the body not so much as 'that which is unified as one' (because of a central nervous system) but much more as 'that which feels as one'.

Damasio's interests go out to neurobiology, but especially the link he makes to Spinoza offers us ways to push this idea of the body as 'that which feels as one' much further. Deleuze already told us that Spinoza offered philosophy a new model: the body,[9] and it is from this model (from the body) that Spinoza allows us to ask key questions of life. Crucial for his model, though developed in the mid-seventeenth century, is on the one hand its fractal logic, which says that any individual is always an aggregate of individuals ad infinitum. On the other hand, the formal element, which Spinoza calls the *conatus*, defines the aggregate as a whole and consequently defines its effectiveness, its power to act. Spinoza himself would consider the conatus the essence of a thing, which is a definition we can only ascribe to if we agree on the fact that 'essence' with Spinoza was never about fixation or about a search for an a priori definition of a being. Essence, on the contrary, as it was developed by Seneca and Cicero, was the present participle of *esse* [to be]: *essens*. It conceptualized the being as an attribute of independency, of an actualization of lifeness as it makes the thing. In short, essence, or conatus, is an *ecology of form*. It searches to conceptualize how that which feels comes to be.

Coming back to Spinoza's conatus, it is vital to understand that it (conatus, but the same goes for essence, of course) has nothing to do with the necessity of the brain. In a famous letter (Letter LXII [LVII]) to G.H. Schaller dated October 1674, Spinoza explains that the conatus is at work *in every possible individual*. Discussing liberty and necessity, he gives us the example of the stone and immediately demystifies the whole idea of consciousness, as it is still so dominant in our days:

> [A] stone receives from the impulsion of an external cause, a certain quantity of motion, by virtue of which it continues to move after the impulsion given by the external cause has ceased. The permanence of the stone's motion is constrained, not necessary, because it must be defined by the impulsion of an external cause. What is true of the stone is true of any individual, however complicated its nature, or varied its functions, inasmuch as every individual thing is necessarily determined by some external cause to exist and operate in a fixed and determinate manner.
>
> Further conceive, I beg, that a stone, while continuing in motion, should be capable of thinking and knowing, that it is endeavouring, as far as it can, to continue to move. Such a stone, being conscious merely of its own endeavour and not at all indifferent, would believe itself to be completely free, and would think that it continued in motion solely because of its own wish. This is that human freedom, which all boast that they possess, and which consists solely in the fact, that men are conscious of their own desire, but are ignorant of the causes whereby that desire has been determined. Thus an infant believes that it desires milk freely.[10]

The conatus with Spinoza is thus not to be located *in* the body; it is what immanently *causes* the body (note that Spinoza keeps stressing [very ecologically] that the chain of causes is infinite [E1P28]), what turns it into one. It is closely linked to Damasio's 'feeling' as it causes a kind of unity or generality to occur. It is the transversal force that actualizes a physical and cognitive assemblage of things not so much in itself but in how *resonances* happen with its outside world. Resonances groove the earth as they form the individual. Resonances cause the Cobozoa's speed, build the *D. coronata*'s house and allow the chlamydomonas to see where they thrive best.

ANOTHER HUMANITY

The times have changed, meaning that in our times 'correlationism', as Meillassoux calls it,[11] has become the standard in academia; starting from the subject–object correlation, 'whatever can be' has been rephrased into 'whatever can be thinkable by us human beings', which is by all means the anthropocentrism dominating also the abovementioned debates. Very much written against these currents, Manuel DeLanda's geological history of life starts with concrete movements and the interplays of matter–energy through which morphogenesis happens. Not taking consciousness, linguistics or any other humanist systematics as its point of departure, rereading paleobiology in line with how Damasio and Conway Morris did this above, DeLanda radically rethinks the notion of life from the autopoietic systems that happen on the surface of the earth.

Interestingly enough, starting from the dynamics of riverbeds, from lava outbursts and thunderstorms, DeLanda leads us back to the human being, human society and, much more in general, to how human life (situated in the earthly currents) arises. But it is a kind of 'humanity' that we are not too familiar with. His non-anthropocentric view on the economy of the human body immediately tells us that the dynamics of life, and the consequences this has for how individual lives take shape, not so much intends to save subjectivity (by ending up with a new type of individuality, a new individual) but rather sets itself to mapping the material resonances by means of which individuality comes to be, or better even, by means of which the 'diffraction patterns', as Karen Barad calls them,[12] and which we refer to as individualities, arise from the material flows.

And thus, in search for a radically different ecological take on what humanity is all about, DeLanda notes that five hundred million years ago a sudden mineralization intruded the soft tissue or at least cooperated with it. The mineral world became part of life ever since as an integral part of its oneness, creating new forms of life previously unknown. A new life should not be reduced to the organic or the inorganic matters from which it came to be. For one, DeLanda notes, '[it] made new forms of movement control possible … freeing them from the constraints and literally setting them [individual living bodies] into motion to conquer every available niche in the air, in water and on land'.[13]

Of course, we should read the dwelling of the *D. coronata* as a similar means for the amoeba to enlarge its power, to increase its strength, its Health (with a capital H, as Nietzsche and later Deleuze talk about this), its oneness. This particular life, in the ongoing experiments of inclusion and exclusion, resonated a(n intricate) new form of movement possible in this particular alliance with the mineral world. The *D. coronata* just as well shows us that life is not locked up in a (thinking) organism but functions in its permeating of the organic and the inorganic (DeLanda himself deliberately uses the term 'nonorganic' in order to confuse the opposition,[14] creating all sorts of zones of intensity through which a oneness comes into being/feels as one [perhaps even well before DeLanda situates it]). If we claim that the *D. coronata* and its dwelling should not be thought of as an opposition (organic versus inorganic), a hierarchy (the organic rules the inorganic) and a correlationist dualism (the organic necessarily has to think the inorganic in order for the inorganic to be true), there is no reason to define extension in terms of us humans by a living organic body (a Subject) separate from that which surrounds it (an Object).

But DeLanda goes even further than this when showing that in many ways the processes of individualization that conclude into the human being are not too different from those that end up with the *D. coronata* since about eight thousand years ago 'human population began mineralizing again when they developed their urban *exoskeleton*'.[15] The mineralization of the earthly grooves can very well be read – with Damasio and perhaps even with Spinoza – as an *improvement* of our body, which means that the invention of sedentary life, similar to the invention of minerals inside us, is once again a quantum leap by means of which humanity hoped to run the economy of its bodies better. Urban tissue should not be considered an 'outside' separate from the organism but actually a folding outside again of the soft tissue and the endoskeleton with which it acts on *the same zone of intensity* (resonating with one another, thus individualizing with one another, similar to how the tissues and the endoskeleton pursued this before). The urban exoskeleton is then also by no means a McLuhanesque 'extension' of the body, which would bring us back again to the wrong kind of bodily essentialism; new series of individualities cause new forms of interference, new diffractions, that cause wholly other forms of life to come into being.

Architectural theorist Lars Spuybroek's abstract materialism (as he himself calls it) practices an ecology of design that wards off the modernist idealism that dominates not only animal architecture but architecture as a whole. Loos and Bauhaus, but also the postmodernist movement that still rules design today, all pledge allegiance to the abstract (Cartesian) line[16] and the white cube that it pushes forward: an idealist space that cannot be felt, that can only be thought. Spuybroek's emphasis on *sympathy* instead, which is a 'form of resonance, a co-movement',[17] or 'what things feel when they shape each other',[18] rewrites architectural history radically, not as a history of the Objects outside us, of the built environment for us to judge, but very much in line with DeLanda's neo-materialism, as a history of the reciprocity between different zones of intensity, of different lives, of different bodies as they form from the surfaces of the earth. '[S]ympathy revolves around a certain immediacy, not the neuroelectrical directness of sensation, however, but the more elastic immediacy of feeling'.[19]

Sympathy searches for a non-human 'aesthetic vitalism' that empowers the ecology of form (noting that his 'sympathy', in the nineteenth-century tradition of the word, is not yet psychologized). Spuybroek's study shows us that Gothic ornamentation *happens-in-matter*, that is, that the Gothic is never idealist (like the neo-gothic or modernist movement); even its two primary forces of the Gothic, being tesselation (from two to one dimension) and ribboning (from one to two dimensions), *make* its very particular spatiality. The resonances steer matter into J curves and S curves and arches and ornaments. That is why the Gothic, unlike idealist architectures, happens all around us, travels in many different unforeseen directions and can realize itself anytime, anyplace. To map vital Gothic energy is to realize the omnipresence of the 'curved gable'.[20] To study the Gothic is then not about analyzing individual dwellings but about mapping the resonance of disparates, as Spuybroek claims: 'It is not only a changefulness of columns, vaults, or traceries in themselves, but also one in which *columns transform into vaults into traceries*'.[21]

The Gothic is a force that traverses matter, causing diffraction patterns, and thus comes to be. It thus produces a Gothic body, a Gothic individual, so to speak, as a material aggregate that functions as one. The very particular resonations resulted in a beautiful zone of intensity that continues to liberate Europe (and the rest of the world) from its Roman regime and the Classicist ideals (including modernism) that followed from it. Gothic craftsmen and architects keep opening themselves up to this immanently new form of life. The Gothic played a crucial role in our history (giving form to it in many ways). It never ceases to haunt the Roman, Cartesian or Bauhausian lines that still organize urban life. The Gothic has always been at work at the margins of our built environment, and especially today, in the age of digital design, the Gothic proves to be more vital than ever before. Spuybroek's own designs are of course a wonderful example of how the Gothic creates the experiments in contemporary digital design (which makes him actually speak of 'the digital nature of the Gothic' [Spuybroek, 2011, chap. 1]). Think for instance of his Water Pavillion at Neeltje Jans in which the ceilings transform into the floor, into the door and into the ornament.

But why would we even limit the Gothic to the architectural? The dominant powers in art history might have made their efforts to capture its elasticity and its variation within the architectural realm, but Worringer already tells us that the Gothic is by no means limited to this particular form of expression. No longer directed towards the purely optical, 'the tactile once again assumes its pure activity'.[22] Gothic art, Worringer (and Deleuze) claim, realize 'a *nonorganic* vitality'.[23] When Deleuze then concludes that 'Neither form nor ground exist any longer ... it is a realism of deformation; and the strokes ... constitute ... zones of indiscernability in the line, insofar as it is common to different animals, to the human and the animal, and to pure abstraction (serpent, beard, ribbon)'.[24] What is left is the 'sensuous-super sensuousness', as Worringer puts it.[25] Pure feeling.

Consequently, its lively tentacles just as easily transform from the ceiling of the Thomaskirche in Leipzig into a Bach cantate. The heavenly circles of the church of *Santo Tome* in Toledo feel El Greco's *The Burial of the Count of Orgaz*. Deleuze and Guattari know that:

> Paul Virilio shows that after the Greek city-state, the Roman Empire imposes a geometrical or *linear reason of State* including a general outline of camps and fortifications, a universal art of 'marking boundaries by lines,' a laying-out of territories, a substitution of space for places and territorialities, and a transformation of the world into the city[26]

And isn't it the Gothic, par excellence, that disrupts these lines, that opens up linear reasoning *as a whole*? Aren't the Gothic tesselations and ribbonings offering us a wholly other terrestriality with their flat layers as well as their wholly other celestiality by continuously pulling up all possible lines high up into the sky?

THE ASCENT OF GOTHIC STONE

The naturalist complexity of the Gothic, the Barbaric as Ruskin (and Worringer) refers to it, is endless! The 'love of *fact*', as Ruskin calls it,[27] which is so central to the Gothic builder, and by means of which he wards off the Classicist or Roman teachers from whom he received the models and the designs, makes the Gothic builder create roundness instead of a circle and alignments instead of a straight line. Even the simplest Gothic lines, as Cimabue, for instance, drew them, find their way into infinity, composing fractellish surfaces to the *n*th dimension. His body of Christ, through the cross (the doubled Gothic line) make 'the fluctuations of the flesh become a play of dermic forces'.[28] Cimabue's cross is by no means a simple body. His cross is radically different from Spinoza's stone and the *D. coronata*. Such a simple body is largely determined by movement from the outside, while its conatus can only be 'the effort to preserve the state to which it has been determined'.[29] What characterizes the Gothic as an individual, as a body *and thus as a conatus*, is not simple at all. Its infinite variability makes it resonate in all directions. The Gothic, Spuybroek claims, is 'more radical than any other architectural style up to the present day'[30] *precisely because of its immanent variation.* Even a single line – the flexible rib – is both ornament and structure and easily turns into a fan fault, a colonnet, a chevet and rose window. When doubled (the cross) an entire ecology opens up.

In his grand book on Spinoza, Deleuze makes a distinction between a simple body's conatus and a composite body's conatus. What makes the Gothic by all means a highly composite body's conatus (especially when compared to a stone or to the *D. coronata*) is that, as Deleuze puts it, its conatus is 'the effort to preserve the relation of movement and rest that defines it, that is, to maintain constantly renewed parts in the relation that defines its existence'.[31] The conatus (or 'desire' as Deleuze translates it here, or 'spirit' as he conceptualizes it elsewhere[32]) of Spinoza's stone affirms its essence into existence. The Gothic stone, however, as it enters into new relations with other stones (of a building), with colours and sounds, realizes the Gothic, continues its existence *by recreating it*.[33] By resonating (movement and rest) with the other parts or disparates that make up the Gothic, the stone realizes infinite variability and complexity. *In its relations*, the Gothic stone immanently gives rise to an individuality, an abstract pattern, that exists in lived perception and that we call the Gothic.

Spuybroek's reappraisal of 'sympathy' already tells us that the Gothic not only consists of stones, of colours, of sounds and the like, but also of us. Sympathy thus reminds us of Whitehead's 'mutual prehensions'[34] as it offers us a way to conceptualize how particular bodies in their nexus (in their actualities and their virtualities) all *feel feelings* and are 'really together'[35] in the event *and* in the futures beyond themselves, in the resonations to come. This 'really togetherness' that makes up the event in which the Gothic stone *and* Gothic sound *and* Gothic humanity take place is what we call the Gothic. Whitehead's 'mutual prehensions' (note the prefix pre-), perhaps even more than Spuybroek's 'sympathy', happens 'with a language that speaks before words, with gestures which develop before organized bodies, with masks before faces, with specters and phantoms before characters'.[36] Gothic creativity happens before cognition, before language. The Gothic thus installs a collectivity that, with Simondon's words, in self-generating ways, desires 'action and emotion to be in resonance with each other'.[37]

The really together actions and emotions that make up the Gothic are its truly unique conatus. The stones, the sounds, the colours, the human flesh and bones, in their resonating togetherness, give rise to a zone of intensity of mutually prehended, unbound creativity. Then when Deleuze notes that 'Bach's ... music is an act of resistance, an active struggle against the separation of the profane and the sacred',[38] this is by all means the Gothic at work. The variability and changefulness that direct our actions and emotions when we feel or even prehend the tenderness in Bach's music (melody transforms into harmony transforms into dissonant transforms into counterpoint) refuse the Roman or Classist rule that cuts, the straight lines that organize, oppose and need to rule not only the built environment but everywhere. With its processes of variation, with the everchanging diffractions caused by the moving of matters and the spatialities thus realized, an *infinite* conatus or spirit is liberated. The rediscovery of the sacred is crucial to the Gothic spirit.

Deleuze's words tell us that Bach's music resonates a spirituality that has nothing to do with the Church as an institute (the true incarnation of the Roman Empire). Ruskin already ensured us that the Gothic did not so much happen in 'those glorious cathedrals', which, on the contrary, *corrupted* Gothic architecture. Ruskin fiercely argues,

> By the monk it was used as an instrument for the aid of his superstition; when that superstition became a beautiful madness, and the best hearts of Europe vainly dreamed and pinned in the cloister, and vainly raged and perished in the crusade – through that fury of perverted faith and wasted war, the Gothic rose also to its loveliest, most fantastic, and, finally, most foolish dreams; and, in those dreams, was lost.[39]

Bach also shows us that this Gothic spirituality has nothing to do with the highest of tones (although with Gothic compositions from Allegri's *Miserere* to Prince's *Purple Rain*, the heights definitely cause a general ascension). That deep spirituality which necessarily resonates with Bach's compositions cannot be pinned down anywhere. It happens in the Gothic *as a whole*, which keeps on installing this new spirituality, this unbound spirituality that is not transcendental but that happens in *all* the actions and emotions that make up its intensity. Thus the Gothic presents us a deeply religious anotherness that fills up a spatio-temporal continuum. This immanent conatus or spirit of the Gothic – these spiritual resonances that create the flattest of serpentine surfaces and the highest of nonorganic structures created by their pure material variation and elasticity – comes with a radically new 'God'.

This *another God* of the Gothic is then the morphogenetic real that we feel or sympathize with in Bach's music, in the Gothic stone, in Cimabue's cross, as well as in the resonances that fill up our body when included by it. Analyzing the already mentioned *Burial of the Count of Orgaz* by El Greco, Deleuze shows this Gothic God and its wholly other actions and emotions, noting that

> With God – but also with Christ, the Virgin, and even Hell – lines, colors and movements are freed from the demands of representation. The Figures are lifted up, or doubled over, or contorted, freed from all figuration. They no longer have anything to represent or narrate, since in this domain they are content to refer to the existing code of the Church. Thus, in themselves, they no longer have to do with anything but 'sensations' – celestial, infernal, or terrestrial sensations. Everything is made to pass through the code; the religious sentiment is painted in all the colors of the world. One must not say, 'If God does not exist, everything is permitted'. It is just the opposite. 'For with God, everything is permitted'.[40]

God, as produced by the Gothic, has the material variations discussed above as its object. It is the lived abstraction set free by the Gothic. It is no different from this object (as with any conatus, they are 'the same'). Its ideas are not limited (by its individuality) but are determined rather by its movements, by the resonances that pattern it. This time it is not the Roman Julius/Jesus, the God that *only* gives us Rules of Language and that Nietzsche and Klossowski (and Artaud) so much detested. The Gothic God is of a wholly other nature. Through architecture, the first of the arts, through the resonances between the clay, the lime and the flint, the ascent of the Gothic stone at the same time gives rise to this wholly other *creative* spirituality.

THE MANY LIVES OF STONES

'The simplest bodies are not absolutely simple and indivisible atoms, but are simple relative to the more composite bodies of which they are part'.[41] Thus stones can be taken up in the grotesque in the resonance of disparates that make up the Gothic, turning their bodies into its variable structures and their minds into its free spirituality. They can also be taken up in the infinitesimal, in the resonance of disparates that make up the *D. coronata*, communicating their motion into the dwelling with which we started. The stones and sands make up the bubble that houses the cytoplasm, which reaches out by means of *pseudopodia*, tentacle-like extensions that just as easily make contact with the inside of the house, thus bringing in organic and inorganic materials. The cytoplasm *feels* the tiniest of stones, sand grains and minerals into a unified core while dissolving its organic prey into the cytoplasm around it. During the process of bud fisson, this core becomes the outside of the daughter bud and forms a surface, a shell, an exoskeleton agglutinated with organic cement.

The house of the daughter does not often resemble the house of the mother. It is built from different stones (different sizes, different surfaces and different materials, of course) which the cytoplasm has to feel with the greatest care in order to create a new surface that suits it. And differences in degree turn into differences in kind. The aperture can have nine denticulate lobes (teeth); it can also have fifteen. Sometimes its dwelling is merely a tube; sometimes it has as much as twenty conical spines. They differ in length, thickness, size and curving; they can end in a (relatively) large chrystal. Ruskin could have referred to this feeling of the earth as 'savageness', a primitiveness that is imperfect, that continues to make mistakes and, thus, that lives. The variability, the primitiveness and the earthliness make the *D. coronata* a small but very complex form that might not have a brain but that in no way prevents it from having complex ideas.

NOTES

1. Mike Hansell, *Built by Animals: The Natural History of Animal Architecture* (New York: Oxford University Press, 2009), 58.

2. When I claim that the brain is still considered the cause of our actions, this includes the recent shift in brain science which questions the idea that the brain stores all the information which it makes use of to the idea that the brain can also store not so much the information itself but rather where it can be found (B. Sparrow, J. Liu and D.M. Wegner, 'Google Effects on Memory: Cognitive Consequences of Having Information at Our Fingertips', *Science,* 333 [2011], 776–778). Though this is by all means a major revolution in the field, it still considers the brain (though necessarily dependent on what lies outside of it) to be the cause of our actions, which I disagree with (see also Massumi, *Parables for the Virtual: Movement, Affect, Sensation* [Durham and London: Duke University Press, 2002]).

3. Dan-E. Nilsson, Lars Gislén, Melissa M. Coates, Charlotta Skogh and Anders Garm, 'Advanced Optics in a Jellyfish Eye', *Nature* (12 May 2005), 202.

4. Simon Conway Morris, *Life's Solution: Inevitable Humans in a Lonely Universe* (Cambridge: Cambridge University Press, 2003), 377.

5. Nilsson et al. 'Advanced Optics in a Jellyfish Eye'.

6. Antonio Damasio, 'How Does the Mind Connect with the Body, Neurologically?' accessed 25 June 2012, http://bigthink.com/ideas/23023.

7. Shaun Gallagher, *How the Body Shapes the Mind* (Oxford: Clarendon Press, 2005).

8. Rosi Braidotti, *The Posthuman* (Cambridge, MA: Polity Press), 158.

9. Gilles Deleuze, *Spinoza: Practical Philosophy.* Trans. Robert Hurley (San Francisco: City Lights), 17.

10. Benedict Spinoza, *The Letters.* Trans. Samuel Shirley (Indianapolis and Cambridge: Hackett), 390.

11. Quentin Meillasoux, *After Finitude: An Essay on the Necessity of Contingency.* Trans. Ray Brassier (New York: Continuum, 2008).

12. Karen Barad, *Meeting the Universe Halfway: Quantum Physics and the Entanglement of Matter and Meaning* (Durham and London: Duke University Press, 2007).

13. Manuel DeLanda, *A Thousand Years of Nonlinear History* (New York: Swerve Editions, 2000), 26–27.

14. Manuel DeLanda, 'Nonorganic Life', in *Incorporations*, Eds. Jonathan Crary and Sanford Kwinter (New York: Zone, 1992), 129–167.

15. DeLanda, *A Thousand Years of Nonlinear History*, 27.

16. Claudia Brodsky Lacour, *Lines of Thought: Discourse, Architectonics and the Origin of Modern Philosophy* (Durham and London: Duke University Press, 1996).

17. Lars Spuybroek, *The Sympathy of Things: Ruskin and the Ecology of Design* (Rotterdam: NAI, 2011), 134.

18. Spuybroek, *The Sympathy of Things,* 9.

19. Spuybroek, *The Sympathy of Things,* 146.

20. John Ruskin, *On the Nature of Gothic Architecture: and Herein of the True Functions of the Workman in Art* (London: Smith, Elder, 1854), 38.

21. Spuybroek, *The Sympathy of Things,* 25.

22. Deleuze, *Francis Bacon: The Logic of Sensation*. Trans. Daniel W. Smith (London and New York: Continuum, 2004), 129.

23. Deleuze, *Francis Bacon*, 129.

24. Deleuze, *Francis Bacon*, 130.

25. Wilhelm Worringer, *Form in Gothic,* Ed. Herbert Read (New York: Schocken, 1964), 158–159.

26. Gilles Deleuze and Félix Guattari, *A Thousand Plateaus: Capitalism and Schizophrenia,* Trans. Brian Massumi (Minneapolis and London: University of Minnesota Press, 1987), 212.

27. John Ruskin, *The Genius of John Ruskin: Selections from His Writings,* Ed. John D. Rosenberg (London and New York: Routledge, 1963), 192.

28. Bernard Cache, *Earth Moves, the Furnishing of Territories.* Trans. Anne Boyman, Ed. Michael Speaks (Cambridge and London: The MIT Press, 1995), 75.

29. Deleuze, *Expressionism in Philosophy: Spinoza.* (New York: Zone Books, 2011), 230.

30. Spuybroek, *The Sympathy of Things,* 26.

31. Deleuze, *The Logic of Sense.* Trans. Mark Lester with Charles Stivale, Ed. Constantin V. Boundas (New York: The Athlone Press, 1990), 230.

32. Deleuze, *Francis Bacon.*

33. This means that the conatus of composite bodies is necessarily creative. Its continuation depends upon the creation of new forms in the Earth. Contrary to Shaviro (*Without Criteria: Kant, Whitehead, Deleuze, and Aesthetics* [Cambridge, MA, and London: The MIT Press], 22), the whole argument constructed here shows that there is no difference between Spinoza's conatus and how Whitehead's 'creative advance', Bergson's 'continuous change' and Simondon's 'processes of individuation' conceptualize material formations.

34. Alfred North Whitehead, *Process and Reality* (New York: The Free Press, 1978), 194.

35. Whitehead, *Process and Reality,* 230.

36. Deleuze, *Difference and Repetition.* Trans. Paul Patton (New York: Columbia University Press, 1994), 10.

37. Gilbert Simondon, *L'individuation psychique et collective* (Paris: Aubier, 1992), 108.

38. Deleuze, *Two Regimes of Madness: Texts and Interviews 1975–1995* (Cambridge, MA and London: Semiotext(e), 2006), 323–324.

39. Ruskin, *The Genius of John Ruskin,* 61.

40. Deleuze, *Francis Bacon,* 9–10.

41. Pauline Phemister, *The Rationalists: Descartes, Spinoza and Leibniz* (Cambridge and Malden: Polity Press, 2006), 129.

BIBLIOGRAPHY

Barad, Karen. *Meeting the Universe Halfway: Quantum Physics and the Entanglement of Matter and Meaning.* Durham and London: Duke University Press, 2007.

Braidotti, Rosi. *The Posthuman.* Cambridge, MA: Polity Press, 2013.

Brodsky Lacour, Claudia. *Lines of Thought: Discourse, Architectonics and the Origin of Modern Philosophy.* Durham and London: Duke University Press, 1996.

Cache, Bernhard. *Earth Moves, the Furnishing of Territories.* Translated by Anne Boyman, edited by Michael Speaks. Cambridge and London: The MIT Press, 1995.

Conway Morris, Simon. *Life's Solution: Inevitable Humans in a Lonely Universe.* Cambridge: Cambridge University Press, 2003.

Damasio, Antonio. *Looking for Spinoza: Joy, Sorrow and the Feeling Brain.* London: William Heinemann, 2003.

———. 'How Does the Mind Connect with the Body, Neurologically?' BigThink.com, accessed 25 June 2012, http://bigthink.com/ideas/23023.

DeLanda, Manuel. 'Nonorganic Life'. In *Incorporations.* Edited by Jonathan Crary and Sanford Kwinter, 129–167. New York: Zone Books, 1992.

———. *A Thousand Years of Nonlinear History.* New York: Swerve Editions, 2000.

Deleuze, Gilles. *Spinoza: Practical Philosophy.* Translated by Robert Hurley. San Francisco: City Lights, 1988.

———. *Cinema 2: The Time Image.* Translated by Hugh Tomlinson. Minneapolis: University of Minnesota Press, 1989.

———. *The Logic of Sense.* Translated by Mark Lester with Charles Stivale, edited by Constantin V. Boundas. New York: The Athlone Press, 1990.

———. *Expressionism in Philosophy: Spinoza.* Translated by Martin Joughin. New York: Zone Books, 1992.

———. *The Fold: Leibniz and the Baroque.* Translated by Tom Conley. Minneapolis: University of Minnesota Press, 1993.

———. *Difference and Repetition.* Translated by Paul Patton. New York: Columbia University Press, 1994.

———. *Francis Bacon: The Logic of Sensation.* Translated by Daniel W. Smith. London and New York: Continuum, 2004.

———. *Two Regimes of Madness: Texts and Interviews 1975–1995.* Cambridge, MA and London: Semiotext(e), 2006.

Deleuze, Gilles and Félix Guattari. *A Thousand Plateaus: Capitalism and Schizophrenia.* Translated by Brian Massumi. Minneapolis and London: University of Minnesota Press, 1987.

———. *What is Philosophy?* Translated by Hugh Tomlinson and Graham Burchell. London and New York: Verso, 1994.

Gallagher, Shaun. *How the Body Shapes the Mind.* Oxford: Clarendon Press, 2005.

Gibson, James Jerome. *The Ecological Approach to Visual Perception.* New Jersey: Lawrence Erlbaum Associates, 1986.

Hansell, Mike. *Built by Animals: The Natural History of Animal Architecture.* New York: Oxford University Press, 2009.

Lyotard, Jean-François. *The Inhuman: Reflections on Time.* Translated by Geoffrey Bennington and Rachel Bowlby. Stanford: Stanford University Press, 1991.

Massumi, Brian. *Parables for the Virtual: Movement, Affect, Sensation.* Durham and London: Duke University Press, 2002.

Meillassoux, Quentin. *After Finitude: An Essay on the Necessity of Contingency.* Translated by Ray Brassier. New York: Continuum, 2008.

Nilsson, Dan-E., Lars Gislén, Melissa M. Coates, Charlotta Skogh and Anders Garm. 'Advanced Optics in a Jellyfish Eye', *Nature* (12 May 2005): 201–205.
Phemister, Pauline. *The Rationalists: Descartes, Spinoza and Leibniz.* Cambridge and Malden: Polity Press, 2006.
Ruskin, John. *On the Nature of Gothic Architecture: and Herein of the True Functions of the Workman in Art.* London: Smith, Elder, 1854.
———. *The Two Paths: being Lectures on Art and Its Application to Decoration and Manufacture.* New York: John Wiley & Sons, 1869.
———. *The Genius of John Ruskin: Selections from His Writings*. Edited by John D. Rosenberg. London and New York: Routledge, 1963.
Shaviro, Steven. *Without Criteria: Kant, Whitehead, Deleuze and Aesthetics.* Cambridge, MA and London: The MIT Press, 2009.
Simondon, Gilbert. *L'individuation psychique et collective.* Paris: Aubier, 1992.
Sparrow, B., J. Liu and D.M. Wegner. 'Google Effects on Memory: Cognitive Consequences of Having Information at Our Fingertips', *Science,* 333 (2011): 776–778. Page numbers quoted from online publication in *Science Express*, www.sciencexpress.org, published 14 July 2011, last accessed 10 October 2011.
Spinoza, Benedict. *Ethics.* Translated by W.H. White. Revised by A.H. Stirling. Ware, Hertfordshire: Wordsworth, 2001.
———. *The Letters.* Translated by Samuel Shirley. Indianapolis and Cambridge: Hackett, 1995.
Spuybroek, Lars. *The Sympathy of Things: Ruskin and the Ecology of Design.* Rotterdam: NAI, 2011.
Wehner, Rüdiger. 'Sensory Physiology: Brainless Eyes', *Nature* (12 May 2005): 157–159.
Whitehead, Alfred North. *Process and Reality.* New York: The Free Press, 1978.
Worringer, Wilhelm. *Form in Gothic*. Edited by Herbert Read. New York: Schocken, 1964.

Part II

AFTER MACHINES

Chapter Six

Media Entangled Phenomenology
Mark B. N. Hansen

ALL MEDIA ARE MEASURING MEDIA

In a crucial passage from his recent essay, 'Experimenting with Media Temporality', German media archaeologist Wolfgang Ernst weaves together all of the ingredients necessary to develop a *physical* approach to the medium:

> So let us investigate the processuality and event nature of media-enhanced experimentation. One level of temporality is the microtemporal behavior of the object in question (that is, 'under experiment'); the second is what it does to (or with) the 'temporal sense' of the human experimenter ... such experimental settings clearly belong to what we call and describe as cultural history (or the 'history of knowledge', in more Latourean terms), but on the other hand (from the point of view of the media themselves, and hence the media-archaeological perspective), there is something *at work* (at the level of both the artifact and the epistemological *dispositif*) that is indifferent to the historical. This I call the 'time-invariant event'. 'Experiment as event' can be reformulated as 'experiencing the event'. The media-archaeological view considers the question of how media temporality, and especially its proper temporal figure of time-critical and microtemporal processes, is experienced through the experiment. In contrast to empirical experience of the observation of primary nature, media-experimental settings perform 'culturalized' experiences of a secondary nature – with measuring media the crucial observers. A media-experimental setting is an artificial configuration based on cultural knowledge – but it is still of a physical nature because there are electro- or even quantum-physical laws at work that are not solely dependent on the respective cultural discourse. The media-experimental event cannot be reduced to discursive effects. There is always the imminent 'veto' that comes from physics.[1]

In this long but crucial passage, Ernst combines a view of medium as a measuring instrument with what he calls a time-critical approach to media, meaning an approach that foregrounds not simply the composition of media operations from time but also the requirement that digital signal processing occur within strict time windows. At the same time, Ernst engages media's specific vocation to mediate between the cultural and the physical, which is equally to say between the macrorealm of experience and the microrealm of quantum processes.

Let me begin my discussion of the physicality of the medium by affirming these commitments of Ernst's: to medium as measurement, to media as time-critical and to time-critical media measurement as the performative hinge linking micro- and macroworlds. As I shall develop them, these commitments are absolutely crucial for understanding the full extent of media's operationality in our world today and, specifically, for appreciating how the medium, that is, the time-critical measuring medium, forms an unavoidable third term – what I have long thought of as a principle of indirection – in the circuit linking human experience and the world.

MEDIUM AS MEASUREMENT

By qualifying media as measuring media, Ernst seeks to divorce media from their cultural and historical overdetermination. His aim in doing so is to liberate the operationality of media from the constraints that human-focused, cultural framings impose on it. A case in point is the archaeology of the acoustic, where human auditory sense, as Ernst diplomatically puts it, just 'does not suffice'. To explore the operation of the sonic beyond the acoustic spectrum of humans, or for that matter, beyond any other delimited acoustic spectrum, we must, Ernst suggests, fully surrender our agency to the agency of the machine: '[T]he real archaeologists in media archaeology', writes Ernst, 'are the media themselves – not mass media, but measuring media that are able to decipher physically real signals technoanalogically'.[2] Media are the 'real archaeologists' for Ernst precisely because they work directly on physical signals prior to their conversion into phenomenologically accessible forms, this work being the very mediation necessary to bring the physical into the domain of experience. With this, we grasp the specificity of Ernst's conception of media archaeology in its full resonance: Rather than focusing on the long history of media devices, as do Erkki Huhtamo and Siegfried Zielinski, certainly two of the most prominent contemporary figures in the discipline of media archaeology, Ernst concentrates his critical gaze on the actual operations of concrete media independently of their cultural functioning. For him, archaeology means the excavation of the affordances of media themselves, prior to any consideration of, and without any reference whatsoever to, their role as agents of cultural life.

Ernst's sustained commitment to this restricted understanding of archaeology – archaeology as excavation of media affordances in themselves – makes common cause with work in science studies and the history of science focused on the role of experiment. In concert with such scholars of science, Ernst insists that physical phenomena like the propagation of ultrafast electromagnetic waves are not invented but discovered and, crucially, are discovered less through the extra-acute vision of the scientist than the superior wisdom of media themselves. When humans set up experiments to tap this superior wisdom of media, they are in effect simply staging the operation of the machine and allowing it to bring to bear its agency on some aspect of the physical world, thereby forging contact between the physical and the experiential domain of cultural life. Noting that 'in the dispositive of human-made experiments media *themselves* have the best media knowledge' ('haben Medien *selbst* das bessere Medienwissen'), Ernst turns to Gaston Bachelard's 'phenomenotechnique' in order to discover a concept capable of grasping the particular positivity of media operationality at issue here. Phenomenotechnique, to cite Bachelard's own elucidating description, 'intensifies that which shines through behind appearance'.[3] That is, phenomenotechnique addresses the *noumenon* behind the phenomenon, though (as we shall see below) less as an unknowable Kantian thing-in-itself than as a fuller grasp – dare I say prehension – of the physical reality addressed by the experimental set-up.

MEDIA TIME-CRITICALITY

By time-criticality, Ernst means something broadly akin to what Husserl meant by time-constituting, as in time-constituting consciousness (or time-consciousness), only with a scope that vastly exceeds the operations of any imaginable consciousness, human or otherwise. Time-criticality thus refers to the time-constituting power of media, a power which – from the study of electricity and electromagnetism onwards – has been exercised predominately at microtemporal scales vastly exceeding the perceptual grasp of human consciousness. In keeping with the specificity of his archaeological practice, Ernst distinguishes time-critical media from 'time-based media', that is, media constituted out of and by time itself. 'Time-critical', Ernst explains, 'does not simply mean that media operations are time-based'. Rather, time-criticality requires that 'the media operations under the condition of digital signal processing must be processed through rigidly determined time windows, in order to work and thereby to bring a message into being in the first place'.[4] Time-criticality would thus designate what, from a Kantian and even from a Deleuzian perspective, we could refer to as a transcendental or transcendental-sensible structure: The operations of time-critical media produce the medium of experience (time and space for Kant, the real conditions of sensibility for Deleuze) and thus form the condition of possibility for experience as such. I use the expression 'would designate' expressly, to mark a certain distance between Ernst's operational account of time-critical processes and any transcendental structure that, like both Kant's and Deleuze's, necessarily takes human experience as its reference point. Ernst's account locates the operations of time-critical media in relation to the physical eventality of the world in and for itself: Media operate directly on the physical, and only subsequently, which is to say, through this very operation, they produce structures that facilitate experience as such, and human experience in particular.

With this point, we can appreciate how Ernst's agenda in his recent study *Chronopoietik* expands upon his earlier reading of media as measuring instruments in the essays cited above. Moving beyond his polemical stance vis à vis history – his career-instigating effort to contrast media givenness via counting against historical narration of all sorts – Ernst turns his attention to the properly ontological dimension of his program: how measuring media constitute time as a medium for experience. As its subtitle – *Zeitweisen und Zeitgaben technischer Medien* (*Temporal Modes and Givens of Technical Media*) – makes clear, Ernst's aim is to excavate the deep affinity between technical (or measuring) media and the medium of time, which is to say, how time's periodicities and givennesses constitute a general medium for experience. Thus, media's operation does not so much seek to isolate time as the target of measurement (as does Aristotle's physical conception of time as the number of movement) so much as it aims to constitute, out of the measuring of time, a medium. Ernst states this quite matter-of-factly: 'Time as the measured value of a movement is here not the goal of measurement, but rather itself a medium'.[5]

Ernst's account of time-critically generated time as general medium involves two fundamental commitments – to implementation and to finitude – that serve to differentiate his approach on the one hand from theoretical invocations of mathematics in the wake of Badiou and on the other from accounts of digital materiality in terms of cultural operations. The fundamental law of Ernst's time-critical media philosophy, if we can speak in these terms, is that mathematics must always be implemented in a physical materiality because every operation of information switching consumes a minimal time interval, 'In-der-Welt-Sein heißt In-der-Zeit-Sein' (Being-in-the-world means Being-in-time). Heidegger's Being-in-the-world is to be understood as and through Ernst's 'Being-in-time',[6] meaning that the technological conditions for being-in-time also condition the experience of being-in-the-world.

This helps to explain why mathematics for Ernst is always and necessarily technomathematics: mathematics implemented through a physical realization, mathematics as phenomenotechnique. And it also explains why technomathematics – that is, measuring media – always operate in the realm of, and can only generate, finite processes.

One could explore the affinity of Ernst's technomathematical insistence on implementation in a physical substrate with recent deployments of mathematical topos theory as a resource for conceptualizing contemporary topological media along lines that diverge fundamentally from Badiou's own deployment of topos theory in *Logic of Worlds*. At the core of such exploration would be the question of the 'intrinsic ontology' that Badiou, despite his own stated intentions, imports from *Being and Event* into its sequel.[7] As Arkady Plotnitsky has pointed out, Badiou turns to topos theory solely to provide a logic for his set theoretical ontology. In no way does Badiou fundamentally rethink his intrinsic ontology or his commitment to 'forcing' as the process whereby the inconsistent multiplicity can generate a break with that which is and thereby produce the new.[8] His overriding aim is, rather, to introduce a concrete site for the happening of the event. As a result, Badiou's deployment of topos theory to supplement his set-theoretical ontology simply neglects the ontological dimension of topos theory as it was developed by Alexandre Grothendieck, a dimension which positions topos theory as a vehicle for ontological enrichment. 'In Grothendieck's hands', Plotnitsky insists, the impoverished concept of relation-in-general 'serves the ontological task of an enrichment of objects of certain categories. Any given object, even a point, becomes multiple, endowed with a multiplicity, because it is defined by arrows, morphisms that link this point to other objects'.[9] What accounts for the richness of this procedure of ontological experimentation is precisely the concrete heterogeneity of the potential relations that not only stands opposed to the purity of Badiou's formalism but also motivates the subordination of the mathematical to the sociological.[10] On this score, it could be shown that the 'sociological infinite' differs fundamentally from Badiou's mathematical infinite precisely because it finds infinity not in the formal non-totalizability of set theory but in the potentiality of concrete relationality where the units at issue are not ordinal numbers and cardinal multitudes but extra-mathematical relational nexuses that are generated through onto-topological experimentation.[11] Developing such a sociological infinite of relational potentiality, which would involve the displacement of the Cantorian continuum by Charles Sanders Peirce's topological continuum, must however remain a task for another time.[12]

For my purposes, the key point is that commitment to implementation in a physical substrate yields a dynamic understanding of the operation of digitization. Contrasting it with sampling as a cultural-aesthetic activity, Ernst links digitization with the sampling of the physical itself, what he calls 'sampling in the technical sense'. Such technical sampling is performative in the sense that it does not sample from a pre-existent and standing time but from the physical processes that are, as it were, underneath time. Its actual operation transforms these physical processes into time, which henceforth cannot exist outside of media operationality, that is, outside the concrete technomathematical operations that materialize time as always and necessarily finite. 'Digitization', explains Ernst,

> is an act of measuring that reacts flexibly to the temporality (frequency) of the signal. World is not thereby submitted to the temporality of enduring and abstract standardized clock pulses; rather technically pulsed time as a function of numerical measurement conforms to the frequency of the signal, and thus to the worldliness of physics itself.[13]

That such flexible measurement necessarily takes place as a compromise between two distinct physical indices – temporal period and signal frequency – only serves to reinforce the onto-performative power of time-critical measuring media. Insofar as they measure 'the rhythm of burst sequences of microtemporal sampling periods', time-critical media operate in the space of indeterminacy between time and frequency. Identified in 1946 by Nobel Prize–winning engineer Dennis Gabor as a mathematically precise extension of quantum-physical indeterminacy, this indeterminacy of time and frequency ultimately explains why media cannot be understood as measuring an externally located and pre-existent time, as all cultural-aesthetic accounts of time-based media would have it. Rather, in the very act of deciding on a correlation of period and frequency, which is precisely what occurs through measurement, measuring media literally produce time-critical phenomena.

Expanding on Gabor, who focused on the domain of sound, Ernst installs quantum-physical indeterminacy at the very core of all time-critical mediations: insofar as it is produced by time-critical measurements, Ernst explains,

> [T]he parameter of time ultimately tips over into quantum physically demonstrated indeterminacy. The smaller the unit of measurement and the higher the exactness with which it is to be measured, the longer the required time of measurement. No time-point, no really extensionless moment can thus be measured. Digital units of measure are never parts of a standing time, but are rather much more time-variable, because every measurement is based on a minimum interval Δt and can in this framework only ever discretely process a finite manifold of information.[14]

The ultimate consequence of this conclusion – namely that there is no real state of affairs prior to the time-critical act of measurement – will prove decisive for how we understand the operational ontology of media in our world today.

TIME-CRITICAL MEDIA MEASUREMENT AS THE PERFORMATIVE HINGE LINKING MICRO- AND MACROWORLDS

Early in his introduction to *Chronopoietik* and by way of what can only be a rhetorical question, Ernst links the determination of time-criticality to the operation of quantum leaps from the microworld of quantum particles to the macroworld of experience. Could it be the case, he wonders, that the 'macrotime of media history relates to the microtime of time-critical processes' in the same way that 'the intact world of classical physics [relates] to the microworld of quantum physics?'[15] This question – and the homology it proposes – allows us to grasp the fundamental time-criticality of the quantum dissolution of physical time, as Ernst himself makes explicit:

> The question concerning the disappearance of discrete time (the *incidental time* of physics) in the quantum mechanical indeterminacy relation is in actual fact time-critical.[16] When particles disappear, with them also disappears the timepoint [Zeitpunkt], and hence the point-oriented concept of the event. Here, media science in the narrow sense comes into play – media science, that is, that does not just deal with mathematical questions, but also with the actual implementation, and thus the temporalization, of mathematics in physical materiality.[17]

With this, the logic of Ernst's argument is laid bare: Quantum mechanics – which is to say, the resolution of quantum indeterminacy – is time-critical because it coincides with, and indeed is simply identical to, the actual implementation of the quantum leap in a material substrate.

HYPEROBJECTS AND HYPEROBFUSCATION

> Quantum theory specifies that quanta withdraw from one another, including the quanta with which we measure them. In other words, quanta really are discrete, and one mark of this discreteness is the constant translation or mistranslation of one quantum by another. Thus, when you set up quanta to measure the position of a quantum, its momentum withdraws, and vice versa. Heisenberg's uncertainty principle states that when an

'observer' – not a subject per se, but a measuring device involving photons or electrons (or whatever) – makes an observation, at least one aspect of the observed is occluded. Observation is as much part of the universe of objects as the observable, not some ontologically different state (say of a subject). More generally, what Bohr called complementarity ensures that no quantum has total access to any other quantum. Just as a focusing lens makes one object appear sharper while others appear blurrier, one quantum variable comes into sharp definition at the expense of others. This isn't about how a human knows an object, but how a photon interacts with a photosensitive molecule. Some phenomena are irreducibly undecidable, both wavelike and particle-like. The way an electron encounters the nucleus of an atom involves a dark side. Objects withdraw from each other at a profound physical level. OOO [Object-Oriented-Ontology] is deeply congruent with the most profound, accurate, and testable theory of physical reality available. Actually it would be better to say it the other way around: *quantum theory works because it's object-oriented*.[18]

Its technical language and level of complexity notwithstanding, this statement is not authored by a quantum physicist but by one of the more prominent adherents of a recent philosophical movement, Object-Oriented Ontology (OOO). The statement comes from the chapter on 'Nonlocality' from Timothy Morton's recent book, *Hyperobjects: Philosophy and Ecology after the End of the World*, and forms part of a larger argument for an ecological account of OOO, whose fundamental concept is the 'hyperobject'. Hyperobjects, in Morton's definition, are 'things that are massively distributed in time and space relative to humans'.[19] Examples of hyperobjects include a black hole, the Lago Agrio oil field in Ecuador or the Everglades; the biosphere, the Solar system, the sum total of all nuclear material on earth or just the plutonium or the uranium; the very long-lasting product of direct human manufacture, such as styrofoam or plastic bags, or the sum of the whirring machinery of capitalism. What makes all of these examples hyperobjects is their status as 'hyper' in relation to some other entity, regardless of whether they are directly manufactured by humans or not.

For the purposes of Morton's ecological take on OOO, two hyperobjects in particular stand out: quantum mechanics and global warming. Both are 'massively distributed in time and space relative to humans', one in the direction of the very small, the other in the direction of the very large. Morton goes so far as to ascribe the impetus behind the concept of the hyperobject to these two examples: 'For sure, the idea of hyperobjects arose because of quantum-theoretical thinking about the nuclei of atoms and electron orbits (nuclear bombs), and because of systems-theoretical approaches to emergent properties of massive amounts of weather data'.[20] What makes these two complementary hyperobjects exemplary and special is the clarity with which they illustrate what will turn out to be the crucial characteristic of hyperobjects: the fact that they 'occupy a high-dimensional phase space that results in their being invisible to humans for stretches of time'.[21] According to Morton, what makes hyperobjects like quantum mechanics and global warming difficult to conceptualize – and indeed, for many, difficult to accept as real – is the fact that they occur in a dimension that is oblique in relation to the everyday world of phenomenal experience. We simply lack any direct means of access to their eventality, which occurs on a scale that exceeds our correlational grasp.

Morton deploys OOO to address this problem. As formulated by Graham Harman, and as taken on board by Morton, OOO postulates that objects are infinitely withdrawn in relation to everything, including themselves. Objects do not enter into causal interrelations and indeed do not, properly speaking, have relations at all; rather, they generate sensible appearances that serve as traces of sorts of their ontological power. In his formulation of the concept of the hyperobject, Morton draws, in particular, on Harman's account of causality as vicarious causality; in the wake of Humean scepticism and Kant's institution of a 'Rift' between thing and appearance,[22] causality no longer concerns objects themselves but rather their appearances. For this reason, Morton dubs causality 'aesthetic', meaning that it is an affair of relations among phenomena, a 'feature of phenomena, rather than things in themselves'.[23] Contextualized against this philosophical backdrop, hyperobjects attain a certain specificity: They are a special kind of object, a particularly visible object that, as Morton puts it, 'force something on us, something that affects some core ideas of what it means to exist, what Earth is, what society is'.[24] Put another, perhaps simpler, way, hyperobjects are objects that compel us to face the 'truth' about objects, namely that they are 'real things whose core reality is withdrawn from access, even by themselves'.[25]

Let us attend more closely to Morton's claim that quantum mechanics has made the withdrawal of the object into an irrepressible reality. The plausibility of this claim stands or falls with the realist interpretation of quantum mechanics that Morton, drawing extensively on David Bohm's account of the Einstein–Podolsky–Rosen theory, simply ratifies as true. At the heart of Morton's account is a conviction that there is such a thing as a quantum entity, that actual photons exist prior to the act of measurement which, on Niels Bohr's account, is responsible for bringing them into existence.

This, indeed, is the deeper truth behind Morton's association of quantum mechanics and OOO: Specifically, when he asserts that 'quantum theory works because it's object-oriented',[26] or, even more consequentially, that quantum theory is a 'valid physical theor[y] to the extent that [it is] object-oriented',[27] he stakes his claims on the validity of the realist interpretation of quantum mechanics, which is to say, on the idea that quantum entities are real in their 'entangled' or 'coherent' states, that is, independently of the act of measurement that resolves quantum indeterminacy. Morton is, or would be, right – right about quantum theory being object-oriented and right that object orientation would provide the ontology for quantum reality – if (and this is a big if) quantum entities were indeed real. Put another way, the reality of quantum entities would make quantum theory a 'valid physical theory', where valid means nothing other than realist, and it would indeed call for an ontology capable of explaining the absolute withdrawal of quantum objects.

Nathan Brown has pointed out that Morton makes no effort to justify his ratification of Bohm's extension of the Einstein–Podolsky–Rosen theory (henceforth EPR) and indeed doesn't even seem to be cognizant that it remains a highly contested theory.[28] This fact should alert us to the more general sleight of hand operating at the core of Morton's argument for the hyperobject: Behind the claim that OOO is the truth of quantum mechanics is a more basic argument, that OOO simply is the truth. In the place of a philosophical argument for the validity of Bohm's realism, Morton offers nothing more than a restatement of the logic of entailment imposed by OOO: Quantum theory is a 'valid physical theor[y]', to repeat some lines just cited, 'to the extent that [it is] object-oriented'.[29] The result is a circular logic that smacks of dogmatism: It is the unquestionable existence of absolutely withdrawn objects – the first principle of OOO – that requires quantum theory to be a realist theory, but this unquestionable existence is at the same time the most powerful argument for why quantum theory is a realist theory. Philosophical logic, as Brown's critique implies and as Morton's repeated belittling of scientists attests, simply trumps science in a way that makes scientific argumentation moot.[30]

Beyond its contribution to ratifying the grandiose ambition of OOO, the aim of Morton's engagement with quantum mechanics is to generalize quantum non-locality such that it, transformed into a core property of hyperobjects, would apply to *all* of reality. Non-locality in this expanded frame is nothing more than a synonym for aesthetic causality: Just as entangled particles enjoy non-local interrelations prior to their disentanglement or decoherence through measurement, so, too, do the particular appearances comprising the aesthetic domain participate in the operationality of a hyperobject whose contours are radically withdrawn from their vantage point. The point, to say it another way, is that the particular aesthetic appearances of, say, global warming – rain in Northern California, the Japan earthquake of 2011, the tsunami churning up La Nina in the Pacific, etcetera – are correlated unknowingly with one another simply in virtue of their belonging to – of their happening within – the hyperobject of global warming.

Once again, however, the logic is circular and points to an underlying dogmatic commitment on Morton's part. For the homology at issue here to work, it has to be the case that the hyperobject is real and that it is real independently of the activity of the particular appearances that unknowingly and partially instantiate it; this in turn means that the non-local situation prior to decoherence or disentanglement, or in other words, prior to measurement, would have to be real. Nothing more nor less is at stake in designating quantum mechanics a hyperobject: On this description, to say it as simply and straightforwardly as possible, quantum non-locality *has to be a real object that is infinitely withdrawn even from itself*. Once again, we are dealing with a situation in which the cart is driving the horse, since it is only the dogmatic imposition of the logic of OOO that justifies the claim for the reality of the non-local.

If Morton's qualifications, and indeed his unequivocal backing-away in *Realist Magic* from the strong reading of quantum reality offered in *Hyperobjects*, suggest that the realist reading of quantum mechanics is unsustainable, it immediately returns us to that crucial element of quantum theory – the measurement problem – that the emphasis on realism allowed Morton largely to bypass. More precisely, we can now clearly discern how Morton's realist reading of quantum non-locality – his postulation that 'something definitely exists before measurement'[31] – aims to access quantum reality 'as it is in itself', which is to say, prior to the collapse of its coherence, superposition or entanglement. 'At the quantum level', Morton argues,

> persisting is simply the way in which quantum events inside an object cancel out. We have arrived at a strange insight. The persistence of a crystal lattice depends upon millions of quantum phenomena that subtend the relatively stable atoms and molecules in the lattice. What are these quantum events? *Nothing but the coherence of the quanta, that is, the way they occupy more than one place at once.* ... At this scale, *physics observes objects that occupy place x and place y at the same time*. These objects are dialetheic.[32]

Faced with this absolutely astounding claim concerning the 'double truth' of the quantum object, one can only wonder by what mechanism physics can perform such observations, given that '"measure" at the quantum level means "alter" (momentum, position) by means of another quantum'.[33] At the very least, we can affirm that observing quantum particles in their dialethic states – an impossibility according to both Bohr and Bohm – would require a suspension of Heisenberg's principle of indeterminacy.

With this conclusion, we come full circle to a point where the violence of Morton's object-ontologizing turns against itself, undermining precisely that quantum-theoretical principle, indeterminacy, from which it claimed to have found inspiration. What is left in its stead is nothing but the hollow ring of the OOO refrain: There are objects, these objects are real and they are infinitely withdrawn from everything, even themselves.

MEASUREMENT AS AN ORIGINARY PHENOMENON

In his recent reconstruction of Niels Bohr's radical non-classical interpretation of quantum mechanics, Arkady Plotnitsky insists on the absolute unknowability of quantum objects:

> The irreducible role of measuring instruments makes mathematically defined quantum states strictly a mathematical tool of our expectations, and nothing else. They do not relate either to the motion of quantum objects themselves or to any properties of these objects at the time of their interactions with measuring instruments. ... Instead, ... quantum states are used to relate to measurements and predictions concerning observations pertaining strictly to certain parts of measuring instruments impacted by their interaction with quantum objects. In other words, quantum states relate physically to no properties of quantum objects at any point, before, during, or after their interaction with measuring instruments. They relate, in terms of probabilistic predictions, only to certain classical physical states of macro-systems (such as measuring instruments) described by means of classical physics, without in any way relating to any dynamics, classical or quantum, responsible for these classical states. There is no physical evolution at any level, quantum or classical, to which quantum states relate, but they, as mathematical objects, enable us ... to make correct probabilistic predictions concerning the outcome of the interactions between quantum objects and measuring instruments, manifested in the classical physical properties of certain parts of these instruments. The mathematics of quantum theory – quantum states as mathematical objects included – enables these predictions but describes nothing physically involved in the situation, and it deprives us of any possible knowledge about the ultimate nature of the physical processes that led to the outcome of the experiments concerning which we make these predictions.[34]

This passage assembles the three crucial features of Bohr's account that inform its ontological radicality: (1) the absolute unknowability, indeed unthinkability, of undisturbed quantum behaviour; (2) the central role played by measuring instruments as the hinge between macro and quantum realms, and thus as sole means of access to the latter and (3) the irreducibly probabilistic nature of predictions concerning quantum phenomena that attest to the 'irreducible role of measuring instruments' in the formation of quantum phenomena.

According to Plotnitsky (whose argument tracks the increasing radicalization of Bohr's thinking in the aftermath of his debates with Einstein), we must make a clear, categorical distinction between quantum objects and quantum phenomena. While the former, quantum objects, are absolutely unknowable, the latter, quantum phenomena, are the result of observation in measuring instruments, and thus are both knowable and part of the classical world. '[Q]uantum objects', explains Plotnitsky,

> are unobservable *as quantum objects.* ... This situation ... compelled Bohr to theorize or idealize *quantum objects,* first, as irreducibly different from what is observed in measuring instruments impacted by quantum objects, which observations define *quantum phenomena;* and second, more radically, as entities placed beyond quantum-theoretical description and even beyond any possible description, knowledge, and ultimately conception.[35]

As the product of interaction between the measuring instrument and quantum objects, quantum phenomena provide the only possible access to the quantum level, an access that is, as we shall see, at best indirect.

Bohr's genius is to have taken this situation for what it is: a radical break with classical ontology and its causal models and an opportunity to rethink basic ontological commitments beginning with the Kantian *noumenon.* Thus, Plotnitsky characterizes the rupture between quantum phenomena and quantum objects as a radicalization of the Kantian distinction between phenomena and *noumena.* Where Kant's noumenon remains thinkable or conceivable, and can indeed be spoken of in the language of metaphysics (Kant himself refers to a 'positive' noumenon as the object of a hypothetical, non-human intellectual intuition), quantum objects in themselves are literally unthinkable by any imaginable form of intuition; they are 'beyond the reach of the theory itself or any possible conception'.[36] Quantum objects only become thinkable, and in a sense only exist, in the form of quantum phenomena, which is to say, as a contribution to or component of the measurement that breaks coherence or entanglement. French philosopher Jacques Garelli takes this logic one step further when he announces that 'the "non-being" of quantum particles' repudiates the 'idea of the noumenon' as such. In a move that will have important consequences for our appreciation of the experimental interface, what takes the place of the noumenon on Garelli's account is the mathematics underpinning the probabilities of experimental outcomes:

> The a priori conditions of possibility of the 'objects' of experience are, in quantum physics, mathematically integrated to the apparatus that elicits the experience, precisely as a priori conditions of its experimental possibility. It is this situation that poses the question of a *Kantianism without noumenon.*[37]

Plotnitsky explains how mathematics can stand in for the noumenon, as Garelli suggests it does, when he writes that mathematics 'allows us to predict the outcomes of quantum experiments in the absence of any knowledge or even conception concerning the actual (independent) physical behavior of quantum objects themselves'.[38] Diverging from Garelli, Plotnitsky plays down the ontological implications of Bohr's radical position; on Plotnitsky's account, it is the pragmatic function of mathematics that is crucial: Mathematics, he suggests, is a 'form of technology, a technology of thought'.[39] With this claim, we are returned to Wolfgang Ernst's emphasis on implementation and what I earlier referred to as 'the fundamental law' of his time-critical philosophy: namely that mathematics must always be implemented in a physical materiality. Bohr makes common cause with Ernst on this point, in the sense that the mathematics describing the probabilistic outcomes of measurement has no existence outside this situation and thus operates as a technology, indeed as a Bachelardian *phenomenotechnique*. As Plotnitsky clarifies,

> The mathematics of quantum theory defines these probabilistic expectations (no other appear possible) in the practice of quantum physics by enabling us to make better predictions concerning what is thus observed in measuring instruments or other macro-objects under the impact of quantum objects. But this is also all that this mathematics does for us, and no other mathematics appears to be able to do more.[40]

Although Plotnitsky insists that 'nonclassical epistemology ... precludes any form of ontology', meaning that the being of quantum objects defies ontological capture, the reference to Ernst points us to a different ontological stratum of quantum theory, namely the event of measurement. In Bohr's understanding, what happens in measurement is a '*reaction* of quantum objects upon other quantum objects', or more precisely, a reaction of quantum objects upon the 'quantum aspects' of the measuring instrument itself. This situation – of experimental contact with quantum objects inside the measuring instrument – definitely absolves Bohr of any charges of humanism or anthropocentrism, for example, those raised by Karen Barad in *Meeting the Universe Halfway*;[41] specifically, it establishes unequivocally that the subject of the measuring experiment *is not* the human observer but the experimental set-up itself. Just as 'media *themselves* have the best knowledge',[42] in Ernst's understanding of media as measurements, so, too, do the experimental measurements – the media, as it were, of quantum physics – produce something – quantum phenomena – that is radically outside the phenomenal grasp of human knowledge, that can in effect only be *known* by media machines.

For Jacques Garelli and his fellow French phenomenologist, Marc Richir, what results from this situation is a generalized conception of the phenomenon, beyond human intentionality, that is resolutely ontological. In his important essay, 'Quantum Mechanics and Transcendental Philosophy', Richir writes:

> [I]t is not the case that the 'real' remains 'hidden' or 'veiled', but rather that there is a physical dimension [*sens physique*] only through being taken up in the

order of the *phenomenon*, in which are included, not observers in the sense of contemplators, but the experimental apparatuses of observation and measure.[43]

When they produce phenomena, these apparatuses are in fact performing ontological work: As the non-causal outcome of contact with the quantum object, quantum phenomena themselves give being to physical reality.

In a more expansive argument, I would here turn to the phenomenological project of the great Czech philosopher Jan Patočka, who sought to reconstruct Husserl's philosophy into an 'asubjective phenomenology of manifestation'. Breaking with the Husserlian topos of 'adumbration' [*Abschattung*] as a partial and unfulfilled presentation of the object, Patočka insists that worldly appearances or manifestations of an object *are the object itself*, in this particular dimension of its being. Put another way, Patočka defines appearances as first and foremost objective, part of the objective being of the world itself; appearances are worldly and objective, that is, before they become subjective, before they become elements in the intentional life of consciousness. Because it collapses the gap between appearance and object, Patočka's philosophy thus offers an important alternative to Graham Harman's object-centred ontology, which is predicated on an irreducible gap or rift between appearance and object. In a way that is not dissimilar to the logic of Bohr's argument for the primacy of measure, Patočka rejects any possibility of access to the objective being of the world that would not take the form of appearances. More radically stated, the world for Patočka simply has no objective being in and of itself; it has no status as an object, independently of its multiplicious modes of appearing. Just as there is no being of quantum objects independently of measurement, there is no being of the world in itself that would be separate from its manifestations.

From this we can conclude that the quantum phenomena produced through the technology of measurement *are ontological*: They are manifestations of the structure of the world as it is, and they are the only way in which the world *is*.

How, we must now ask, does this ontological account of the phenomenon correlate with the renunciation of causality that Bohr believes is necessary in the wake of the quantum revolution? Because our access to the quantum domain is restricted to the results of quantum measuring experiments – because access is only possible, as it were, *from inside* the apparatus of experiment – we must forsake any lingering hope of independent access to the quantum object, and indeed, as we have seen, we must simply renounce any and all invocation of the quantum domain in itself. In the 1937 essay 'Complementarity and Causality', where he first formulates his ultimate, radically non-classical view, Bohr takes stock of this momentous task and its irreducible necessity:

> The renunciation of the ideal of causality in atomic physics which has been forced on us is founded logically only on our not being any longer in a position to speak of the autonomous behavior of a physical object, due to the unavoidable interaction between the object and the measuring instruments which in principle cannot be taken into account, if these instruments according to their purpose shall allow the unambiguous use of the concepts necessary for the description of experience.[44]

In closing this discussion of the quantum-theoretical concept of the phenomenon, and the crucial role played by the measuring experiment in its production, let me emphasize how radically different this renunciation of causality is from that animating Morton's aesthetic theory of causality. Whereas in Morton's account the absolute withdrawal of the hyperobject effectively guarantees that all of its phenomenal or aesthetic manifestations are interconnected and are indeed manifestations of the hyperobject under consideration, even though this cannot be perceived from any phenomenal point of view, in Bohr's account, there can be no reference beyond what is given in the measuring experiment.

That is precisely why Bohr's understanding of causality after Hume differs radically from Morton's. Indeed, by dissolving the gap between phenomenon and thing that Kant institutes as a way to overcome Humean skepticism – and that OOO hypostatizes as the deep ontology of the object – Bohr in effect returns us to the situation described by Hume: There simply is no basis in reality for causal analysis. What we are left with is a probabilistic analysis of the possible outcomes of quantum experimentation, where, in contradistinction to classical physics, probability does not index a closed set of variables that can, at least ideally, be fully known but rather an open, and radically indeterminate, set of possible outcomes that not only do not correlate sequentially with one another (as do, for example, coin flips) but that can differ even across identically prepared experiments. The deep reason for the shift from causal to probabilistic analysis does not have to do with any lack of knowledge, as it still arguably does on Morton's aesthetic account; rather, it directly concerns the radical randomness of the quantum domain as this manifests, through experiment, in the form of quantum phenomena: '[O]ur predictions are unavoidably probabilistic', Plotnisky explains, 'because identically prepared experiments in general lead to different outcomes even in the case of individual quantum events'.[45] If what accounts for the different outcomes of individual quantum events is the interaction that occurs within the measuring apparatus, would we be wrong to attribute ontological power to the experimental operation of measurement and the probabilities associated with it? And if it is the case that experiment produces quantum phenomena as an ontological operation, wouldn't the data generated through experiment, which correlate with the probabilities associated with it, themselves possess such ontological power?

THE ETHICS OF CLIMATE SIMULATION

Climate is what you expect, weather is what you get.[46]

Austrian media theorist Claus Pias contextualizes his exploration of climate simulation in relation to the very same disjunction – between weather and climate – that animates Morton's account of global warming. Yet, whereas Morton immediately enters the domain of abstraction, Pias turns to the practical problem of experiencing climate change. Engaging the work of one pair of climate scientists, he affirms the disconnect between the opacity of climate and the exigencies of real life:

> Humans are strange. Although we cannot (yet) predict future climate conditions, we act as if we can. Every day, political and development policies are defined and business, financial or even personal decisions are made, as if we knew which future climate conditions we will face.[47]

This is the practical reality of life in a world of climate change, where our possibilities for knowledge are limited. What we know are weather conditions that we can loosely rely on, at least for a span of a few days, but this knowledge does not translate in any direct or compelling way into predictions about climate in the future. We are thus faced with an impasse: either we act as if today's weather predictions are in fact indicators of future climate conditions or we face the difficulty of trusting the results of climate research that, as data of complex computer simulations, seem very far removed indeed from our daily experience. In the one case, we act as if there were no disjunction whatsoever between weather and climate, while in the other, we experience the disjunction between them to be so vast that we simply cannot find any way of mediating between them.

In response to this dilemma, Pias emphatically enjoins us to adopt a media-theoretical approach to climate simulation:

> The following exploration proceeds from the assumption, on one hand, that the status of scientific knowledge has been fundamentally modified with and through computer simulation, and, on the other, also that the science-critical concepts of 'actor networks' and 'heterogeneous collectivities' have always

already owed a debt to a cybernetic 'archive of knowledge'. The problematic of computer simulation is grounded in this double turn to a changed object and a ... changed mode of critique. The question concerning climate should henceforth be regarded not as a scientific-political problem, but rather as a media-technical-epistemological one. It is less a question of what to do, than of what can be known. How does computer simulation procure its specific form of knowledge? And in what ways have computer simulations fundamentally reconstructed scientific knowledge in the past half-century? ... Computer simulations possess a medial specificity that categorically differentiates them from other writing systems as well as from older forms of models and simulation. ... [This specificity concerns] the level of code, which will be translated into scientific knowledge just as it has long been translated into mathematics, with the difference that such scientific translation differs categorically from mathematical translation because of its temporality. ... Computer simulations ... operate ... with the self-understanding that their knowledge is always already associated with a hypothetical index, that they learn about themselves through their fictionality, that they thematize their performance, that they know about their problematic genesis and that they specify their limited value.[48]

A media-theoretical approach promotes an experimental deployment of computer simulation that pushes it into a position beyond the traditional categories of theory and experiment: Understood as a 'temporalizing imitation of system behavior through the medium of the computer', computer simulation is able to render phenomena that are 'not analytically accessible' – phenomena like climate – addressable.

In support of this claim, Pias cites four characteristics of computer simulation that are responsible for the transformation it brings in the object of scientific knowledge: First, computer simulation separates the performance of the model from the exactness of the results and lays emphasis on the former. Second, computer simulation deals less with laws than with rules, which means that it is not bound by the limitations of contemporary scientific knowledge of nature and is thus free to speculate about what is not (or not yet) known.

> Rules have ... a different relation to the future [than laws] and to the cases of natural laws they produce. In climate research this situation is expressed in particular through parametricization, in which it is a question of operational dealings with the not-known. ... [T]he rule proves itself as a form in which something that is not-understood in the strong sense of the term can nonetheless be dealt with.[49]

Third, computer simulations are not concerned with proof but rather with the demonstration of adequateness. This characteristic stipulates that simulations must be run in real time, for it is only on this condition that simulations can embrace what remains beyond prediction even in deterministic systems when these latter are implemented physically. Once again, the payoff is that climate simulations are able to simulate phenomena that are analytically very difficult to access or indeed beyond analytical access as such. Fourth, computer simulations are concerned less with truth than with correctness. Emancipated from the need to decide on a true reality, simulations are able to embrace a 'plurality of realities', each of which is possible and each of which has a distinct probability. With reference to our earlier discussion of probability in quantum measurement, what Pias's analysis makes clear is the fact that it is the entire set of probabilities, the full conjunction of possible realities, that makes up the phenomenon produced by experimental measurement or simulation.

Pias's account of climate simulation thus comes to fruition precisely when he affirms its status as what we might call an 'objective phenomenon'.[50] Despite its apparent disjunction from phenomenological experiences of the weather, the data generated through climate simulation is itself a phenomenological presentation of climate, in the strong ontological sense that Patočka lends the term. The data of climate simulation, in other words, *simply is the phenomena of climate.* There is no true climate, no real climate, no climate qua hyperobject, that stands behind these phenomena. Affirming this situation, Pias's position ultimately takes the form of an ethical claim: We must accept the data of climate researchers, the phenomena of climate, not as a mere representation that will forever be inadequate to its alleged cause but as climate itself. Such a claim requires a profound ethical shift, for it involves embracing the domain of probability – or more precisely, the set of probabilities associated with any given measurement – as the phenomenon of climate, indeed, as climate tout court.

That such an ethical shift is now required can be seen by way of contrast with Morton's account of the impasse of global warming, that is, the disjunction between weather and climate. 'Global warming plays a very mean trick', Morton writes:

> It reveals that what we took to be a reliable world was actually just a habitual pattern – a collusion between forces such as sunshine and moisture and humans expecting such things at certain regular intervals and giving them names, such as Dog Days. We took weather to be real. But in an age of global warming we see it as an accident, a simulation of something darker, more withdrawn – climate.[51]

'Global warming is really here', he continues,

> even more spookily, it was already here, already influencing the supposedly real wet stuff falling on my head and the warm golden stuff burning my face at the beach. That wet stuff and that golden stuff, which we call weather, turns out to

have been a false immediacy, an ontic pseudo-reality that can't stand up against the looming presence of an invisible yet far more real global climate. Weather, that handy backdrop for human lifeworlds, has ceased to exist, and along with it, the cozy concept of *lifeworld* itself.[52]

Despite the rhetorical twists and turns of Morton's mode of argumentation, the logic underlying this claim is the same one we examined above: There is a radical rift between the phenomenon and the thing. Weather, along with climate simulation and any other experimental production of data, is a phenomenon and thus necessarily a false immediacy that cannot lead back to an embrace of 'climate in general'; climate, by contrast, is a thing, a hyperobject, that is radically withdrawn from its appearances, including all weather events and all computer simulations.

If Morton is able to dismiss data and simulation in this way, it is due to the same logic. In the face of a hyperobject that is infinitely withdrawn, even from itself, simulation and data are confounded: Climate as a hyperobject can neither be modelled in real time (since it operates in a non-local and atemporal way) nor equated with the massive datasets and computing power necessary to model climate. Indeed, Morton goes so far as to suggest that climate simulations – understood as a phenomenal or aesthetic appearance of the hyperobject climate – are needed to supplement human perceptions precisely because of the withdrawal of the object. By contrast, for Pias, simulations are necessary precisely *because there is no real climate in itself, no hyperobject called global warming*. Rather, global warming simply is the conjunction of models of climate, a set that encompasses the host of humanly perceived weather events along with all available climate simulations that produce data about the probability of incompossible future possibilities. Thinking about climate in this way – which is to say, thinking about climate ethically and conceiving of experimentation, following Ernst, as implementation – is to restore the possibility of engaging with it, to turn our new mode of knowledge into the basis for new forms of practical intervention. On this score, Morton is not only wrong to characterize global warming as a wicked problem (a problem one can understand perfectly, but for which there is no rational solution); he is effectively complicit *in making global warming a wicked problem*. Indeed, Morton's analysis of global warming as a hyperobject is precisely what makes it into a wicked problem: By instituting a radical rift between the hyperobject, global warming and its worldly effects, Morton destroys any chance for us to come into touch with it and thus to act in ways that might forestall its future advent.

I can thus agree with Morton that global warming is 'not a function of our measuring devices', but not for the reasons he offers: Far from being radically disjunct from some real object called global warming, our measuring devices literally produce global warming as a phenomenon, indeed, as the originary phenomenon, of climate. Outside of our perceptions and our data concerning climate, both of which offer access to climate, there simply is no such thing as global warming.

Let me reiterate the practical ethical implications of my criticism of Morton and of my effort to generalize and render objective the phenomenon. Morton's hypertheoretical transmutation of global warming into an infinitely withdrawn hyperobject effectively eliminates all possibility for engaging its operationality. From his standpoint – a standpoint that itself performs the transmutation of global warming into a 'wicked problem' – no weather phenomenon and no climate simulation can tell us anything real about the hyperobject climate. As a result, all manifestations of global warming are simply appearances of false immediacy that have absolutely no bearing on and no capacity to inform us about their underlying, infinitely withdrawn cause. Not only do we face a radical impasse concerning any possible practical engagement aimed at alleviating global warming, but we are left wondering how Morton can be so confident that, as he puts it, 'global warming is really here' (or 'was already here'). It appears that Morton is stuck between a rock and a hard place: for by discounting the validity of weather phenomena and climate simulations while at the same time insisting on the 'looming presence of an invisible yet far more real global climate', he must conjure up some kind of magical access to the real that is, in reality, nothing other than blind dogmatism – a dogmatism that simply repeats, without any proof and without any possibility of proof, the familiar refrain of OOO, which stipulates that the (hyper)object (i.e. climate) is infinitely withdrawn, even from itself.

Given this situation, it becomes clear why it is so crucial to affirm the validity and irreducibility of the phenomenal and to generalize the concept of the phenomenon itself to encompass not simply what humans (and other perceivers) experience as weather events but also what computers can simulate as probabilistic outcomes of concrete scenarios. The experience of weather and the probabilistic simulation of climate constitute the sole means of access to global warming and, as such, can and must be understood – following Patočka's great insight concerning the reality of manifestation – as consubstantial with climate itself. There is no looming invisible real operating beneath these manifestations; they are, rather, necessarily partial and perspectival manifestations of the reality of global warming that do not aspire to capture what global warming *really is*, what it is as a totality, but rather *what it is phenomenally*, which is to say, what it does. This practical shift to a position capable of acting on the incomplete knowledge generated by such manifestations is precisely what defines media entanglement. In stark contrast to OOO, medium-entangled phenomenology insists on the objective reality of the phenomenal and insists that this constitutively partial and perspectival reality is consubstantial with reality as such, without having to ask what any given phenomenon really is. Precisely this capacity to refrain from posing a certain kind of ontological question underscores why the practical shift to a medium-entangled phenomenology is crucial for any ethical engagement with global warming: For it is only by engaging the concrete operationality of global warming – which medium-oriented ontology understands to be global warming itself –that we can aspire, however tentatively and unsurely, to influence the course of its futurity.

NOTES

1. Wolfgang Ernst, 'Experimenting with Media Temporality: Pythagoras, Hertz, Turing'. In *Digital Memory and the Archive,* Ed. Jussi Parikka (Minneapolis and London: University of Minnesota Press, 2013), 185.

2. Ernst, 'Toward a Media Archaeology of Sonic Articulations'. In *Digital Memory and the Archive,* Ed. Jussi Parikka (Minneapolis and London: University of Minnesota Press, 2013), 178.

3. Gaston Bachelard, *The New Scientific Spirit*, quoted in Ernst, *Chronopoietik: Zeitweisen und Zeitgaben technischer Medien* (Berlin: Kulturverlag Kadmos, 2012), 73.

4. Ernst, *Chronopoietik*, 29.

5. Ernst, *Chronopoietik*, 27.

6. Ernst, *Chronopoietik*, 18.

7. The term 'intrinsic ontology' was first used by Jean-Toussaint Desanti in his response to Badiou's *Being and Event*. See Desanti, 'Some Remarks on the Intrinsic Ontology of Alain Badiou'. Trans. Ray Brassier, in *Think Again: Alain Badiou and the Future of Philosophy,* Ed. Peter Hallward (London and New York: Continuum, 2004), 63–64.

8. Arkady Plotnitsky, 'Experimenting with Ontologies: Sets, Spaces and Topoi with Badiou and Grothendieck', *Environment and Planning D: Society and Space,* 30 (2012): 351–368.

9. Plotnitsky, 'Experimenting with Ontologies', 362.

10. From a categorical or topos-theoretical perspective one starts with a certain, arbitrarily chosen space, X, potentially any space, without initially specifying it mathematically. Indeed, one can start with an object, say, a set of numbers, that is not spatial in any given sense and only becomes spatialized by virtue of its relations to other objects of the same kind, analogous to the relationships between conventional spatial objects. What would be specified, at first, are the relationships between spaces, such as categorical arrows, Y, mapping one space by another space or multiplicity of other spaces. This procedure enables one to specify a given space not in terms of its intrinsic structure, say, as a set of points with relationships among them, but, in Yuri I. Manin's terms, 'sociologically' – through its relationships with other spaces of the

same category. An intrinsic structure – set-theoretical or other, say, topological, as the number of holes in a given space – is then derived from this 'sociology' (Plotnitsky, 'Experimenting with Ontologies', 357).

11. 'Contrary to Badiou's view that any ontology rigorously considered by philosophy should be mathematical, ... ontology – that which "pronounces what is expressible about being qua being" – need not always be and *even cannot always be* mathematical, or only mathematical. Indeed, ... this is true even in mathematics itself: No matter how we try to configure it mathematically (via set theory, topos theory, or otherwise), any rigorously established mathematical ontology *always has a nonmathematical residue*' (Plotnitsky, 'Experimenting with Ontologies', 362).

12. For a first step toward such an account, see my chapter 'Topology of Sensibility', in Jay David Bolter et al., *Ubiquitous Computing, Complexity and Culture* (New York: Routledge, 2016, 33–47). A longer discussion of Badiou and topos theory and a discussion of the relation between Peirce's topological continuum and his phenomenology will be included in my book *Topology of Sensibility: Towards a Speculative Phenomenology*.

13. Ernst, *Chronopoetik*, 250.
14. Ernst, *Chronopoetik* , 250–251.
15. Ernst, *Chronopoetik* , 18.
16. 'Incidental Time' is in English in the original.
17. Ernst, *Chronopoetik*, 18.
18. Timothy Morton, *Hyperobjects: Philosophy and Ecology After the End of the World* (Minneapolis and London: University of Minnesota Press, 2013), 40–41, emphasis added.
19. Morton, *Hyperobjects*, 1.
20. Morton, *Hyperobjects*, 48.
21. Morton, *Hyperobjects*, 1.
22. 'It is Kant who shows, at the very inception of the Anthropocene, that things never coincide with their phenomena. All we need to do is extend this revolutionary insight beyond the human-world gap. Unlike Meillassoux, we are not going to try to bust through human finitude, but to place that finitude in a universe of trillions of finitudes, as many as there are things – because a thing just is a fit between what it is and how it appears, for any entity whatsoever, not simply for that special entity called the (human) subject' (Morton, *Hyperobjects*, 18).
23. Morton, *Hyperobjects*, 16.
24. Morton, *Hyperobjects*, 15.
25. Morton, *Hyperobjects*, 15.
26. Morton, *Hyperobjects*, 41.
27. Timothy Morton, *Realist Magic: Objects, Ontology, Causality* (Ann Arbor: Open Humanities Press, 2013), 31.
28. The problem with Morton's account of quantum mechanics, as Brown sees it, 'is that the interpretation of phenomena like entanglement, superposition, and action at a distance – particular their ontological interpretation – is itself a matter of debate both in quantum physics and in philosophy of science. But there is no

96   Chapter Six

real engagement with these debates in Morton's book' (Nathan Brown, 'The Nadir of OOO: From Graham Harman's Tool-Being to Timothy Morton's Realist Magic: Objects, Ontology, Causality', *Parrhesia,* 17 [2013]: 65).

29. Morton, *Realist Magic,* 31.

30. For a different version of this same criticism of OOO, see N. Katherine Hayles, 'Speculative Aesthetics and Object Oriented Inquiry (OOI)', *Speculations: A Journal of Speculative Realism,* 5 (2014), accessed 29 July 2014, http://www.speculations-journal.org/storage/06_Hayles_Speculative_Aesthetic_and_Object_Oriented_Inquiry_OOI.pdf.

31. 'The measurement of a quantum destroys its "coherence", namely its existence in a dialetheic state in which different positions and momenta are "superposed" one on the other. Something definitely exists before measurement, which is why measurement can happen at all. We are not dealing with *esse est percipi* here. Yet measurement destroys the fragile, wavering quality of an object as it oscillates and not-oscillates'. Morton, *Realist Magic,* 209.

32. Morton, *Realist Magic,* 174–175, emphasis added.

33. Morton, *Realist Magic,* 96. It should be noted that Morton is here citing Bohm, a fact that is not without consequence for his allegiances. This is a point that Brown also raises in his review, noting how Morton seems to embrace Bohm's position only to go on to criticize it. One particularly revealing instance of Morton's confusion concerning Bohm comes when he cites Bohm's account of quantum probability in the service of an argument for the reality of the electron: 'Just as there is no top level, there may be no bottom level that is not a substantial, formed object. Electrons come and go, change into other particles, radiate energy. An electron is real. Yet in the act of becoming or unbecoming an electron, it's a statistical performance: [citing Bohm] "Quantum theory requires us to give up the idea that the electron, or any other object has, by itself, any intrinsic properties at all. Instead, each object should be regarded as something containing only incompletely defined potentialities that are developed when an object interacts with an appropriate system"' (Morton, *Hyperobjects,* 44). How this argument merits the following development is entirely beyond my comprehension: 'To argue thus approaches Harman's image of the withdrawn-ness of objects as a "subterranean creature". Thus, the "something deeper" from which the electron unfolds is also withdrawn' (44).

34. Arkady Plotnitsky, *Epistemology and Probability: Bohr, Heisenberg, Schrödinger, and the Nature of Quantum-Theoretical Thinking* (New York: Springer, 2010), 175–176.

35. Plotnitsky, *Epistemology and Probability,* 6.

36. Plotnitsky, *Epistemology and Probability,* 6.

37. Jacques Garelli, *Rhythmes et mondes: Au revers de l'identité et de l'altérité* (Grenoble: Editions Jérôme Millon, 1991), 248.

38. Plotnitsky, *Epistemology and Probability,* 129.

39. Plotnitsky, *Epistemology and Probability,* 133.

40. Plotnitsky, *Epistemology and Probability,* 136.

41. Karen Barad, *Meeting the Universe Halfway: Quantum Physics and the Entanglement of Matter and Meaning* (Durham: Duke University Press, 2007), chapter 7.

42. Ernst, *Chronopoietik*, 73.
43. Marc Richir, *Mécanique quantique et philosophie transcendantale*, 209, quoted in Garelli, 248.
44. Bohr, quoted in Plotnitsky, *Epistemology and Probability*, 344.
45. Plotnitsky, *Epistemology and Probability*, 19.
46. Robert Heinlein, *Time Enough for Love: The Lives of John Lazarus* (New York: Putnam, 1973).
47. McGuffie and Henderson-Sellers, quoted in Claus Pias, 'Klimasimulation', in *Das Wetter, der Mensch und sein Klima* (Göttingen: Wallstein, 2008), 108.
48. Pias, 108, 115.
49. Pias, 113.
50. I explore this concept in my essay 'Appearance In-Itself, Data-Propagation, and External Relationality: Towards a Realist Phenomenology of "Firstness"', *Zeitschrift für Medien- und Kulturforschung*, 7.1 (2016): 45–60.
51. Morton, *Hyperobjects*, 102.
52. Morton, *Hyperobjects*, 103.

BIBLIOGRAPHY

Barad, Karen. *Meeting the Universe Halfway: Quantum Physics and the Entanglement of Matter and Meaning*. Durham: Duke University Press, 2007.
Brown, Nathan. 'The Nadir of OOO: From Graham Harman's Tool-Being to Timothy Morton's Realist Magic: Objects, Ontology, Causality', *Parrhesia*, 17 (2013): 62–71.
Desanti, Jean-Toussaint. 'Some Remarks on the Intrinsic Ontology of Alain Badiou'. In *Think Again: Alain Badiou and the Future of Philosophy*. Translated by Ray Brassier, edited by Peter Hallward. London and New York: Continuum, 2004.
Ernst, Wolfgang. 'Experimenting with Media Temporality: Pythagoras, Hertz, Turing'. In *Digital Memory and the Archive*. Edited by Jussi Parikka. Minneapolis and London: University of Minnesota Press, 2013.
———. 'Toward a Media Archaeology of Sonic Articulations'. In *Digital Memory and the Archive*. Edited by Jussi Parikka. Minneapolis and London: University of Minnesota Press, 2013.
———. *Chronopoietik: Zeitweisen und Zeitgaben technischer Medien*. Berlin: Kulturverlag Kadmos, 2012.
Garelli, Jacques. *Rhythmes et mondes: Au revers de l'identité et de l'alterité*. Grenoble: Editions Jérôme Millon, 1991.
Hansen, Mark B.N. 'Appearance In-Itself, Data-Propagation, and External Relationality: Towards a Realist Phenomenology of "Firstness"'. *Zeitschrift für Medien- und Kulturforschung* 7.1 (2016): 45–60.
———. 'Topology of Sensibility'. In *Ubiquitous Computing, Complexity and Culture*. Edited by Jay David Bolter et al., 33–47. New York: Routledge, 2016.

Hayles, N. Katherine. 'Speculative Aesthetics and Object Oriented Inquiry (OOI)'. *Speculations: A Journal of Speculative Realism,* accessed 29 July 2014. http://www.speculationsjournal.org/storage/06_Hayles_Speculative_Aesthetic_and_Object_Oriented_Inquiry_OOI.pdf.

Heinlein, Robert. *Time Enough for Love: The Lives of John Lazarus.* New York: Putnam, 1973.

Morton, Timothy. *Hyperobjects: Philosophy and Ecology After the End of the World.* Minneapolis and London: University of Minnesota Press, 2013.

———. *Realist Magic: Objects, Ontology, Causality.* Ann Arbor: Open Humanities Press, 2013.

Pias, Claus. *Das Wetter, der Mensch und sein Klima.* Göttingen: Wallstein, 2008.

Plotnitsky, Arkady. *Epistemology and Probability: Bohr, Heisenberg, Schrödinger, and the Nature of Quantum-Theoretical Thinking.* New York: Springer, 2010.

———. 'Experimenting with Ontologies: Sets, Spaces and Topoi with Badiou and Grothendieck'. *Environment and Planning D: Society and Space,* 30 (2012): 351–368.

Chapter Seven

On Reason and Spectral Machines
Robert Brandom and Bounded Posthumanism
David Roden

BOUNDED POSTHUMANISM

Surveying the contemporary philosophical landscape, it seems that anthropocentrism remains relatively entrenched, if under stress. Post-Rawlsian political theory, for example, is largely concerned with distributing rights and entitlements to creatures supposed morally equal on the grounds of their humanity or personhood. The bioethics of technological enhancement and transhumanism is dominated by partially theorized assumptions about the moral priority of human-like persons.[1] Even left accelerationism, acutely sensitive to the ontological potential of drastic techoscientific change, pays lip service to anthropocentric notions of rational 'self-mastery'.[2]

However, anthropocentrism is not confined to practical philosophical sub-disciplines like ethics or political theory. Following Kant, modern transcendental thinkers propound a strong anti-naturalistic humanism for which humans are distinguished by the capacity to organize the world conceptually and semantically. According to these 'transcendental humanists', the world is not structured independently of the concept-wielding activity that makes it an object of representation or practical agency.

A milder – that is, avowedly realist, or not ostensibly *anti*-realist – version of transcendental humanism is evident in the work of pragmatist readers of Kant such as Wilfred Sellars and Robert Brandom, for whom real intentionality and autonomy are ineluctably tied to the human capacity to follow public inferential proprieties. Brandom's analytic pragmatism, as we shall see, draws a clear distinction between the ascribed intentionality of merely sentient beings, such as parrots, and the authentic intentionality of humans, whose capacity to institute and abide by shared norms rescue them from the pre-signifying state of nature.

Posthumanists are united by their rejection of philosophical anthropocentrism but tend to do so in different settings. In particular, critical posthumanism (CP) is concerned with the post-human as a social and intellectual condition, while speculative posthumanism (SP) asserts the possibility of technologically made non-human agents. In other words, SP holds that *there could be post-humans*, where post-humans would be 'wide human descendants'[3] of current humans that have become non-human in virtue of some process of technical alteration.[4,5]

Nonetheless, CP and SP have a convergent interest in refuting a transcendental humanism that casts us as demigods, uniquely equipped to interpret a mute, unmeaning nature. Human life may be distinctive in many ways, but nothing obviously precludes comparable ontological novelty (arising, perhaps, from a biotechnological convergence) in the near or deep future. Accordingly, future life may diversify into alien forms quite different from those that 'our' cultural and evolutionary history equips us to understand. Exploring the implications of this 'unboundedly weird' SP exposes the metaphysical commitments of anthropocentrism and thereby equips us to confront the ethical dilemmas posed by long-term technoscientific change.[6]

In *Posthuman Life*, I frame the tension between anthropocentricism and SP by distinguishing two claims about notional successors to current humans: an *anthropologically bounded posthumanism* (ABP) and an *anthropologically unbounded posthumanism* (AUP).

ABP is a strong corollary of transcendental humanism since it requires future agents to satisfy the conditions of current human agency. This position can be spelt out as follows:

1. There are unique constraints, 'C's, (on cognition and agency) that all agents satisfy.
2. Any agent that knows it is an agent can correctly infer that the Cs apply to all agents (the Cs are transcendental conditions).
3. Human agents know they are agents.
4. Human agents can correctly infer that all agents satisfy the Cs.
5. Post-humans (if such existed) would be agents.[7]

Human agents can correctly infer that post-human agents would satisfy the Cs.

ABP's purport becomes clearer if we consider the collection of histories whereby post-human wide descendants of humans could feasibly emerge. In *Posthuman Life*, I refer to this set as Post-human Possibility Space (PPS).[8] Given that post-humans would be agents of *some* kind (see chapter 6 in *Posthuman Life*) and given ABP, members of PPS would have to satisfy the same transcendental conditions (C) on agency as humans.

Daryl Wennemann assumes something along these lines in his book *Posthuman Personhood*. He adopts the Kantian idea that agency consists in the capacity to justify one's actions according to reasons and shared norms. For Wennemann, a person is a being able to 'reflect on himself and his world from the perspective of a being sharing in a certain community'.[9] This is a condition of post-human agency as much as of human agency. This implies that, whatever the future throws up, post-human agents will be social and, arguably, linguistic beings, even if they are robots or computers, have strange bodies or even stranger habits. If so, PPS cannot contain non-anthropomorphic entities whose agency is significantly non-human in nature. ABP thus implies a priori limits on post-human *weirdness*.

AUP, by contrast, leaves the nature of post-human agency to be settled *empirically* (or technologically). Post-humans might be social, discursive creatures, or they might be different from us in ways that we cannot envisage, short of making some post-humans or becoming post-human ourselves. AUP thus extends the critical posthumanist rejection of anthropocentrism to the deep time of the technological future.

In *Posthuman Life*, I defend AUP via a critique of Donald Davidson's work on intentionality, coupling this with a 'naturalistic deconstruction' of transcendental phenomenology in its Husserlian and Heideggerian forms.[10] Some of these arguments, I believe, carry over to Brandom's overtly normativist philosophy.

The account of the relationship between normativity, social practice and intentionality that Brandom offers in *Making It Explicit*, and in other writings, is one of the most impressively detailed, systematic and historically self-aware attempts to explain subjectivity, agency and intentionality in terms of social practices and statuses. Moreover, contemporary proponents of philosophical realism and naturalism have praised Brandom for purging the Kantian tradition of anti-naturalistic, idealist and subjectivist deviations. If this is right, then Brandom's views merit appraisal by posthumanists *since they represent a comprehensive and powerful argument in favour of privileging anthropoform subjectivity and agency in the face of their speculative assaults on human-centred thinking*. This is what I will attempt to undertake here, at least in a preliminary form. My aim is to show that despite the rigour and constructive brilliance of Brandom's thinking, his thought fails to circumscribe notions of agency or meaning that could thwart the fissiparous decentrings of the human undertaken by SP and CP.

FIRST- AND SECOND-CLASS AGENTS

I will begin with a thumbnail sketch of how Brandom derives conditions of possibility for agency and meaning from a theory of social practices. Then I will consider whether its foundations are capable of supporting this transcendental superstructure.

Brandom is a philosophical pragmatist. He claims that our conceptual and intellectual powers are grounded in our practical abilities rather than in relations between mental entities and what they represent.[11, 12] His pragmatism implies a species of interpretationism with regard to intentional content. Interpretationists, such as Daniel Dennett, claim that intentional notions such as 'belief' do not track inner vehicles of content but help us assess patterns of rational activity on the part of other 'intentional systems'.[13] Belief–desire talk is not a folk-psychological 'theory' about internal states but a social 'craft' for evaluating and predicting other rational agents.

For Dennett, an entity qualifies as an agent with reasons if predicting its behaviour requires interpreters to attribute to it the beliefs and desires it ought to have, given its nature and environment. A being whose behaviour is 'voluminously predictable' under this 'intentional stance' is called an 'intentional system' (IS). In IS theory, there is no gap between predictability under the intentional stance and having real intentionality.[14, 15]

Brandom endorses Dennett's claim that intentional concepts are fundamentally about rendering agency intelligible in the light of reasons, but he argues that IS theory furnishes an incomplete account or intentionality. Interpretation is, after all, an *intentional* act; thus interpretationists need to elucidate the relationship between attributed intentionality and *attributing* intentionality. If we do not understand what counts as a prospective interpreter, we cannot claim to have understood what it is to attribute intentionality in the first place.[16]

Brandom goes one step further. The intentionality attributed to intrinsically meaningless events or linguistic inscriptions seems entirely derived from interpreters. Similarly, with relatively simple ISs. Maze-running robots or fly-catching frogs can properly be understood from the intentional stance – making them true believers by Dennett's lights. But their intentionality seems likewise observer-relative, *derived* from attitudes of *interpreting* ISs.[17] To hold otherwise, he argues, is to risk a disabling regress. For, if intentionality is derivative all the way up, there can be no real intentional attributions and thus no derivative (non-observer relative) intentionality.[18]

Brandom claims that his theory can be read as an account of the conditions an organism must satisfy to qualify as an *interpreting IS* – that is, to warrant attributions of *non-derived* intentionality rather than the 'as-if' intentionality we can attribute to simpler organisms or complex devices:

> The theory developed in this work can be thought of as an account of the stance of attributing original intentionality. It offers an answer to the question, What features must one's interpretation of a community exhibit in order properly to be said to be an interpretation of them as engaging in practices sufficient to confer genuinely propositional content on the performances, statuses, attitudes, and expressions caught up in those practices?[19]

Whatever else the capacity for original or 'first-class' intentionality includes, it must involve the ability to evaluate the cognizance and rationality of their actions and the actions of other beings.[20,21] Entities with the capacity to assess and answer to reasons in this way are referred to by Brandom as *sapient*. Entities with only derived intentionality may exhibit the *sentient* capacity to react in discriminating and optimizing ways to their environment, but the conceptual content of these responses is attributed and observer-relative.

The claim that intentionality (or the capacity for objective thought) implies the capacity to evaluate reasons obviously has a rich post-Kantian lineage. However, one of the clearest arguments for connecting intentionality and the capacity for other-evaluation is provided by Donald Davidson in his essay 'Thought and Talk'.[22] Davidson begins with the assumption that belief is an attitude of 'holding' true some proposition: for example, that there is a cat behind that wall. If belief is holding true, it entails a grasp of truth and the possibility of being mistaken and, thus, a concept of belief itself. We cannot have a concept of belief without exercising it. Thus we cannot believe anything without the capacity to attribute to others true-or-false beliefs about the same topic.[23] This capacity presupposes linguistic abilities, according to Davidson, because attributing contents to fellow creatures requires a common idiom of expression. Absent this, the possession of a concept of belief and, thus, the very *having of beliefs*, is impossible.[24]

> Our manner of attributing attitudes ensures that all the expressive power of language can be used to make such distinctions. One can believe that Scott is not the author of Waverley while not doubting that Scott is Scott; one can want to be the discoverer of a creature with a heart without wanting to be the discoverer of a creature with a kidney. One can intend to bite into the apple in the hand without intending to bite into the only apple with a worm in it; and so forth. The intentionality we make so much of in the attribution of thoughts is very hard to make much of when speech is not present. The dog, we say, knows that its master is home. But does it know that Mr. Smith (who is his master), or that the president of the bank (who is that same master), is home? We have no real idea how to settle, or make sense of, these questions.[25]

Brandom agrees! We need language to have and attribute beliefs and, by extension, practical attitudes corresponding to desires and intentions.[26] However, his official account avoids talk of beliefs or intentions in order to steer clear of the picture of beliefs and so on as 'inner' vehicles of content (sentences in the head, say) rather than social statuses available to discursive creatures like ourselves.

For Brandom, the primary bearers of propositional content are public assertions. Thus he bases his elaborate theory of intentionality not on a theory of mental representations or sub-propositional concepts but on a pragmatic account of the place of assertions within the social game of 'giving and asking for reasons'. Correlatively, Brandom's semantics begins with an explanation of how assertions – and their syntactical proxies, sentences – acquire propositional content.[27] Like Sellars's brand of functional semantics, it is framed in terms of the normative role of utterances within social practices that determine how a speaker can move from one position in the language game to another (language transition rules), assume an 'initial position' (language entry rules) or exit the game.[28]

In the case of assertions, the language transition rules correspond to materially correct inferences, such as the inference that *x is coloured* from *x is red*. Language entry rules are non-inferential since they are made on the basis of reliable dispositions to discriminate the world in inferentially consequential ways.[29] As Brandom puts it, statements like 'This is red' (uttered in response to red things) are 'non-inferentially elicited but inferentially articulated'.[30] Finally, 'language exit rules' correspond to practical commitments disposing one to forms of non-linguistic action.

Thus Brandom agrees with other post-Wittgensteinian pragmatists that linguistic practices are governed by public norms, as well as by reliable differential responsive dispositions (RDRDs). However, he follows Davidson in rejecting the 'I–we' conception of social structure.[31] If meanings are inferential roles (as Dummett and Sellars also claim), then the content attributable to expressions will dance in line with the doxastic commitments of individual speakers.

Suppose one observes a masked figure in a red costume clambering up a skyscraper. The language entry rules you have internalized may entitle you (by default) to claim that Spiderman is climbing the building. However, you are unaware that Spiderman is none other than Peter Parker. So you are not yet entitled to infer that *Peter Parker* is climbing the building – although the 'substitution-inferential' rules of English would entitle you to that further claim if (say) some reliable authority informed you of this fact.[32]

This simple example shows that the inferential roles – thus meanings – of expressions like 'Spiderman' are not fixed communally but vary with auxiliary assumptions, sensitivities and dispositions of individual speakers. Understanding or interpreting the utterances and beliefs of others is a matter of *deontic scorekeeping* – that is, keeping track of the way social statuses alter as speakers update their inferential commitments.[33, 34] *Thus semantic and intentional content are co-extensive with the normative-functional roles of states and actions.* It follows that what a belief or claim 'represents' or is 'about' is fixed by the status it can be ascribed from the perspective of various deontic scorekeepers (including the believer or claimant).

Functional semantics can be thought of as a philosophical appropriation of the formal conception of computation as automated symbol manipulation developed in the early part of the twentieth century.[35] In its purely mathematical form a computational engine can be understood as a set of 'state transitions' fixing how the data stored in some memory location determines consecutive states of the machine. A Turing machine's table, for example, 'completely determines' how it would behave when reading a particular symbol at a particular memory location on its 'tape' while in a particular state.[36, 37]

The obvious attraction of this socio-mechanical metaphor to contemporary philosophical materialists like Ray Brassier is that it promises to cash out abstract notions such as 'meaning' or 'representation' in terms that are, at first sight, closer to home: people uttering and inscribing marks, responding and acting to the impulsions of a shared natural world.[38]

However, with Brandom's social machines the inferential transitions are not formally or causally determined but *required or permitted*. As we shall see in the following two sections, this network of proprieties (and thus the social apparatus they compose) is somewhat spectral and elusive since Brandom does not consider them to be factually real but spun from the passing attitudes of the scorekeepers.

Brandom, like Davidson, argues that the ascription and adoption of such states is only possible if the scorekeepers can practically express them in a structured language with components such as predicates and singular terms.[39] Thus, as advertised, Brandom's account suggests a pragmatic-semantic story with which to transcendentally partition PPS. If post-humans are to be intentional agents in thrall to concepts, they will be subjects of discourse assessing one another according to public inferential proprieties.

THE NORM-GROUNDING PROBLEM

However, we have grounds for partitioning PPS along these lines only if normativism can contend with some difficult foundational issues deriving from the aforementioned spectrality of inferential roles. I will refer to the most pressing of these as 'the norm-grounding problem'.

Brandom's pragmatics implies that the rules that furnish deontic statuses are implicit in *what we do*: in our linguistic and non-linguistic performances rather than in some explicit set of semantic rules. But what does it mean for a norm to be implicit in a practice?[40] What is it about what we *do* that constitutes our observance of one norm rather than another? Are norms a special kind of fact, to which our practices conform or fail to conform? If there were normative facts that transcended our actions, this could at least explain how our inferences can be held to account by them.

Brandom rejects factualism regarding norms. They are not, he claims, 'part of the intrinsic nature of things, which is entirely indifferent to them'.[41] This seems wise on the face of it. If there are Platonic norms, it is far from clear how animals like us, or our evolutionary forebears, could come to be aware of them. Brandom thus adopts a non-factualist or 'phenomenalist' position regarding norms. Non-normative reality is 'clothed' in a weave of normative statuses when speakers treat public actions as correct or incorrect, permitted or entitled.[42]

However, before considering Brandom's non-factualist account of norms in greater detail, it is instructive to consider a superficially appealing position that he rejects: *regularism*. Regularism is the claim that norms are regularities. To act according to a norm (or follow a rule) is simply to conform with a regularity.[43] Regularism is consonant with pragmatism because one can conform to a regularity without having explicit knowledge of it. This avoids the vicious regress that ensues if we require that semantical rules need to be explicitly grasped by speakers.[44] Regularism also appeals to philosophical naturalists because it explains how norms depend (or supervene) on facts about the physical state and structure of individual speakers.

However, Brandom rejects this attempt to ground normative claims in factual claims. Here he follows Kripke's seminal reading of Wittgenstein's discussion of rule-following: pointing out that any finite sequence of actions will conform to a possibly infinite number of regularities. Thus suppose, as in Kripke's original example, that all the addition sums I performed involve values less than 57. My addition behaviour is consistent with the function that always maps two values onto their sum. But it is also consistent with the function 'quus' that maps two numbers onto their sum if each is less than 57 and onto 5 otherwise.[45]

There will be an infinite number of such interpretations of my arithmetical practice, no less consistent with it than with the plus function. And this situation will apply for any maximum summed values.[46] So any episode of my supposed 'additive' behaviour will be equally interpretable as quaddative. Similar considerations apply for any maximum of summed values and extend to empirical concepts, as the easy definition of 'gruesome' predicates illustrates. Thus historical applications of the term 'horse' to its instances are behaviourally consonant with the rule for the predicate 'shmorse' – which applies to a thing if it is observed before the year 30,000 and is a horse, or if it is not observed and is a cat.

The take-home moral is that there is no such thing as the unique regularity that a finite performance conforms to. Moreover, for any continuation of that performance 'there is some regularity with respect to which it counts as "going on in the same way"'.[47] There are just too many ways of *gerrymandering regularities* for any given continuation of a performance, and the simple regularity view provides no basis for selecting between them. So the simple regularity account fails to explain how a determinate norm can be implicit in practice.

One appealing response to the failure of the simple regularity view is to shift attention from finite stretches of performance 'to the sets of performances (for instance, applications of a concept) the individual is *disposed* to produce'.[48] The appeal of unpacking the idea of grasping a rule in terms of dispositions is that it might be that one could be disposed to do an infinite number of things that one never gets round to doing due to lack of time or the absence of triggering input.[49] So a dispositional analysis[50] seems to get at the infinitary nature of concepts in naturalistically admissible ways.

So it appears that we can avoid the gerrymandering objection by saying that different agents A and B grasp the same rules where they are disposed to perform identically given the same triggering inputs. However, Brandom rejects the dispositionalist account of rule-following. Following Kripke, he claims that dispositionalism is unable to account for misapplications of a rule. Abiding by a rule has to be compatible with errors in performance.[51] One can violate a norm. But one cannot, he claims, act in violation of one's dispositions. For example, A might be disposed to behave identically under the same triggering conditions as B. But whereas A is correctly applying the adding rule, B could be incorrectly *quadding* or misapplying some other rule.[52] If a dispositionalist grounding of norms treats dispositions counterfactually, then it will be unable to account for the mismatch between the rule followed and its application. So dispositions (at least, if counterfactually conceived) do not help solve the norm-grounding problem.[53, 54]

DEONTIC STATUSES AND DEONTIC ATTITUDES

As advertised, Brandom's favoured account of norms is non-factualist. We 'clothe' a non-normative world in deontic statuses, he claims, by *taking* certain actions or utterances to be correct or incorrect.[55] Normative statuses arise only insofar as there are creatures that can treat *one another as committed or entitled to do this or that*. In Brandom's terminology, deontic statuses are assigned when creatures adopt *deontic attitudes* towards one another.

> Looking at the practices a little more closely involves cashing out the talk of deontic statuses by translating it into talk of deontic attitudes. Practitioners take or treat themselves and others as having various commitments and entitlements. They keep score on deontic statuses by attributing those statuses to others and undertaking them themselves. The significance of a performance is the difference it makes in the deontic score – that is, the way in which it changes what commitments and entitlements the practitioners, including the performer, attribute to each other and acquire, acknowledge, or undertake themselves.[56]

But what are deontic attitudes? If – like *propositional* attitudes – they are inherently intentional, Brandom is stuck in a regress. The philosophical attraction of normative functionalism is that it promises to reduce intention talk to norm talk. If deontic attitudes are necessarily intentional, however, he has made little progress in explaining interpreting intentionality in terms of social practices. Moreover, his account would fail to accord with a modest Darwinian naturalism regarding the emergence of the intentional. The requirement I have in mind is Darwinian in the loose sense that it holds that the intentional and the mental are not basic features of the world but depend on the way heterogeneous arrangements of mindless (or less minded) things interact with one another.[57] Note that this commitment is not restricted to analytic naturalists like Dennett or Jerry Fodor. It applies to continental materialists and critical posthumanists who, in Pramod Nayar's words, seek 'the radical decentering of the traditional sovereign, coherent and autonomous human in order to demonstrate how the human is always already evolving with, constituted by and constitutive of multiple forms of life and machines'.[58] They have to deny the existence of basic psychological properties for such a project to have any prospect of decentring *anything*. The decentring effect of the claim that humans are constituted by congeries of machines and life forms presupposes that these heterogeneous entities are not themselves the kind of things that possess autonomy or subjectivity as classically conceived.

However, such positions need to go further and provide explanations for the emergence of mental properties in a non-mental world or (if they are deflationary) for the emergence of systems that can attribute such psychological states to arise. This is because they must deny that such powers emerge 'spookily' – that is, in ways that are recalcitrant to explanation. This point is recognized, for example, by Manuel DeLanda, a Deleuzian philosopher of science, who proposes that any explanation of emergent behaviour in a given system should have a mechanistic component framed in terms of its constituents and the ecological relations they enter into: for example, a system of chemical reactants far from equilibrium or a population of individuals in a pre-state society.[59, 60] Spooky or strong emergence would defang the decentring effect by allowing subjectivity to jump fully formed out of the slime of heterogeneity even where these attributes do not form part of the basic furniture of the world.

Naturalists, materialists and posthumanists should, then, require that our theories of intentionality be compatible with some gradualist explanation of the development of intentional systems from non-intentional ones – in this instance, that norm-instituting powers cannot have appeared fully formed but must have emerged gradually from the scum of sentience.[61]

Brandom is properly sensitive to these requirements. As he puts it, 'It is clear that there were nonlinguistic animals before there were linguistic ones, and the latter did not arise by magic'.[62] The capacity to ascribe deontic and practical commitments in discourse presupposes a story whereby 'suitably social creatures can learn to distinguish in their practice between performances that are treated as correct by their fellows'. Darwinian naturalism thus enjoins Brandom to show how deontic attitudes can occur in 'prelinguistic communities' that lack full noetic and agential powers.[63]

The simplest model of deontic attribution that he provides is one in which performances are assessed as something the performer is authorized to do by the withholding of sanctions – where sanctioning behaviour, here, is 'compounded out of reliable dispositions to respond differentially to linguistic and non-linguistic stimuli', not florid interpretative powers.[64] For example, the deontic status of being *entitled* to pass through a door might be instituted by a ticketing system in which 'the ticket-taker is the attributer of authority, the one who recognizes or acknowledges it and who by taking the ticket as authorizing, makes it authorizing, so instituting the entitlement'.[65] This account can be complicated if we introduce deontic attitudes that institute responsibilities on the part of agents. For example, taking the Queen's shilling makes one liable to court martial if certain military duties are not undertaken.[66]

According to Brandom these cases illustrate how social actors can partition 'the space of possible performances into those that have been authorized and those that have not, by being *disposed* to respond differently in the two cases'.[67] Does this model show that Brandom's account can satisfy the minimal naturalist constraints that he recognizes?

A number of commentators – including Daniel Dennett and Anandi Hattiangadi – have argued that it succumbs to the same gerrymandering objections that Brandom cites against regularism.[68] If so, any performative regularities (actual or counterfactual) exhibited by actors and sanctioners in this simple model will be consistent with *multiple normative readings of either behaviours* – including interpretations that render the 'deontic attitudes' mistaken.

The response of a ticket-taker towards ticket holders for some prelinguistic social event might be to open a door, physically permitting entry. However, this is consistent with multiple deontic statuses, including 'entry permitted unconditionally', 'entry permitted [mistakenly] according to a rule barring ticket holders and non-holders alike', 'entry permitted, conditional upon possession of a ticket and having a birth place within a five-mile radius' and so on. Thus if deontic attitudes have to be *compounded only from reliable dispositions to respond to stimuli*, each such response is consistent with the attribution of many, many mutually exclusive statuses.

Just as there is nothing corresponding to *the regularity* exhibited by a given stretch of sign-using behaviour, there is nothing corresponding to the *deontic status* exhibited by any finite episode of what (at first sight) appears to be sanctioning behaviour. Otherwise put, *if regularism fails to supply the constitutive ground for meanings (as Brandom claims) it fails just as spectacularly to supply the constitutive ground for deontic status ascriptions.*

As Hattiangadi points out, beefing up the mental powers of instituters would avail Brandom little, or rather too much. If we furnish sanctioners with the power to make contentful judgements (about whether an agent is entitled to pass through the door, for example) we are already in the realm of the intentional.[69] This indeterminacy ramifies equally if we suppose the sanctioning behaviour extended to something resembling sign use. Suppose prelinguistic Emma sanctions prelinguistic John by kicking him when the latter points to something saying 'That's red'.

> The question is what has John been punished for? Has Emma attributed the commitment to say 'that's not blue', or has she attributed the commitment to say 'that's not grue'? Which of these commitments has John violated?[70]

Again, we cannot attribute contentful attitudes regarding the regularity that John failed to follow here without attributing the florid intentional and agential powers whose emergence was to be accounted for by their prelinguistic analogues. If regularism is false, reliable responses alone do not suffice to furnish contentful attitudes regarding correctness or incorrectness of others' performances.[71] Thus – prior to the emergence of sapience – there can be no deontic statuses at all.

It follows that a naturalistically constrained normativism does not appear able to explain how social but non-linguistic beings can institute norms, thus normative statuses, without a vitiating appeal to florid intentional powers. But this explanatory gap implies that Brandom cannot provide an explanatory framework in which the emergence of intentionality and sapience are non-magical.

THE INTERPRETATIONIST DEFENCE

Can Brandom's account be repaired in a way that meets his minimal naturalist commitment? Well, one defence that seems consistent with Brandom's avowals elsewhere is to follow Davidson and Dennett by claiming that certain kinds of social behaviour are norm-governed if (1) members of our speech community would properly interpret them as normative or (2) if an ideally rational interpreter privy to all the relevant behavioural facts would read them as normative. This response has something to recommend it. When interpreting alien social practices, we are liable to appeal to our own background assumptions about what performances belong to the kind 'social practice'.

Moreover, appealing to the notion of an ideal interpreter can be of value when trying to understand the theoretical and empirical constraints on attributions of semantic or normative content.

However, as Hattiangadi remarks, this response misses the point of the dispositional analysis of deontic attitudes. This was to explain how a non-sapient community could bootstrap itself into sapience by setting up a basic deontic scorekeeping system.[72] Appealing to actual or ideal interpreters simply replicates the problem with Dennett's intentional stance approach since it tells us nothing about the conditions under which a creature qualifies as a potential interpreter and thus little about the conditions for meaning, understanding or agency.

A similar problem afflicts Joseph Heath's proposal[73] that Brandomian norms emerge from reciprocal expectations supported by sanctions. The idea is that a first person acts in a certain way while expecting a sanctioning response from a second person. The second person, meanwhile, is disposed to respond to certain performances with sanctioning behaviour while the first person recognizes this. Where this minimal intersubjective couple converges towards a single pattern of behaviour over time, Heath argues, we are entitled to treat their activity as implying a norm.

Heath's proposal may be fine if we assume that certain intentional powers are already in place – for example, that each individual both expects and sanctions the activity of the other. However, as Hattiangadi's appeal to the gerrymandering argument shows, this structure presupposes beings capable of intentional states such as expecting and sanctioning. This is presumably what distinguishes it from simpler cases of dynamical coupling where two physical systems converge towards a single pattern of behaviour. But if the normativist is serious about explaining the intentional in normative terms, they are not entitled to these assumptions.

UNBOUNDED POSTHUMANISM

If Brandom is right about the defects of Dennett-style or Davidson-style interpretationism, the tendency for his own account to regress to those positions is most telling. It suggests that interpretationist accounts cannot explain the semantic or the intentional without regressing to assumptions about ideal interpreters or background practices whose scope they are incapable of delimiting: '[In] principle interpretability is ill defined unless we have some conception of what is doing the interpreting'.[74]

The point is *not* that interpretationism is false but that it is unilluminating. It is empirically unproblematic that we interpret other speakers, texts, cultural artifacts and so on. However, if in-principle interpretation according to the intentional stance fixes the content of intentional discourse, but the nature of such interpretation is ill defined, we have merely satisfied our curiosity about the nature of mindedness by appealing to local mind-reading techniques. We do not yet know what the invariants (if any) of intentional interpretation are.

Another way of putting this is that our practices of interpretation and deontic assessment are phenomenologically 'dark'.[75] The fact that we have them and have a little empirical knowledge of them leaves us ignorant both of their underlying nature and (by extension) of the space of interpretative and psychological possibility. Normativist ABP and its interpretationist variants thus provide no future-proof constraints on the space of possible minds or possible agents. AUP is not seriously challenged by the argument that mind and meaning are constituted by social practices. *AUP implies that we can infer no claims about the denizens of PPS a priori, by reflecting on the pragmatic transcendental conditions for semantic content.* We thus have no reason to suppose that post-human agents would have to be subjects of discourse or members of communities.

For example, it is conceivable that there might be beings that are far more capable of altering their physical and functional structure than current humans. I call an agent 'hyperplastic' if it can make arbitrarily fine changes to its structure without compromising its agency or its capacity for hyperplasticity. A modest anti-reductionist materialism of the kind embraced by Davidson and (arguably) Brandom implies that such agents would be uninterpretable using an intentional idiom because intentional discourse could have no utility for agents who must predict the effects of arbitrarily fine-grained self-interventions upon future activity. However, the stricture on auto-interpretation would equally apply to hetero-interpretation. Were such hyperplastics possible, they would not be interpretable for discursive creatures, which is not to say that they would be uninterpretable tout court.[76, 77]

As Scott Bakker and I have argued, this position is fatal for the ambitious rationalist or 'Promethean' projects of thinkers such as Brassier and Reza Negarestani.[78] These are *inhumanist* insofar as they reject the claim that a commitment to Enlightenment entails a commitment to any ontological or theological conception of the human subject. Inhumanism proposes that all meaningful intelligence is artificial insofar as it involves the unbounded extension of discursive practices: Humanity *just is* the revisionary power to redefine humanity within the discursive space of reasons.[79] However, AUP implies that there is no warrant for the claim that any serious intelligence must be a 'subject of discourse' able to measure its performances against public standards. So the space of possible intelligences and agents is notionally far larger *and stranger* than can be accommodated by Brassier and Negarestani's bounded inhumanism.

By extension, the politics of posthumanism cannot be fixed by the structure of discursive agency either. We have no future-proof grasp of how strange post-humans (our wide descendants) might be, so we lack any basis for adjudicating the moral status of such beings. We may buy into a parochial humanism which accords human subjects a level of moral consideration that is greater than the non-human creatures we know about. But this does not entail that there are not ethically considerable states of being in PPS that have little in common with the modes of being accessible to current humans. If post-human politics is anthropologically unbounded, in this way, any ethical assessment of the post-human must follow upon its historical emergence. If we want to do serious post-human ethics, we need to *make* post-humans, or *become* post-human.

NOTES

1. David Roden, *Posthuman Life: Philosophy at the Edge of the Human* (London: Routledge, 2014), 5, 97–98, 166–193; Rosi Braidotti, *The Posthuman* (Cambridge: Polity), 38–39.

2. Ray Brassier, 'The View from Nowhere', *Identities: Journal for Politics, Gender and Culture,* 17 (2011): 7–23; Reza Negarestani, 'The Labor of the Inhuman, Part I: Human', *E-flux,* accessed 30 April 2014, http://www.e-flux.com/journal/the-labor-of-the-inhuman-part-i-human/; 'The Labor of the Inhuman, Part II: Inhuman', *E-flux,* accessed 30 April 2014, http://www.e-flux.com/journal/the-labor-of-the-inhuman-part-ii-the-inhuman/; Alex Williams, 'Escape Velocities', *E-flux,* 46 (2013), accessed July 2013, http://worker01.e-flux.com/pdf/article_8969785.pdf.

3. I've coined the term 'wide descent' because exclusive consideration of biological descendants of humanity as candidates for posthumanity would be excessively restrictive. Post-human-making technologies may involve discrete biotechnical modifications of the reproductive process such as human cloning, the introduction of transgenic or artificial genetic material or seemingly exotic processes like mind uploading. Thus entities warranting our concern with the post-human could emerge via modified biological descent, recursive extension of artificial intelligence technologies (involving human and/or non-human designers), quasi-biological descent from synthetic organisms, a convergence of the above or via some technogenetic process yet to be envisaged! (Roden, 2012, 2014: 22).

4. Roden, 'The Disconnection Thesis', in *The Singularity Hypothesis: A Scientific and Philosophical Assessment,* Eds. Amnon H. Eden, Johnny H. Soraker, James H. Moor and Eric Steinhart (London: Springer, 2012): 281–298; *Posthuman Life,* chapter 5.

5. This formulation allows that post-humans could be descended from technological assemblages that are existentially dependent on servicing 'narrow' human goals. Becoming non-human in this sense is not a matter of losing a human essence but of ceasing to belong to a human-oriented sociotechnical system which I call the 'Wide

Human' (Roden, 'The Disconnection Thesis', *Posthuman Life,* 109–113). I refer to the claim that becoming post-human consists in becoming independent of the Wide Human as 'the Disconnection Thesis'. Several critical discussions of the disconnection thesis and related themes in *Posthuman Life* are archived at http://www.philpercs.com/2015/07/posthuman-life-reading-group-summer-2015.html.

6. See Roden, *Posthuman Life,* chapters 7 and 8.
7. See Roden, *Posthuman Life,* chapters 5 and 6.
8. Roden, *Posthuman Life,* 53.
9. Vincent C. Punzo, *Reflective Naturalism: An Introduction to Moral Philosophy* (New York: Macmillan, 1969), cited in Daryl Wennemann, *Posthuman Personhood* (New York: University Press of America, 2013), 47.
10. See also Roden, 'Nature's Dark Domain: An Argument for a Naturalised Phenomenology', *Royal Institute of Philosophy Supplements,* 72 (2013): 169–188.
11. Robert Brandom, 'Kantian Lessons About Mind, Meaning, and Rationality', *Southern Journal of Philosophy,* 44 (2006): 49–71.
12. Brandom also follows Kant in trying to understand semantic notions like reference and truth in terms of their roles in articulating judgements rather than as semantic or representational primitives (Brandom, *Making It Explicit: Reasoning, Representing, and Discursive Commitment* [Cambridge, MA: Harvard University Press, 1994], 79–80).
13. Jeremy Wanderer, *Robert Brandom* (Montreal: McGill-Queens University Press, 2008): 29–30.
14. Daniel C. Dennett, *The Intentional Stance* (Cambridge, MA: MIT Press): 13–42.
15. Intentional systems are unlikely to contain just sawdust or stuffing, but IS theory is agnostic regarding their internal machinery. Thus it undercuts both eliminativism and reductionism while providing a workable methodology for investigations into the mechanisms that actuate intentional systems.
16. Brandom, *Making It Explicit,* 59.
17. Brandom, *Making It Explicit,* 60.
18. Brandom, *Making It Explicit,* 60, 276.
19. Brandom, *Making It Explicit,* 60.
20. Brandom, *Making It Explicit,* 61.
21. 'The key to the account is that an interpretation of this sort must interpret community members as taking or treating each other in practice as adopting intentionally contentful commitments and other normative statuses' (Brandom, *Making It Explicit,* 61).
22. Donald Davidson, 'Thought and Talk', in *Inquiries into Truth and Interpretation* (Oxford: Clarendon Press, 1984): 155–170.
23. Davidson, 'Thought and Talk', 169.
24. Roden, *Posthuman Life,* 62.
25. Davidson, 'Thought and Talk', 163.
26. Brandom, *Making It Explicit,* 231–232.
27. His subsequent, very rich analysis of subsentential expressions is necessarily *decompositional* rather than compositional (Brandom, *Making It Explicit,* 79–82). For example, the difference between a predicate and a singular term is understood

in terms of the different inferential consequences which follow from their inter-substitution within sentences (368).

28. Wilfrid Sellars, 'Some Reflections on Language Games', *Philosophy of Science,* 21.3 (1954): 204–228; 'Meaning as Functional Classification (A Perspective on the Relation of Syntax to Semantics)', *Synthese* 3/4 (1974): 417–437.

29. Sellars, 'Some Reflections on Language Games', 209–210.

30. Brandom, *Making It Explicit,* 235, 258.

31. Brandom, *Making It Explicit,* 39–40; Davidson, 'A Nice Derangement of Epitaphs', in *Truth and Interpretation,* Ed. Ernest Lepore (Oxford: Blackwell, 1986): 433–446.

32. That is, the fact that the inferential move in the language game from 'Spiderman is climbing the building' to 'Peter Parker is climbing the building' is materially valid.

33. Brandom, *Making It Explicit,* 142.

34. The point of attributions of belief or desire, for example, is to determine what an agent is committed or entitled 'to say or do'. Likewise, the point of affixing truth values to beliefs or statements is to assess or endorse their propriety within the game of giving and asking for reasons. Is the claimant entitled to make their assertion? Are the inferential consequences acknowledged by the claimant its actual consequences? (17, 542).

35. Sellars, for example, is happy to accept that learning to infer is, at base, a matter of internalizing formal transformation rules. (Sellars, 'Some Reflections on Language Games', 209.)

36. Jack B. Copeland, 'What is Computation?' *Synthese,* 108.3 (1996): 341–343.

37. The table specifies which operation the machine carries out when in a particular machine state (say, q0) and when a particular symbol is lying on the square currently being scanned. The table may, for example, specify that if the machine is in q0 and a '0' is on the current square, then it should erase '0', replace it with a '1', move right and enter another state (e.g. q2). These simple 'read', 'erase' and 'write' operations can manipulate the contents of the tape and generate an output corresponding to the value of a function when appropriately choreographed by the machine table – for example, a the binary expression of a fraction (see Petzold, 2008).

38. Brassier, 'Nominalism, Naturalism, and Materialism: Sellars' Critical Ontology', in *Contemporary Philosophical Naturalism and its Implications,* Eds. Bana Bashour and Hans D. Muller (London: Routledge, 2013): 101–114.

39. Brandom, *Making It Explicit,* chapter 6.

40. Brandom, *Making It Explicit,* 29–30; Anandi Hattiangadi, 'Making It Implicit: Brandom on Rule Following', *Philosophy and Phenomenological Research,* 66.2 (2003): 419–431; Gideon Rosen, 'Who Makes the Rules Around Here?' *Philosophy and Phenomenological Research,* 57.1 (1997): 163–171.

41. Brandom, *Making It Implicit,* 48; Rosen, 'Who Makes the Rules Around Here?', 163–164.

42. Brandom, *Making It Implicit,* 48.

43. Brandom, *Making It Implicit,* 27.

44. Brandom, *Making It Implicit,* 24–25.

45. Saul Kripke, *Wittgenstein on Rules and Private Language* (Oxford: Blackwell, 1982), 9.

46. So in addition to *quus*, we can define the function *wuss*. Where
x wuss $y = x + y$ if $x, y < 58$
else, x wuss $y = 5$
and so on!

47. Brandom, *Making It Explicit*, 28.

48. Brandom, *Making It Explicit*, 28: emphasis added.

49. So it is not necessary for the rule user to have all the triggering instances 'before his mind' to have grasped how to perform in any of these instances.

50. John Heil and C.B. Martin, 'Rules and Powers', *Philosophical Perspectives*, 12.12 (1998): 284.

51. Brandom, *Making It Explicit*, 29, 31.

52. By extension, a straight dispositional analysis would not distinguish someone who means *grue* by 'green' but has been neurologically interfered with so that they would apply it (incorrectly) to green things after the year 2010 and a user of 'green' who would be disposed to apply it to exactly the same items.

53. Martin and Heil, 'Rules and Powers', 284–285.

54. In 'Rules and Powers', Martin and Heil present a very interesting case for holding that dispositional accounts of rule-following can avoid Kripkensteinian sceptical conclusions if dispositions are construed realistically rather than in terms of statements about counterfactual behaviour. Then it could be true of A and B that they would perform identically, even though A is disposed to follow the plus rule whereas B is disposed to follow the quus rule. This is because B's disposition could be 'blocked' in some way, accounting for the error. Howhy (2003) develops a similar account.

55. Brandom, *Making It Explicit*, 161.

56. Brandon, *Making It Explicit*, 166.

57. Levi R. Bryant provides a useful summary of how this kind of naturalism can be cashed as a Deleuzian Machine-Oriented Ontology (MOO) in 'The Gravity of Things: An Introduction to Onto-Cartography', *Anarchist Developments in Cultural Studies*, 2 (2013): 10–30.

58. Pramod K. Nayar, *Posthumanism* (Oxford: Polity, 2013).

59. Manuel DeLanda, *Philosophy and Simulation: The Emergence of Synthetic Reason* (London: Bloomsbury Academic, 2011): 13–15.

60. In DeLanda's account, the second component corresponds to the Deleuzian Idea: the specification of singularities reflecting that same system's tendency to slip into distinctive portions of its state space.

61. Rosen, 'Who Makes the Rules Around Here?'

62. Brandom, *Making It Explicit*, 155.

63. Brandom, *Making It Explicit*, 161.

64. Brandom, *Making It Explicit*, 156.

65. Brandom, *Making It Explicit*, 161.

66. Brandom, *Making It Explicit*, 163.

67. Brandom, *Making It Explicit*, 161–162: emphasis added.

68. Daniel C. Dennett, 'The Evolution of "Why?": An Essay on Robert Brandom's Making It Explicit', 2006, http://ase.tufts.edu/cogstud/dennett/papers/Brandom.pdf/, accessed 24 November 2010; Hattiangadi, 'Making It Implicit'.
69. Hattiangadi, 'Making It Implicit', 428.
70. Hattiangadi, 'Making It Implicit', 426.
71. Hattiangadi, 'Making It Implicit', 427.
72. Hattiangadi, 'Making It Implicit', 429.
73. Joseph Heath, 'Brandom et les sources de la normativité', *Philosophiques*, 28.1 (2001): 27–46.
74. Roden, *Posthuman Life*, 128.
75. See Roden, 'Nature's Dark Domain', *Posthuman Life*, 82–104.
76. Roden, 'Reduction, Elimination and Radical Uninterpretability', https://www.academia.edu/15054582/Reduction_Elimination_and_Radical_Uninterpretability; *Posthuman Life*, 101.
77. I've argued that Neil Cassidy, the rogue neuroscientist of Richard Scott Bakker's ultra-dark thriller *Neuropath*, becomes a 'beta test' hyperplastic from the moment that he turns his radical neurotechnology on himself (Bakker, *Neuropath* [New York: Tor, 2010]); Roden, 'Aliens Under the Skin: Serial Killing and the Seduction of Our Common Inhumanity', in *Serial Killing: A Philosophical Anthology*, Eds. Edia Connole and Gary J. Shipley (Schism Press, 2015).
78. Bakker, 'The Blind Mechanic II: Reza Negarestani and het Labor of Ghosts: Three Pound Brain', accessed 30 April 2014, https://rsbakker.wordpress.com/2014/04/13/the-blind-mechanic-ii-reza-negarestani-and-the-labour-of-ghosts; 'Interview with David Roden', *Figure/Ground*, http://figureground.org/interview-with-david-roden; Brassier, 'The View From Nowhere'; Negarestani, 'The Labor of the Inhuman, Part I: Human'; 'The Labor of the Inhuman, Part II: The Inhuman'; Williams, 'Escape Velocities'.
79. Negarestani, 'The Labor of the Inhuman, Part II: The Inhuman'.

BIBLIOGRAPHY

Bakker, Richard Scott. *Neuropath*. New York: Tor, 2010.

———. 'The Blind Mechanic II: Reza Negarestani and the Labor of Ghosts'. *Three Pound Brain* (blog), 4 April 2014, https://rsbakker.wordpress.com/2014/04/13/the-blind-mechanic-ii-reza-negarestani-and-the-labour-of-ghosts/, accessed 30 April 2014.

———. 'Phenomenology: Zahavi, Dennett, and the End of Being'. *Three Pound Brain* (blog), 22 October 2014, https://rsbakker.wordpress.com/2016/05/28/zahavi-dennett-and-the-end-of-being/, accessed 2 November 2014.

———. 'Interview with David Roden'. *Figure/Ground* (2015), http://figureground.org/interview-with-david-roden/.

Braidotti, Rosi. *The Posthuman*. Cambridge: Polity, 2013.

Brandom, Robert. *Making It Explicit: Reasoning, Representing, and Discursive Commitment*. Cambridge, MA: Harvard University Press, 1994.

———. *Articulating Reasons: An Introduction to Inferentialism*. Cambridge MA: Harvard University Press, 2001.

———. *Tales of the Mighty Dead: Historical Essays in the Metaphysics of Intentionality*. Cambridge: Cambridge University Press, 2002.

———. 'Kantian Lessons about Mind, Meaning, and Rationality'. *Southern Journal of Philosophy*, 44 (2006): 49–71.

———. 'Inferentialism and Some of Its Challenges'. *Philosophy and Phenomenological Research*, 74.3 (2007): 651–676.

Brassier, Ray. 'The View from Nowhere'. *Identities: Journal for Politics, Gender and Culture*, 17 (2011): 7–23.

———. 'Nominalism, Naturalism, and Materialism: Sellars' Critical Ontology'. In *Contemporary Philosophical Naturalism and Its Implications*, edited by Bana Bashour and Hans D. Muller, 101–114. London: Routledge, 2013.

Bryant, Levi R. 'The Gravity of Things: An Introduction to Onto-Cartography'. *Anarchist Developments in Cultural Studies*, 2 (2013): 10–30.

Copeland, B. Jack. 'What is Computation?' *Synthese*, 108.3 (1996): 335–359.

Davidson, Donald. 'A Nice Derangement of Epitaphs'. In *Truth and Interpretation*, edited by Ernest LePore, 433–446. Oxford: Blackwell, 1986.

———. *Inquiries into Truth and Interpretation*. Oxford: Clarendon Press, 1984.

———. 'Thought and Talk'. In *Inquiries into Truth and Interpretation*, edited by Donald Davidson, 155–170. Oxford: Clarendon Press, 1984.

DeLanda, Manuel. *Philosophy and Simulation: The Emergence of Synthetic Reason*. London: Bloomsbury Academic, 2011.

Dennett, Daniel C. *The Intentional Stance*. Cambridge, MA: MIT Press, 1989.

———. 'The Evolution of "Why?": An Essay on Robert Brandom, *Making It Explicit*', 2006, http://ase.tufts.edu/cogstud/dennett/papers/Brandom.pdf, accessed 24 November 2010.

Hattiangadi, Anandi. 'Making It Implicit: Brandom on Rule Following'. *Philosophy and Phenomenological Research*, 66.2 (2003): 419–431.

Heath, Joseph. 'Brandom et les sources de la normativité'. *Philosophiques*, 28.1 (2001): 27–46.

Heil, John and C.B. Martin. 'Rules and Powers'. *Philosophical Perspectives*, 12 (1998): 283–312.

Hohwy, Jakob. 'A Reduction of Kripke-Wittgenstein's Objections to Dispositionalism About Meaning'. *Minds and Machines*, 13.2 (2003): 257–268.

———. 'Internalized Meaning Factualism'. *Philosophia*, 34.3 (2006): 325–336.

Kraut, Robert. 'Universals, Metaphysical Explanations, and Pragmatism'. *Journal of Philosophy*, 107.11 (2010): 590–609.

Kripke, Saul A. *Wittgenstein on Rules and Private Language*. Oxford: Blackwell, 1982.

Lauer, David. 'Genuine Normativity, Expressive Bootstrapping, and Normative Phenomenalism'. *Ethica and Politica/Ethics & Politics*, 11.1 (2009): 321–350.

Lewis, Kevin. 'Carnap, Quine and Sellars on Abstract Entities'. 2013, https://www.academia.edu/2364977/Carnap_Quine_and_Sellars_on_Abstract_Entities, accessed 12 July 2014.

Nayar, Pramod K. *Posthumanism*. Cambridge: Polity, 2013.

Negarestani, Reza. 'The Labor of the Inhuman, Part I: Human'. *E-flux*, (2014), http://www.e-flux.com/journal/the-labor-of-the-inhuman-part-i-human/, accessed 30 April 2014.

———. 'The Labor of the Inhuman, Part II: The Inhuman'. *E-flux*, (2014), http://www.e-flux.com/journal/the-labor-of-the-inhuman-part-ii-the-inhuman/, accessed 30 April 2014.

Petzold, Charles. *The Annotated Turing: A Guided Tour through Alan Turing's Historic Paper on Computability and the Turing Machine*. Indianapolis: Wiley, 2008.

Punzo, Vincent C. *Reflective Naturalism: An Introduction to Moral Philosophy*. New York: Macmillan, 1969.

Roden, David. 'The Disconnection Thesis'. In *The Singularity Hypothesis: A Scientific and Philosophical Assessment*, edited by Amnon H. Eden, Johnny H. Søraker, James H. Moor and Eric Steinhart, 281–298. London: Springer, 2012.

———. 'Nature's Dark Domain: An Argument for a Naturalised Phenomenology'. *Royal Institute of Philosophy Supplements*, 72 (2013): 169–188.

———. *Posthuman Life: Philosophy at the Edge of the Human*. London: Routledge, 2014.

———. 'Aliens Under the Skin: Serial Killing and the Seduction of Our Common Inhumanity'. In *Serial Killing: A Philosophical Anthology*, edited by Edia Connole and Gary J. Shipley. USA: Schism Press, 2015.

———. 'Reduction, Elimination and Radical Uninterpretability', 2015, https://www.academia.edu/15054582/Reduction_Elimination_and_Radical_Uninterpretability, accessed 2 October 2015.

Rosen, Gideon. 'Who Makes the Rules Around Here?' *Philosophy and Phenomenological Research*, 57.1 (1997): 163–171.

Sellars, Wilfrid. 'Some Reflections on Language Games'. *Philosophy of Science*, 21.3 (1954): 204–228.

———. 'Meaning as Functional Classification (A Perspective on the Relation of Syntax to Semantics)'. *Synthese*, 3/4 (1974): 417–437.

Wanderer, Jeremy. *Robert Brandom*. Montreal: McGill-Queens University Press, 2008.

Wennemann, Daryl J. *Posthuman Personhood*. New York: University Press of America, 2013.

Williams, Alex. 'Escape Velocities'. *E-flux*, 46 (2013), http://worker01.e-flux.com/pdf/article_8969785.pdf, accessed July 2013.

Chapter Eight

Circuits of Desire

Cybernetics and the Post-natural According to Lyotard and Stiegler

Ashley Woodward

One approach to a 'philosophy after nature' is that which follows the breakdown of the oppositional distinction between nature and a variety of other terms – the human, the cultural, the technical, the artificial – which serve to give the concept 'nature' a meaningful consistency. We can see such a breakdown in the theories of cybernetics and systems which developed in the twentieth century, in the 'general physics' discussed by Jean-François Lyotard, and in Bernard Stiegler's 'general organology'. Despite their differences, each of these approaches shows how new ways of thinking become possible as old distinctions are broken down and connections between areas previously separated are developed. More specifically, each of these approaches proposes to think these possibilities in terms of the way energy moves in systems (thus as an economy). With these displacements, a 'philosophy after nature' can no longer appeal to familiar metaphysical hierarchies in order to understand the world and develop principles for acting in it. How, then, are we to think ourselves and the world in terms of energy and systems?

I wish to highlight some of the issues at stake in such considerations by critically contrasting the thought of the two above-mentioned French philosophers. Both Lyotard and Stiegler are concerned with how technology in particular impels us to think beyond the natural/artificial opposition and opens up the possibility of thinking the physiological, the technical and the psychosocial organizations as systems. Moreover, and crucially, both are concerned with how we can think such systems critically in terms of how energy, understood as *libidinal* (the energy of desire), circulates in such systems. While both philosophers present *descriptively* comparable analyses, they appear to be *prescriptively* at odds regarding how we should evaluate the flows of desire in the contemporary information networks. The critical contrast I wish to stage here thus allows a clarification of what is at stake in thinking about a broad range of issues concerning contemporary systems, focused on how we understand desire and – as we will see – with implications for 'what makes life worth living'. Before moving to this critical comparison, let us examine what has brought about the collapse of the separation between the natural, the technological and the social, and thus what has led to the contemporary situation they both engage.[1]

SYSTEMS

The conception of nature as distinct from the artificial and the cultural was progressively displaced in the twentieth century by the new sciences of cybernetics and systems theory. Founded by Norbert Wiener, cybernetics was a paradigm-shifting way of thinking functions of communication and control analogously in both organic and non-organic systems (animal and machine). This model, the result of truly interdisciplinary collaborations, flourished in a wide variety of fields in the mid-twentieth century. While cybernetics, as a research model understood in terms of a particular methodology, did not meet expectations and was superseded by artificial intelligence and cognitive science, as Mohammed-Ali Rahebi argues, this did not prevent it from having a broad 'ideological' impact which remains influential.[2] Adam Curtis's 2011 documentary *All Watched Over by Machines of Loving Grace* traces the development of just such a cybernetic ideology, giving a clear picture of the origins of dominant and persistent ideas about ecology and economy which have a grounding in cybernetics and systems theory and are united by what he calls 'the machine paradigm'.

This paradigm views all systems, including animals and machines, ecology, economy and human social systems in general, as *self-regulating*, naturally inclined towards homeostasis or equilibrium. While the idea of the world as a harmonious, self-regulating system is a very ancient one,[3] Curtis argues that what is new in the twentieth century is the claim to establish this scientifically. The basis of this claim is the identification of the *mechanism* of self-regulation: feedback. What is new in this situation, then, is that our policies in areas like ecological, economic and social management – our ideas about what *ought* to be the case – come to be based on claims about what is believed to have been scientifically 'proven' *to be* the case. Curtis claims that scientifically, such assumptions have proven false, yet the ideologies they have spawned continue to persist, contributing to a dehumanized, mechanical world in which human individuality is crushed.

In brief, here is the story Curtis tells in episode two, 'The Abuse of Vegetative Concepts'. The biologist Arthur George Tansley, intrigued by one of his dreams, began reading Freud and was captivated by Freud's model of the mind as a system regulated by laws similar to the principles of thermodynamics, in which the system maintains its equilibrium by discharging build-ups of energy. Tansley postulated that the ecological system of the natural world should be understood according to this principle, which he called the 'Great Universal Law of Equilibrium'.[4] Jay Wright Forrester, a computer scientist who became a professor of management at MIT, developed a theory called 'Systems Dynamics', which generalized the concept of system such that the same basic principles could be applied to both technical systems and complex social systems. Forrester claimed that the mechanism responsible for equilibrium is *feedback*: an output of the system which is then fed in as a new input, such that the system can regulate itself on the basis of information about itself.[5]

This idea of feedback was taken up and developed in cybernetics by Norbert Weiner and others.[6] The brothers Howard and Eugene Odum then applied cybernetic principles to ecology, in some classic statements of nature as a self-regulating system, as expressed in the well-known term 'the balance of nature'.[7] The idea that cybernetic principles could be applied to *human social systems* was enthusiastically embraced by anthropologists such as Gregory Bateson and Margaret Mead.[8]

However, Curtis points out the failure of this cybernetic model of the system which regulates itself in order to reach equilibrium. First, the science in the realm of ecology turns out to be wrong. The 'system-equilibrium' model, which reigned unquestioned throughout much of the twentieth century, was effectively falsified by the most ambitious attempt to prove it through the computer modelling of a grassland environment in the 1970s. The data which emerged from this and other studies pointed to the contrary, namely that ecological systems are unstable; they tend towards instabilities and catastrophes, after which the system 'resets' itself and changes, rather than returning to its previous state. Thus nature does not preserve itself in equilibrium; it is prone to disasters and the eradication of species.[9] Moreover, as alluded to in the title of episode three, Curtis points to the potential of these ideas to be ideologically abused. Tansley's ideas of nature as system were applied to social systems by Jan Smuts, a governor in South Africa, who argued that in order for the social system to function correctly, natural roles must be respected and whites (naturally) must have the role of superiors. Tansley accused him of 'the abuse of vegetational concepts'.[10]

What we learn from following Curtis's exploration of the emergence of 'the machine paradigm' in the twentieth century is that this paradigm placed at its centre the idea of *a self-regulating system in a constant state of equilibrium*. This paradigm erased differences between natural, technological and social systems, even as it allowed a central understanding of how systems should operate to become dominant. While on the one hand this paradigm seemed to break down traditional metaphysical distinctions, with their hierarchical privileges, in another sense it kept them very much alive: the old idea of a balanced, harmonious nature came to be understood on a technoscientific model, and the combined ideological force of a supposed 'natural order' and 'scientific verification' was brought to bear on the organization of social systems. In differing ways, Lyotard and Stiegler both accept that after the developments of twentieth-century thought, we must develop a philosophy after nature – that is, without appeal to the supposedly natural order of things – and are critically aware of how the machine paradigm is itself open to such ideological abuses. Both offer alternative evaluative models for thinking systems in terms of the economies of desire operative in them, but with strikingly different conclusions. Let us turn now to the detail of their critical encounters.

ENTROPY

Lyotard's thought reacts to a cybernetic ideology– which he often refers to simply as 'the system' or 'development' – explicitly and extensively in his later work around the idea of the inhuman[11] but also implicitly in his earlier work on libidinal economy.[12] His strategy amounts to a critical reconsideration of the *values* which underlie the drives operative in libidinal economy and, by analogical extension, in cybernetics and the machine paradigm generally. (We have already seen how Freud's work on psychic economy influenced Tansley's ecological model which fed into this paradigm.) Lyotard effectively 'revalues' the drives by reading Freud through Nietzsche, giving value to the death drive (read as the Dionysian and as a repetition of affects akin to the eternal return) as the motive force for artistic creativity, political transformation and everything which he terms 'events'. Lyotard emphasizes the deregulating function of the death drive, which would do justice to the existence of instabilities and 'events' in systems.

Lyotard's philosophy of libidinal economy, developed in the early 1970s, is an extension of the concept Freud uses to describe the movements and transformations of libidinal energy (or desire) in the psyche. For Lyotard, it is a description of social reality which allows him to map its stabilities and instabilities from the perspective of relatively kinetic or quiescent energies.[13] Freud indicates two types of desire: wish-desire and libido-desire. Wish-desire is teleological and negative; it aims to possess something that is felt lacking. Libido-desire is a positive force of transformable energy. For Lyotard, libido-desire is itself divided according to two regimes: Eros and the death drive. Eros contributes to the stable functioning and regulation of a system and operates according to Freud's principle of constancy (energy maintained at a low, stable level). The death drive deregulates the system and works against its unity and stable functioning: It produces intensities at very high or very low levels of energy, which Lyotard characterizes as 'events'.[14]

In general, Lyotard applies Nietzschean-inspired values in his libidinal economy by criticizing the quiescence of libidinal energy maintained at low levels in bound wholes and stable systems governed by Eros as a kind of nihilistic depression and privileging the transformative potential of libidinal intensities. The aim of the libidinal economist is to encourage a life-affirmative, creative flow of energy *within* systems, encouraging them to change and to produce new intensities. He sees the intensities produced by the desublimation of libido as a constructive power which is the source of art, political motivation and the positive, affirmative force which makes life worth living.

As is well known, Lyotard had distanced himself from his libidinal economics by the time he began to pay serious attention to technoscientific development in the 1980s. Nevertheless, the critical categories he developed with the Freudian drives continued to find expression through explicit appeal to the thermodynamic principles which had to some extent inspired Freud, negentropy (Eros) and entropy (the death drive). In this period, Lyotard developed a critical model of 'the system' of 'development', which he saw as functioning, after the end of metanarratives and the collapse of belief in the perfection of the human subject of history, according to the sole value of negentropy (the establishment and development of order). He suggests that the current complex of technoscientific and capitalist development can be modelled according to a metaphysics of energy, which he explicitly associates with cybernetics and systems theory (and thus links directly with the machine paradigm discussed above).

Lyotard outlines this in the short essay '*Oikos*'.[15] He argues that the man/nature opposition belongs to the speculative tradition (Marx/Hegel) and the inside/outside opposition belongs to the tradition of *the metaphysics of the subject*. But there is another tradition where these distinctions are not relevant: *the metaphysics of energy*. What counts in this tradition is the opposition between *matter* and *form*. Leibniz is an extreme expression of this philosophical tradition, while cybernetics is its more recent form. This tradition suppresses the outside/inside border in favour of different degrees of complexity. Lyotard describes this as a

> general physics which stretches from astrophysics to particle physics (electronics, information technology, and cybernetics are only aspects of this general physics) and of course also in economic terms. In this description, the alive or the human appear as particular cases, very interesting cases of complex material systems. This means that, from this perspective, conflict (and ultimately war) does not arise between human and nature; rather, the struggle is between more developed systems and something else that is necessarily less developed and that the physicists know as entropy, the second principle of thermodynamics.[16]

Crucially for our interests here, then, Lyotard suggests that the shift to a view of reality as a material system of energetic transformations characterized by greater or lesser degrees of complexity results in a view of history no longer as a conflict between man and nature ('civilization') but between negentropy (the principle of increasing complexity, or order) and entropy (the principle of decreasing complexity, or increasing disorder).

In essays collected in *The Inhuman*, Lyotard describes the variations in complexity which affect systems in more detail using Leibnizian and Bergsonian concepts. In Leibniz's 'monadology', reality is described as consisting of monads (simple substances) of varying complexity, ranging from a bare material point which stores virtually no information to God as the ideal monad which contains all the information of the cosmos within itself. Lyotard suggests that the contemporary system of technological development aims towards the great monad (God) as its ideal. Lyotard explains complexity itself as consisting in the capacity of a monad or system to process new input by passing it through retained memories, which operate on and transform it before translating it into output (a process not unlike the feedback loop in cybernetics and systems theory).[17] A similar picture is given in Bergson's redefinition of the relation between matter and mind as one of increasing complexity, where mind emerges from the capacity of matter to memorize past states and compare new states to them in increasingly circuitous paths. The more complex the system, the longer the circuit.[18]

According to Lyotard, the contemporary system of development is 'the realization of metaphysics as a general physics under the name of cybernetics'.[19] While Lyotard accepts that the scientific developments charted in the previous section above are legitimate, and that we must cease to think in terms of oppositions such as the human/nature and so on, he also critiques the implicit values in the ideological forms of cybernetics, specifically around the supposed equilibrium state of a system which minimizes entropy. His fear is that '[f]rom the point of view of development ... the Third World is nothing but a source of entropy for the *autopoesis* [sic] of the great monad'[20] – and would be better eliminated so as not to be an inefficient energy drain on the system. Lyotard suggests that his own philosophical work could be characterized as a defence of *entropy*, understood as that which resists the negentropic programming of the system of development – art, thought, the unconscious, the singularity of the event and so on. Stiegler gets this precisely wrong when he writes that 'calculation is that which eliminates all *negentropy*, all singularity, all opacity, as Jean-François Lyotard saw very well'.[21] Knowingly or unknowingly, here he is (mis)translating Lyotard's thought into the terms of his own, to which we now turn.

NEGENTROPY

Bernard Stiegler's works have contributed to a 'philosophy after nature' since the publication of his seminal thesis, in *Technics and Time 1: The Fault of Epimetheus*,[22] that the human is fundamentally constituted by the relation to technics. Stiegler posits an 'originary technicity' in which the human's relation to technics is effectively that of a *supplement* understood in the Derridean sense: technics are prosthetics insofar as they are something exterior to humans, added on, but this exteriorization is also internalized in a process through which humans are constituted by something which nevertheless remains other to them.

Stiegler's work has drawn heavily on, though also modified, Gilbert Simondon's, and he has developed a 'general organology' which deploys the Simondonian notion of individuation (the process through which things take on consistency and are organized in relation to their *milieu*) as it takes place at three principal levels: the physiological, the technical and the social.[23] This general organology cuts through old oppositions such as the artificial and the natural, the individual and society, and allows a theorization of the links between minds, bodies, social organizations and technologies. It also allows a thinking of values in terms of more or less successful processes of individuation. Despite Stiegler's thesis of originary technicity – and in a precise way because of it – he is highly critical of the effects of contemporary technologies on the processes of psychic and collective individuation as they function in consumer capitalism. In various ways, he has argued that the contemporary developed world is a deeply nihilistic epoch affected by a generalized *loss of individuation*.

Since the first volume of his *Disbelief and Discredit* series,[24] Stiegler has trained his critical focus on the *libidinal economy* operative in general organological systems. Desire, he explains, inscribes itself in 'grammatizations'.[25] Grammatization is a type of formalization which consists in the division of continuous processes into discrete units ('grammes'), 'the finite number of components forming a system'.[26] For Stiegler, the generalization of information technologies constitutes a decisive revolution in the history of grammatization, after the alphabet and the printing press. Grammatization affects the way that symbolic systems, and therefore cultural meanings, operate and circulate, and in this way it affects desire. A libidinal economy operates in symbolic systems, conditioned by the grammatizations of information and communication technologies. Libidinal economy is thus a way for Stiegler to think the problems of existence in the contemporary information society in terms of how we value things – or, significantly, fail to do so – according to our libidinal attachments and investments. Stiegler has increasingly focused on the nature of technics as a *pharmakon*, both poison and cure, and for him these are the two tendencies of libidinal economy, Eros and the death drive. As he phrases it, these tendencies may be understood as two circuits of desire operating in all organized systems, both caused by the *pharmakon* of technics: 'on the one hand it produces long circuits through which it becomes care, entering into the service of the libido orientated through sublimation, that is, the binding of the drives. Long circuits connect or bind the drives that are disconnected or unbound by short-circuits'.[27]

Drawing heavily on the work of Donald Winnicott,[28] Stiegler associates the work of Eros in the construction of 'bound wholes' or consistent objects with the capacities of humans to become psychically individuated in a healthy sense by shifting attachments from the mother to reality through *transitional objects* at an early age, a process responsible for *instilling the feeling that life is worth living*. Stiegler associates the establishment of 'long circuits' of desire with motivation and the capacity to set long-term goals and the 'short-circuiting' of desire with the erosion of motivation and attention span produced by consumer culture with its insistence on immediate short-term satisfaction, facilitated by the speed of information and communication technologies. According to him, the grammatization effected by information technologies allows unprecedented control over symbolic meanings, which have been co-opted by marketing. This results in the short-circuiting of desire by channelling it into immediate, fleeting consumer satisfactions, undermining processes of healthy individuation.

Stiegler's response to the contemporary nihilism of the libidinal economy involves an invocation of what he calls a 'negentropology'.[29] As this term suggests, Stiegler frequently characterizes the problem of nihilism – the failure of processes of individuation – as entropic and successful individuations as negentropic. Technics are pharmacological for him because they both contribute to the entropic effects of consumer society and also have the potential for contributing to new modes of negentropic individuation. Stiegler's call to arms is inventive or constructive, in opposition to what he sees as the reactive and nihilistic quality of the old form of politics as 'resistance'.[30] He calls for a new politics which will take care of libidinal economy in the structures of general organology by promoting the processes of individuation he sees as necessary to produce the feeling that life is worth living.

METASTABILITY

Both Lyotard and Stiegler engage with the 'post-natural' conception of the world as a generalized system, through which movements of energy flow, and both develop critical approaches by focusing on the transformations of the energy of desire in this system. But we can immediately see an apparent conflict between their positions with respect to the values accorded to the major principles of the movements of desire and energy in the system in general: Eros/negentropy and Thanatos/entropy. In contrast to Stiegler's alarm at the increase of entropic processes and defence of negentropic individuations, which we have just seen, Lyotard's critique is trained on the negentropic tendencies of the system, and he defends the value of entropic processes. For him, the more complex, the more negentropic the system, and the longer the circuit through which 'input' is processed (in Stiegler's terms, the more one is 'individuated'), the less likely something is to strike us with the singular force of an event or to allow a libidinal intensity which will deregulate the system and open it up to dynamic change. What Stiegler calls the 'short-circuits' of desire, and castigates as consumerist decadence, seem close to what Lyotard privileges in his version of libidinal economy as 'sterile consumptions', singular intensities consisting of jouissance for its own sake, rather than contributing in utilitarian fashion to a productive libidinal or capitalist economy.[31]

Despite the apparently stark contrast between their views, however, both Lyotard and Stiegler in fact acknowledge the necessity of *both* negentropy and entropy, Eros and the death drive, in the healthy functioning of systems. This is evident in what is arguably the central principle of Lyotard's libidinal economy, *dissimulation*: the necessary mutual co-implication of Eros and the death drive.[32] While Lyotard emphasizes intensive singularities and transformative effects on structures, he insists that there are no libidinal energies free from structuration, no death drive except in operation as the deregulation of structures governed by Eros. Moreover, the outcomes of such deregulating forces are always the reinscriptions of energies into new bound wholes, new structures.[33]

Stiegler, for his part, at points acknowledges the importance of both entropic and negentropic tendencies in the process of individuation: Both tendencies are seen as essential to the *metastability* which properly characterizes this process.[34] In 'To Love, to Love Me, to Love Us', we read the following:

> Life is a crystal that does not reach crystallization, caught in a process of *metastable equilibrium*.[35]
> [...]
> It is a metastable process precisely in that it is not stable: if it was, it would be a totally ossified crystal, without future or temporality; if it was totally unstable, it would lead to an explosion of the group – atomization, pulverization, entropy, absolute disequilibrium. A group is always between equilibrium and disequilibrium, neither in equilibrium nor in disequilibrium, but rather always at the border of both: at the border of pure equilibrium, which is called pure synchrony, the crystal being purely synchronic; and of disequilibrium, that is, of pure diachrony, total atomization, completed *diabelein*. Disequilibrium exists in groups, and it is called madness. Madness is *at the heart* of the process of individuation,

but it is an energy that must be, precisely, *calendarized and cardinalized* to be channeled and to form something that creates movement without leading to disintegration. Metastability produces movement. Pure disequilibrium is the collapse of movement. Pure equilibrium is immobility preceding movement. Between these two is fragile metastability.[36]

Similarly, in a passage of *Symbolic Misery Volume 1: The Hyperindustrial Epoch*, he acknowledges the necessary value of both Eros and Thanatos in processes of individuation, processes undermined by hyperindustrial consumer capitalism:

> the consumer, consumed by what he consumes, is *vampirized*, and this development is that of an *(almost) perfect control* leading to the annulment of Eros and Thanatos. Their annulment, that is, as tendencies which – in the tension between them, in the play of effective repetitions – together composed the dynamic of individuation (of difference).[37]

What Stiegler fears, and believes is the threat of what he calls our 'hyperindustrial epoch', is precisely an excess of madness, leading to the breakdown of the metastable process through excess of entropic disequilibrium. By contrast, Lyotard (and others of his 'poststructuralist' generation), while also effectively acknowledging the necessity of both entropy and negentropy, privileged entropy because he saw it as what was in danger of being eradicated by the hegemonic system of development obsessed with equilibrium. What is at issue is not only a possibly different emphasis regarding values but also primarily the question of how the complex contemporary sociopolitical situation is to be interpreted.

This preliminary sketch of an encounter between Lyotard and Stiegler[38] suggests a method of reading in which each can be used as a corrective to the other. Lyotard tends to treat processes of individuation, the formation of systems, as processes which will take care of themselves, and Stiegler's concern that we need to seriously think about and take care of these processes, because they are under threat, is essential. Stiegler's concerns with such individuation processes, however, seem to ignore the dangers of privileging negentropy that Lyotard saw, as well as to significantly undervalue the entropic processes which he nevertheless acknowledges as essential to individuation itself.

This kind of conclusion – a 'balanced' one – can seem disappointing, for reasons Stiegler notes when he suggests that any discourse of the 'golden mean' seems to be a discourse of 'reformism and adaptation' which 'systematically ignores radical questions'.[39] Yet Stiegler insists that there is nothing more radical than thinking in terms of complex tendencies rather than simple oppositions. A philosophy which attempts a political and cultural critique must do more than simply adopt scientific principles such as entropy and negentropy as avatars of 'good' and 'evil' – this is precisely the lesson of the misplaced faith in the negentropic equilibrium of systems Curtis charts and Lyotard critiques. Rather, such evaluative categories can only be provisional concepts used in the service of sensitive judgements regarding complex interactions of tendencies in an increasingly complex world system. In contributing different perspectives on how to evaluate the circulations of desire in the networks of our information society, Lyotard and Stiegler both aid our capacity to reflect on the complexity of such tendencies and illuminate important aspects of what is at stake in formulating a 'philosophy after nature'.

NOTES

1. A critical comparison of the thoughts of Lyotard and Stiegler deserves much more attention than I am able to afford it in the limited space available here. Lyotard was evidently the first philosopher to engage with Stiegler's thought in print, in several essays collected in *The Inhuman* (1988). These papers were originally presented at conferences where Stiegler also presented in the 1980s, well before the publication of any of his major works (starting with the first volume of *Technics and Time* in 1991). Stiegler, for his part, has increasingly engaged with Lyotard, notably in *For a New Critique of Political Economy* and in chapter 4 of *States of Shock*. What I hope to achieve here is therefore only a prolegomenon to more extensive analysis, which would be valuable in illuminating the timely issues they both engage.

2. Mohammed-Ali Rahebi, 'The Cybernetic Organon and the Obsolescence of the Subject of Knowledge'. Unpublished.

3. John Kricher finds versions of it in the Ionian pre-Socratic philosophers. See *The Balance of Nature: Ecology's Enduring Myth* (Princeton and Oxford: Princeton University Press, 2009), 33.

4. See Arthur George Tansley, *Elements of Plant Biology* (Lenox, MA: HardPress, 2012 [1922]).

5. Forrester explains that '[a] feedback system, which is sometimes called a "closed" system, is influenced by its own past behaviour. A feedback system has a closed loop structure that brings results from past action of the system back to control future action'. *Principles of Systems* (Sheffield: Pegasus Communications, 1968), 1–5 [chapter one, page 5, following the pagination used in the text].

6. Norbert Wiener, *Cybernetics, or Control and Communication in the Animal and the Machine* (Cambridge, MA: MIT Press, 1968 [1948]).

7. Eugene Odum and Howard T. Odum, *Fundamentals of Ecology,* 2nd edition. (Philadelphia: W.B. Saunders, 1959).

8. Gregory Bateson, *Steps to an Ecology of Mind* (Chicago, IL: Chicago University Press, 1999).

9. According to one study written in the 1960s, there was already ample evidence that this thesis was false. See P.R. Ehrlich and L.C. Birch, 'The "Balance of Nature" and "Population Control"', *The American Naturalist,* 101.918 (1967): 97–107. For a recent popular overview of the issue, see John Kricher's *The Balance of Nature: Ecology's Enduring Myth*. Kricher presents the discrediting of the 'myth'

132　　　　　　　　　　　　　*Chapter Eight*

of the balance of nature in ecology less dramatically than Curtis, as the result of a gradual accumulation of data from a broad range of studies.

10. Arthur G. Tansley, 'The Use and Abuse of Vegetational Terms and Concepts', *Ecology*, 16.3 (1935): 284–307.

11. Jean-François Lyotard, *The Inhuman: Reflections on Time*. Trans. Geoffrey Bennington and Rachel Bowlby (Cambridge: *Polity Press*, 1991).

12. Lyotard, *Libidinal Economy*. Trans. Iain Hamilton Grant (London: Athlone, 1993).

13. A concise outline of Lyotard's conception of a social system as a libidinal economy can be found in the section 'The System and the Event' in his essay 'March 23', collected in *Jean-François Lyotard: Political Writings*. Trans. Bill Readings and Kevin Paul (Minneapolis: University of Minnesota Press, 1993).

14. The *locus classicus* of Freud's concepts of Eros and the death drive is of course the paper in which he first proposes the latter, 'Beyond the Pleasure Principle'. See Sigmund Freud, *Beyond the Pleasure Principle, Group Psychology, and Other Works*. Trans. and Ed. James Strachey. *The Standard Edition of the Complete Psychological Works of Sigmund Freud, Volume 18* (New York: Vintage, 2001). Lyotard gives a concise outline of his heterodox reading of these drives in 'Painting as Libidinal Set-up' in *The Lyotard Reader and Guide*, Eds. Keith Crome and James Williams (Edinburgh: Edinburgh University Press, 2006).

15. In Lyotard, *Jean-François Lyotard: Political Writings*. Trans. Bill Readings and Kevin Paul (Minneapolis: University of Minnesota Press, 1993).

16. Lyotard, '*Oikos*', in *Jean-François Lyotard: Political Writings*, 98–99.

17. See Lyotard, 'Time Today', in *The Inhuman*.

18. Lyotard, 'Matter and Time', in *The Inhuman*.

19. Lyotard, '*Oikos*', 101.

20. Lyotard, '*Oikos*', 99.

21. Bernard Stiegler, *The Decadence of Industrial Democracies: Disbelief and Discredit 1*. Trans. Daniel Ross (Cambridge: Polity, 2011), 86: italics added.

22. Stiegler, *Technics and Time 1: The Fault of Epimetheus*. Trans. George Collins and Richard Beardsworth (Stanford: Stanford University Press, 1998).

23. Stiegler writes, 'The programmatologies through which physiological, technical, and social programmes are arranged together, programmes that are established and implemented by physiological, technical and social systems of organs and organizations, constitute a complex and multi-dimensional organological milieu. This mileu is woven by transductive relations knitted together on all three organological levels through the play of the tendencies and counter-tendencies they harbor. And they thus metastabilize, through a horizon of meaning, that 'understanding that being-there has of its being' that constitutes what Simondon named the transindividual'. *What Makes Life Worth Living: On Pharmacology*. Trans. Daniel Ross (Cambridge: Polity, 2013), 119.

24. Stiegler, *The Decadence of Industrial Democracies: Disbelief and Discredit 1*. Trans. Daniel Ross (Cambridge: Polity, 2011).

25. Stiegler with Frédéric Neyrat, 'Interview: From Libidinal Economy to the Ecology of the Spirit'. Trans. Arne De Boever, *Parrhesia*, 14 (2012), 3.

26. Stiegler, *Symbolic Misery Volume 1: The Hyperindustrial Epoch*. Trans. Barnaby Norman (Cambridge: Polity, 2014), 54. Stiegler adopts the concept of

grammatization from Sylvain Auroux. See his *La Révolution technologique de la grammatization* (Brussels: Mardaga, 1993).

27. Stiegler, *What Makes Life Worth Living*, 25.
28. See Donald Winnicott, *Playing and Reality* (London and New York: Routledge, 2005).
29. This was developed in Stiegler's presentation, titled 'Anthropocene and Negentropology', at a recent conference devoted to his work, 'General Organology: The Co-individuation of Minds, Bodies, Social Organisations and Techne' at the University of Kent, 20–22 November 2014.
30. He writes, 'an obsolete idea of politics, that is, one founded on the discourse of "resistance": holding on to such a politics could only mean becoming ensnared in one more delusion. One must struggle against this tendency by *inventing* rather than by resisting. Resistance can only ever be *reactive* and, as such, it belongs to *nihilism* – in the Nietzschean sense of these words'. *The Decadence of Industrial Democracies*, 37.
31. See Lyotard, 'Acinema' in *The Lyotard Reader,* Ed. Andrew Benjamin (Oxford and Cambridge: Basil Blackwell, 1989).
32. James Williams argues this in *Lyotard and the Political* (London: Routledge, 2000).
33. Lyotard writes, for example, 'Let us be content to recognize in dissimulation all that we have been seeking, difference within identity, the chance event within the foresight of composition, passion within reason – between each, so absolutely foreign to each other, the strictest unity: dissimulation'. *Libidinal Economy*, 52.
34. Metastability, like entropy and negentropy, is another term adopted from thermodynamics and is developed by Gilbert Simondon as an integral aspect of his theory of individuation. Jean-Hugues Barthélémy explains that 'it is a state that transcends the classical opposition between stability and instability, and that is charged with potentials for a becoming'. For Simondon, '[t]he difference between the physical individual and the living individual is [...] that the second entertains within it a metastability, whereas the first has become stable and has exhausted its potentials'. 'Fifty Key Terms in the Works of Gilbert Simondon', in *Gilbert Simondon: Being and Technology*, Ed. Arne De Boever, Alex Murray, Jon Roffe and Ashley Woodward (Edinburgh: Edinburgh University Press, 2012), 217.
35. Stiegler, *Acting Out*, 78.
36. Stiegler, *Acting Out*, 79–80.
37. Stiegler, *Symbolic Misery Volume 1: The Hyperindustrial Epoch*, 64.
38. See note 1.
39. Stiegler, *Acting Out*, 74.

BIBLIOGRAPHY

Auroux, Sylvain. *La Révolution technologique de la grammatization.* Brussels: Mardaga, 1993.

Barthélémy, Jean-Hugues. 'Fifty Key Terms in the Works of Gilbert Simondon'. In *Gilbert Simondon: Being and Technology*. Edited by Arne De Boever, Alex

Murray, Jon Roffe and Ashley Woodward, 203–231. Edinburgh: Edinburgh University Press, 2012.

Bateson, Gregory. *Steps to an Ecology of Mind.* Chicago: Chicago University Press, 1999.

Cordeschi, Roberto, 'Cybernetics'. In *The Blackwell Guide to the Philosophy of Computing and Information.* Edited by Luciano Floridi, 186–196. Malden: Wiley-Blackwell, 2003.

Curtis, Adam, *All Watched Over by Machines of Loving Grace.* London: BBC, 2011.

Ehrlich, P.R. and L.C. Birch. 'The "Balance of Nature" and "Population Control"'. *The American Naturalist,* 101.918 (1967): 97–107.

Forrester, Jay Wright. *Principles of Systems.* Sheffield: Pegasus Communications, 1968.

Freud, Sigmund. *Beyond the Pleasure Principle, Group Psychology, and Other Works.* Edited and translated by James Strachey. *The Standard Edition of the Complete Psychological Works of Sigmund Freud, Volume 18.* New York: Vintage, 2001.

Kricher, John. *The Balance of Nature: Ecology's Enduring Myth.* Princeton and Oxford: Princeton University Press, 2009.

Lyotard, Jean-François. *The Lyotard Reader.* Edited by Andrew Benjamin. Oxford and Cambridge: Basil Blackwell, 1989.

———. *The Inhuman: Reflections on Time.* Translated by Geoffrey Bennington and Rachel Bowlby. Cambridge: Polity Press, 1991.

———. *Libidinal Economy.* Translated by Iain Hamilton Grant. London: Athlone, 1993.

———. *Jean-François Lyotard: Political Writings.* Translated by Bill Readings and Kevin Paul. Minneapolis: University of Minnesota Press, 1993.

———. 'Freud, Energy and Chance: A Conversation with Jean-François Lyotard'. *Tekhnema: Journal of Philosophy and Technology,* 5 (1999). (Interview with Richard Beardsworth) http://tekhnema.free.fr/5Beardsworth.html.

Odum, Eugene and Howard T. Odum. *Fundamentals of Ecology.* 2nd edition. Philadelphia: W.B. Saunders, 1959.

Rahebi, Mohammed-Ali. 'The Cybernetic Organon and the Obsolescence of the Subject of Knowledge'. 2014, Unpublished.

Stiegler, Bernard. *Technics and Time 1: The Fault of Epimetheus.* Translated by George Collins and Richard Beardsworth. Stanford: Stanford University Press, 1998.

———. *Acting Out.* Translated by David Barison, Daniel Ross and Patrick Crogan. Stanford: Stanford University Press, 2009.

———. *Technics and Time 2: Disorientation.* Translated by Stephen Barker. Stanford: Stanford University Press, 2009.

———. *For a New Critique of Political Economy.* Translated by Daniel Ross. Cambridge: Polity, 2010.

———. *The Decadence of Industrial Democracies: Disbelief and Discredit 1.* Translated by Daniel Ross. Cambridge: Polity, 2011.

———. *What Makes Life Worth Living: On Pharmacology.* Translated by Daniel Ross. Cambridge: Polity, 2013.

———. *Symbolic Misery Volume 1: The Hyperindustrial Epoch.* Translated by Barnaby Norman. Cambridge: Polity, 2014.

———. *States of Shock: Stupidity and Knowledge in the 21st Century.* Translated by Daniel Ross. Cambridge: Polity, 2015.

Stiegler, Bernard with Frédéric Neyrat. 'Interview: From Libidinal Economy to the Ecology of the Spirit'. Translated by Arne De Boever. *Parrhesia*, 14 (2012): 9–15.
Tansley, Arthur George. 'The Use and Abuse of Vegetational Terms and Concepts'. *Ecology*, 16.3 (1935): 284–307.
———. *Elements of Plant Biology.* Lenox, MA: HardPress, 2012 [1922].
Wiener, Norbert. *Cybernetics, or Control and Communication in the Animal and the Machine.* Cambridge, MA: MIT Press, 1968 [1948].
Winnicott, D.W. *Playing and Reality.* London and New York: Routledge, 2005.

Chapter Nine

History as an Ecological Niche
Beyond Benjamin's Nature
Damiano Roberi

Regarding topics which currently need philosophical reflection most urgently, the relationship between History and Nature is surely at the forefront. This is true despite (or, possibly, precisely because of) the almost unavoidable impression of untimeliness (*Unzeitgemäßigkeit*) of this statement. In less philosophical terms, this could seem a sort of rearguard action, given the omnipresent discourses on economy on the one hand and the increasingly accurate amount of data arriving from the natural sciences regarding our planet's state in relation to human actions on the other. Perhaps, though, the search for an *ubi consistam* of philosophical discussion on these themes, able to defeat this negative starting observation, can find some precious help in Walter Benjamin's thinking: One of his main concerns is in fact the radical intertwining of History and Nature within capitalism. We will try and show how the reasons for the collapse of this economic system are intrinsically bound to its relationship with the natural dimension. The current significance of these reflections, though, will not prevent us from considering the problematic roots of the Benjaminian thoughts, that is, the radical perturbation inflicted on Nature by Man's Original Sin. At the same time, we will see how Benjamin pays great attention to the *connection* between Man, Nature and Technology; this will serve as a starting point for considering a model able to support the positive aspects of the Benjaminian reflections. The concept of ecological niche, based on the idea of interconnectedness between the organisms and their environment, will proceed (in its connection to History) beyond Benjamin's Nature, contributing to the aim of this book – the search for a new 'philosophy after Nature'.

THE BREATH OF CAPITALISM

Walter Benjamin's thinking presents (when compared to the *communis opinio* regarding the crisis of the philosophy of history)[1] a dual advantage. Not only does it develop a harsh critique against what we could call, to borrow an expression from Karl Löwith, 'the fatality of progress' (*das Verhängnis des Fortschritts*) but, more importantly, it does so by analysing the repercussions on Nature of this ideology. It is however necessary to be clear from the outset: The Benjaminian reflections do not represent a naive ecologist thought, which could perhaps present an immediate appeal. It seems, on the contrary, that Benjamin tries to help us understand a simple fact: that such a reflection about Nature is, quite paradoxically, one of the few (possibly the only?) serious philosophical attempts *and not* an unaffordable luxury (Morton would say that we have to develop an 'ecology without Nature').[2]

This statement can be explained by looking at the analysis of capitalism within the unfinished *Passagenwerk*, where the city of Paris, as the capital of the nineteenth century, figures at the same time both as a paradigm and anticipation of contemporary high capitalism. This task could however seem difficult to perform, since Benjamin writes in a fragment 'the experience of our generation: that capitalism will not die a natural death'.[3] The difficulties do not end here: in his eleventh thesis *On the Concept of History* he fights the social-democratic idea of a 'nature that [...] exists gratis',[4] which he considers fundamentally equivalent to the capitalistic vision and warns against the deceptive and tempting belief of being swept along on the tide of Nature towards revolution. Despite this, it is possible to identify three fundamental steps in order to describe the collapse which is the result of the breath of capitalism.[5] First, the city absorbs Nature from a quantitative point of view[6] (for example, extension). In order to fight the decline of their class, the bourgeois try to build their own *intérieur* wherein they can leave their traces. On another scale, the city itself represents an *intérieur*, a womb, within the whole universe, which is, however, more similar to an enormous ecological footprint.[7] All of Nature is swallowed up by the capitalist city, literally or figuratively, be it through the exploitation of resources or the representation of the advertisement of the universal exhibitions: these 'propagate the universe of commodities. Grandville's fantasies [a famous publicist of that era] confer a commodity character on the universe'.[8] In this way, the capitalist tendency to build comfortable, protective internal spaces reaches its apex, building the world interior of the capital.[9] This greenhouse, though, hides its own rifts, that is, the *passages*: These ephemeral commercial galleries (at first glance, a simple failed economical experiment of the early nineteenth century) represent, according to Benjamin, the privileged hunting ground of an attempt to wake up Europe from its nightmares. 'Capitalism was a natural phenomenon with which a dream-filled sleep came over Europe, and, through it, a reactivation of mythic forces'.[10]

The reappearance of Nature, precisely within this context, represents the second step. As a disquieting, damaging toxin, it also constitutes the inevitable product from the chain of distribution of goods. This time Benjamin uses the image of the Sphinx, which is no longer the terrible mythological monster defeated by Oedipus but rather something akin to Kafka's Odradek: the discarded good, waste in its disquieting inutility. Nature is, at most, a stock fund: indeed, 'un vieux sphinx ignoré du monde insocieux'.[11] The *passages* thus reveal themselves to be akin to a dump, within which the capitalist *promesse de bonheur* shows itself as broken.

It is not by chance, then, that this capital of the nineteenth century tried to hide the ultimate expression of the 'bad conscience'[12] of capitalistic modern mythology, embodied by the prostitute, our third and last passage. What is at stake here is not just colonial exploitation – 'when he went to meet the consumptive Negress who lived in the city, Baudelaire saw the true 'aspect of the French colonial empire'[13] – but a perversion of the very essence of Nature, that is, its character of a benefactress. Benjamin had already underlined this aspect in his *Childhood in Berlin*, where the waste of resources appeared in the image of the scraps at a covered market that he visited as a child. The character of the prostitute, though, goes beyond this as it represents the *ultimate* incarnation of the goods. 'So long as there is semblance in history, it will find in nature its ultimate refuge. The commodity, which is the last burning glass of historical semblance [*Schein*] celebrates its triumph in the fact that nature itself takes on a commodity character. It is this commodity appearance [*Warenschein*] of Nature that is embodied in the whore'.[14]

Benjamin's description of these figures allows us to interpret the essentially instable character of the city of Paris, of the dream world proper to capitalism from the point of view of Nature: The connection of the metropolis with its surrounding environment is not able to reach a point of equilibrium, a homeostatic condition. The relation between City and Nature leads in the direction of the latter, but only in the disquieting form of the ever-same, of the regression. In this sense, progress appears as the mask of a silent death drive, as outlined by Freud in his *Beyond the Pleasure Principle*, which Benjamin quoted in some loci of his analysis (for example, '"Beyond the pleasure principle" is probably the best commentary there is on Proust's works').[15] The capitalist society, observing that model, works in a way really akin to primitive organisms, to which the conclusive remarks of that work are dedicated: They are forced to renew themselves by combining with other entities akin to them, or even by performing phagocytosis on the excrements of other species. Otherwise, there is 'a natural death from the imperfect disposal of its own metabolic products'[16]: that is to say, in Marcuse's terms, that 'the return of the repressed makes up the tabooed and subterranean history of civilization'.[17] The city of Paris, as a prophecy of the twentieth century when it reaches the extreme limit of its capacity of expansion, cannot but perish since it is not able to change the very principle of its existence, its character of 'entropic empire'.[18]

ROOTS AND PROBLEMS

Benjamin, however, does not only develop what could be called an *ecological genealogy of high capitalism* – he also leads it right back to its very roots.[19] The problem of the relationship between History and Nature appears evident already looking at the beginning of modernity, at the German Baroque Drama.[20] In these forgotten works of the seventeenth century, Benjamin finds a petrified Nature on which History has collapsed: the landscape of the *facies hippocratica*. The problem of the exploitation of natural resources, of the inclusion of Nature within History, thus finds a more radical precedent here. In the middle of Destiny's web, interpreted as 'guilt complex of the living [*Schuldzusammenhang des Lebendigen*]',[21] not only does History assume the rigidity of Nature but also this appears marked in its very being: 'the word "history" stands written on the countenance of nature in the characters of transience'.[22] This absorption of the whole being within Destiny is quite clearly wider, more encompassing, if compared to that already analysed.

The ultimate roots of these reflections by Benjamin are to be found in the essay 'On Language as Such and on the Language of Man', where he recalls Genesis 3 and its narration of the Original Sin, which he interprets as linguistic.[23] Man abandons his original task,[24] the imposition of names, as he establishes a difference between Good and Evil and thus lets Judgment arise along with its magic. Nature is therefore condemned by human signification to dumbness: 'the sadness of Nature makes her mute'.[25] The irremediably historical character of Nature finds its origin precisely here, with the birth of human language: 'Nature finds itself betrayed by language. [...] History becomes equal to signification in human language'.[26] From this point onward (not chronologically, however) it will be impossible to distinguish properly between History and Nature; rather, pure Nature will disappear[27] within what will be the baroque (but more generally modern) *Naturgeschichte*. For certain aspects, it could thus be said that the problems analysed before must be seen as different consequences of this turning point.[28]

From a certain point of view, however, the same Benjamin seems to find himself in a tight spot. On the one hand, he criticizes the capitalist view of a gratis-existing nature, but on the other hand he recognizes that a positive connection between a Man who is no longer enslaved and a Nature which is no longer exploited still needs to be identified. How could this be possible if, as we have just seen, with the birth and concomitant fall of human language, Nature seems to be included within the 'more encompassing'[29] entity (here I quote from the essay 'The Task of the Translator')[30] represented by History? If, in other words, Nature has always been exploited through human signification? This other kind of relationship would, in any case, have to be considered in relation to History and human language; but how? The same Benjamin has to face this 'encompassing-problem'.

In this sense, though, it seems that we are led back to a situation similar to the one highlighted in the opening of this chapter, marked by the difficulty for philosophy to develop such themes. The most common attitudes, in fact, fluctuate mainly between a suppression of the problem (TINA, i.e. There Is No Alternative to this system) and the extemporary explosions of catastrophism in the occasion of natural catastrophes attributable to human behaviour. This is instead what we need to keep in mind when looking at Benjamin's legacy: Human history, even though it represents an insignificant time lapse compared to that of the whole planet,[31] requires nonetheless philosophical reflection able to recognize the radical interference of Man in Nature, *now more than ever*. This is precisely one of the political tasks (or, rather, *the* political task) of our times, indeed a 'new axial age'.[32]

HISTORY AS AN ECOLOGICAL NICHE

If Walter Benjamin's thinking limited itself to a form of natural messianism, this would bring it (despite all its theoretical importance) to a consistent loss of actuality. Even assuming that each and every moment could be the small gate through which the Messiah may enter, at least prima facie, this does not really represent a great source of consolation in light of the exponential growth of population and global climate change (it is sufficient to recall here the *Limits to Growth* series).[33] However, the objections made to Benjamin's thinking remain faithful to its inner meaning. A comparison with Benjamin unable to build a constellation between his reflections and our time would make him appear only as an exponent of the 'cultural history' (apparently neutral, but actually an expression of dominance) that he himself harshly criticized. However, another topic that Benjamin constantly returns to is the pursuit of happiness on the part of Mankind *through* a relationship with Nature mediated by technology. The latter is thus not considered as a negative fate which would hang on humanity, nor should Man feel a 'prometheic shame'[34] towards the machines; quite on the contrary, in the *Passagenwerk* we read that the revolutions are 'an innervation of the technical organs of the collective'.[35] In a juvenile fragment (*Schemata zum psychophysischen Problem*) dedicated to the problem of the relationship between mind and body, Benjamin talks about a collective body, *Leib*, constituted by Mankind, Nature *and* Technology: The historical presence of Man on the planet is indeed determined by *all* three of these factors. This perspective, then, leaves really no place for a contraposition between these dimensions but rather, given their necessary reciprocal reference, hints at a thought of the interconnectedness. *Only through* technology would it be possible to realize an 'othering of nature',[36] no longer considering it either as a looming threat or an amount of exploitable resources. The task of the 'true politician'[37] will consist in the creation of a playful relationship with Nature, characterized by a childish gaze, able to recognize the potentialities which are at hand.[38] This, according to Benjamin, was exemplified by Fourier and Scheerbart: Both wanted to help Nature to 'give birth to the creations that now lie dormant in her womb'.[39]

This perspective should nevertheless be put into effect, taking into account also the problem of the radical perturbation inflicted by Man on Nature, as it becomes more and more evident nowadays. Once more, we have to deal with the problem of the collocation of/within Nature, particularly with the diachronic aspects of this topic. Benjamin's view, as we have just seen, is – given its allegorical character – ready to highlight the degradation inflicted by Man on Nature. At the same time, however, the Benjaminian thinking is also willing to detect and underline the positive potentialities of Nature itself.[40] Both of these undertones appear essential to a reflection about the relationship between Man and Earth; my (not so modest) proposal, in order to lose neither of them, would consist in a substitution of the concept of Original Sin with that of ecological fault,[41] or at least an integration between the two. In this way it could be possible to retain a sense of the gravity of acts of interference (such as the fundamental example of the birth of language) of Man in Nature without forgetting, however, that the effects of this interference cannot be valued equally from their very beginning. In this sense the critical evaluation by Marx, in his *Economic and Philosophical Manuscripts*, on the concept of the Fall proves its great value: Original Sin hypostatizes in an initial state something which should be rather explained as a process (as he shows at the end of the first book of *Capital*, talking about the original accumulation).[42] Recalling Benjamin once more, the aspect of Nature will appear petrified only at the end of a series of wicked actions by Man, which can be described as an ecological fault which has evolved (and worsened) as time has gone by. The task would be, in brief, to write (after a natural history) *a philosophical history – a philosophy of history – of the ecological fault.*

This attempt, though, should find its own collocation, which on the one hand has to be different from the world interior of the capital, yet on the other hand be able to avoid the risks implied by an over-metaphysical perspective. It is necessary to learn how to think of – and thus hopefully to deal better with – a *real* relationship, neither as collapse nor redemption, with Nature.

A plausible solution to this could be represented by a consideration of History as an ecological niche 'within' Nature (but we will immediately see how it is not exactly so). The notion of ecological niche, developed in the 1920s in the field of biology and ecology, designates the environment and parameters required for the survival of a species. Authors like Achille Varzi and Barry Smith have paved the way with articles about the ontology of the niche for the use of this concept also in other fields.[43] Their 'theory of niches [...] is of course no more than just a first, provisional chapter of a formal ontology of ecological phenomena'[44]; however, their acquisitions could serve, despite the difference of our approach, as a starting basis. The presupposition of my argument is that Man cannot help but dwell in a historical way.[45] The historical niche does not represent – unless from a speculative point of view (which, however, encounters the difficulties just outlined) – something as broad as Nature from the very beginning. It has rather become so as time and human actions have gone by, resulting finally in something similar to a 'hyperobject'.[46] Surely, we have to reflect upon the fact that we are here in front of a niche whose status is quite peculiar. Not only has Man, starting from a biological basis, built upon it a different, namely cultural, dimension not attributable to the former, but this process has also been characterized by a positive feedback: 'in humans, culture has greatly amplified our capacity for niche construction and our ability to modify selection pressures'.[47] Moreover, and most importantly, how can we talk about a 'niche', as it seems there is no longer a space external to it?[48] Nature is not properly 'outside' History, nor is History 'within' Nature, since they are truly entangled. However, by adopting the concept of niche we can show better how the (at least) *two-way*[49] *connection* between History and Nature functions (or should function). This representation can also prove useful in letting us figure out how a correct or incorrect planning of this link can decide between Man as the *ultimate* or *last*[50] niche constructor, between a realized, efficient niche and one which is collapsing. 'Niche construction [...] may promote the kind of equilibria with functional integration that renders ecosystems orderly and which at the largest scale is exemplified by the Gaia hypothesis. However, under different circumstances, the feedback generated by niche construction [...] could generate chaotic interactions'.[51] For all the reasons I have just briefly outlined, I believe that these reflections can represent not only a contribution to the critique of the system we live in nowadays but also, and above all, a first step towards the theoretical foundation of a new kind of thought (marked by sustainability) about History. It may be argued that having started with a negative observation, by passing through Benjamin's analyses, we have finally reached a positive and forward-thinking untimeliness. This could be seen as the hallmark of a philosophy finally aware of the problem represented by its own *coming after* Nature, and which thus *looks after* Nature.

NOTES

1. An overview on the origins of this discipline can be cast – respectively from a philological and philosophical point of view, to adopt the distinction typical of Vico – through the analysis of Reinhart Koselleck and Karl Löwith. In his *Futures Past: On the Semantics of Historical Time*, the former has shown how the process of temporalization (*Verzeitlichung*), which would have reached its apex with the rise of the philosophies of history, entailed a detachment from Nature: 'the naturalistic basis vanishes' (Reinhart Koselleck, *Futures Past: On the Semantics of Historical Time*. Trans. Keith Tribe (New York: Columbia University Press, 2004), 37). Löwith, on the other hand, believes that the union of the premises of the *Heilgeschichte* and of a *Weltgeschehen* completely absorbed within a fated progress shows 'modern history in a paradoxical light: it is Christian by derivation and anti-Christian by consequence' (Karl Löwith, *Meaning in History: The Theological Implications of the Philosophy of History* (Chicago: University of Chicago Press, 1949), 202). It is particularly interesting to notice how Nietzsche tries to bring back the dimension of History to Nature. Here the 'fundamental conflict in the relationship of man and world' (Löwith, *Meaning in History*, 10) which has plagued the whole of modernity becomes explicit: 'since Descartes's doubt [...] up to Nietzsche's attempt [...] philosophy has been one single attempt to regain a lost world' (Karl Löwith, *Nietzsche's Philosophy of the Eternal Recurrence of the Same*. Trans. J. Harvey Lomax (Berkeley and Los Angeles: University of California Press, 1997), 95).

2. See Timothy Morton, *Ecology without Nature: Rethinking Environmental Aesthetics* (Cambridge, MA: Cambridge University Press, 2009).

3. Walter Benjamin, *The Arcades Project*. Trans. Howard Eiland and Kevin McLaughlin (Cambridge, MA and London: The Belknap Press of the Cambridge University Press, 1999), 667.

4. Walter Benjamin, *Selected Writings Volume 4: 1938–1940*, Eds. Howard Eiland and Michael W. Jennings (Cambridge, MA and London: The Belknap Press of the Harvard University Press, 2006), 394.

5. Benjamin in fact uses this image: 'the lung as the seat of desire is the boldest intimation of desire's unrealizability that can be imagined' (Walter Benjamin, *The Arcades Project*, 349).

6. Regarding this topic in the works of Benjamin, see for example Susan Buck-Morss, *The Dialectics of Seeing: Walter Benjamin and the Arcades Project* (Cambridge, MA: MIT Press, 1989) and Graeme Gilloch, *Myth & Metropolis: Walter Benjamin and the City* (Cambridge: Polity Press, 1997).

7. See Mathis Wackernagel and William Rees, *Our Ecological Footprint: Reducing Human Impact on the Planet* (Gabriola Island: New Society, 1998). This idea does not seem completely unrelated to an image used by Benjamin: 'what I propose is to show how Baudelaire lies embedded in the nineteenth century. The imprint he has left behind there must stand out clear and intact, like that of a stone which, having lain in the ground for decades, is one day rolled from its place' (Walter Benjamin, *The Arcades Project*, 321).

8. Walter Benjamin, *The Arcades Project*, 8.

9. About Benjamin, see particularly Peter Sloterdijk, *Im Weltinnenraum des Kapitals* (Frankfurt am Main: Suhrkamp, 2005), 265–276.
10. Walter Benjamin, *The Arcades Project*, 391.
11. Charles Baudelaire, *Oeuvres completes. Volume 1: Les Fleurs du Mal* (Paris: Gallimard, 1918), 112.
12. Irving Wohlfarth, 'On Some Jewish Motives in Benjamin', in *The Problems of Modernity: Adorno and Benjamin,* Ed. Andrew Benjamin (London and New York: Routledge, 1989), 190.
13. Walter Benjamin, *The Arcades Project*, 327.
14. Walter Benjamin, *The Arcades Project*, 345.
15. Walter Benjamin, *The Arcades Project*, 547.
16. Sigmund Freud, *Beyond the Pleasure Principle.* Trans. C.J.M. Hubback (London and Vienna: The International Psycho-Analytical Press, 1992), 39.
17. Herbert Marcuse, *Eros and Civilization* (Boston: Beacon Press, 1966), 34.
18. Lieven De Cauter, *Entropic Empire: On the City of Man in the Age of Disaster* (Rotterdam: NAI, 2013).
19. It is not possible here to discuss the important fragment *Kapitalismus als Religion*, where Benjamin compares his own theories not only with the hypothesis of Max Weber on the birth of capitalism in relation to Protestantism but also with Freud, Marx and Nietzsche. See for example Samuel Weber, *Benjamin's Abilities* (Cambridge, MA: Harvard University Press, 2010), 250–280.
20. For an introduction to this text, see Bettine Menke, *Das Trauerspiel-Buch. Der Souverän – das Trauerspiel – Konstellationen – Ruinen* (Bielefeld: Transcript, 2010).
21. Walter Benjamin, *Selected Writings Volume 1: 1913–1926,* Eds. Marcus Bullock and Michael W. Jennings (Cambridge, MA and London: The Belknap Press of the Cambridge University Press, 2004), 204.
22. Walter Benjamin, *The Origin of German Tragic Drama.* Trans. John Osborne (London and New York: Verso, 1998), 177.
23. On this essay see, for example, Peter Fenves, *Arresting Language. From Leibniz to Benjamin* (Stanford: Stanford University Press, 2001), 174–227.
24. It is dubious, however, whether one can properly talk of a task and thus of a sin or whether (more probably) the instability of this situation cannot but lead to the fall (see Werner Hamacher, 'Affirmative, Strike. Benjamin's "Critique of Violence"', in *Walter Benjamin's Philosophy: Destruction and Experience,* Eds. Andrew Benjamin and Peter Osborne (New York: Routledge, 1994), 137).
25. Walter Benjamin, *Selected Writings Volume 1: 1913–1926*, 73.
26. Walter Benjamin, *Selected Writings Volume 1: 1913–1926*, 60.
27. This seems to recall the *German Ideology*, 'the nature that preceded human history ... today no longer exists anywhere (except perhaps on a few Australian coral-islands of recent origin)': Karl Marx and Friedrich Engels, *A Critique of the German Ideology* (Marx-Engels Internet Archive, 2000), accessed 19 February 2015, http://www.marxist.org/archive/marx/works/download/Marx_The_German_Ideology.pdf.
28. 'If this paradigm provides the underlying structure of Benjamin's subsequent materialism, it will also be profoundly altered by what it anticipates. The difficulty lies in deciding which of the two is the "substructure" of the other. The devious

answer contained in Benjamin's closing statement on the matter seems to be: both and neither' (Wohlfarth, 'On Some Jewish Motives in Benjamin', 165–166).

29. Walter Benjamin, *Selected Writings Volume 1*: 1913–1926, 255.

30. Benjamin, within this passage, tries to extend *positively* the notion of life, beyond a mere biological dimension, to literary works. See for example Eli Friedlander, *Walter Benjamin: A Philosophical Portrait* (Cambridge, MA, and London: Harvard University Press, 2012), 115–116. It is, however, possible, in my opinion, to develop a negative lecture of this assumption, which tries to highlight how Man forces Nature to be always a *Naturgeschichte*.

31. See Walter Benjamin, *Selected Writings Volume 4: 1938–1940*, 396.

32. See Robert N. Bellah and Hans Joas (Eds.), *The Axial Age and Its Consequences* (Cambridge, MA: Belknap Press, 2012).

33. See for example Jorgen Randers, *2052: A Global Forecast for the Next Forty Years* (White River Junction, VT: Chelsea Green, 2012).

34. See Günther Anders, *Die Antiquiertheit des Menschen. Über die Seele im Zeitalter der zweiten industriellen Revolution* (München: Beck, 1956).

35. Walter Benjamin, *The Arcades Project*, 631.

36. Andrew Benjamin, *Working with Walter Benjamin: Recovering a Political Philosophy* (Edinburgh: Edinburgh University Press, 2013), 149.

37. See Uwe Steiner, 'The True Politician: Walter Benjamin's Concept of the Political', *New German Critique,* 83 (2001): 43–88.

38. See Carlo Salzani, 'Experience and Play: Walter Benjamin and the Prelapsarian Child', in *Walter Benjamin and the Architecture of Modernity,* Eds. Andrew Benjamin and Charles Rice (Melbourne: re.press, 2009), 175–198.

39. Walter Benjamin, *Selected Writings Volume 4: 1938–1940*, 394.

40. See Andrew Benjamin, *Working with Walter Benjamin*, 3.

41. See Guido Chelazzi, *L'impronta originale. Storia naturale della colpa ecologica* (Torino: Einaudi, 2013).

42. Once more Wohlfarth notes that there could be a connection between Original Sin as meant by Benjamin and the original accumulation (Wohlfarth, 'On Some Jewish Motives in Benjamin', 162).

43. See at least Barry Smith and Achille Varzi, 'The Niche', *Noûs,* 33.2 (1999): 214–238; 'Surrounding Space. The Ontology of the Organism-Environment Relations', *Theory in Biosciences,* 121.2 (2002): 139–162; Barry Smith, 'Toward a Realistic Science of Environments', *Ecological Psychology,* 21.2 (2009): 121–130.

44. Smith and Varzi, 'The Niche', 234.

45. This idea, obviously, is no real recent acquisition, since it can be traced back as far as Heidegger's *Being and Time*. See for example §72–77: 'factically, Da-sein always has its "history", and it can have something of the sort because the being of its being is constituted by historicity' (Martin Heidegger, *Being and Time.* Trans. Joan Stambaugh [Albany: State University of New York Press, 1996], 350) and Dilthey. However, in looking for the origin of this idea, one would eventually have to return to Giambattista Vico's *New Science* and its 'eternal and never-failing light of a truth beyond all questions: that the world of civil society has certainly been made by men'

(Giambattista Vico, *The New Science of Giambattista Vico*. Trans. T. Goddard Bergin and M.H. Fisch [Ithaca, NY: Cornell University Press, 1948], 85).

46. See Timothy Morton, *Hyperobjects: Philosophy and Ecology after the End of the World* (Minneapolis: University of Minnesota Press, 2013). Within Morton's brilliant book, what he calls 'the end of the world' seems particularly interesting. 'We still believe that Nature is "over there" – that it exists apart from technology, apart from history. Far from it. Nature is the stockpile of stockpiles' (Morton, *Hyperobjects*, 113). Many of the topics developed in this book are in accordance with the ones we are trying to develop here starting from Benjamin. For example, it is necessary, once more according to Morton, to abandon the concepts of Nature and Sustainability, insofar as they fluctuate between capitalist and catastrophist meanings. The presence of these terms in this last part of our argument does not conflict with his position, with which we completely agree. However, the model represented by the niche could serve as a different approach to the problem discussed by Morton – and thus perhaps help to combat some of the confusion introduced into our lives by the advent of the era of hyperobjects.

47. K.N. Laland, J. Odling-Smee and M. Feldman, 'Cultural Niche Construction and Human Evolution', *Journal of Evolutionary Biology*, 14.1 (2001): 22. See also J. Odling-Smee, K.N. Laland and M. Feldman, *Niche Construction: The Neglected Process in Evolution* (Princeton: Princeton University Press, 2003).

48. In this sense, it would be interesting to compare the concept of niche with Agamben's 'threshold of indistinction' (see Giorgio Agamben, *Homo Sacer: Sovereign Power and Bare Life*. Trans. Daniel Heller-Roazen [Stanford: Stanford University Press, 1998]), as a possible, positive counterproposal to it. If it is true also that ecology has become a part of a global state of exception, it is necessary to find a way to deal with this condition – which is surely related to Power, however only *on the basis of* natural laws.

49. It must be stressed that this connection is multi-dimensional rather than simply two-way (see once more Timothy Morton, *Hyperobjects*, 73). The very niche is a *n*-dimensional object, where *n* stands for the number of parameters taken into account.

50. See Guido Chelazzi, *L'impronta originale*, 173.

51. K.N. Laland, J. Odling-Smee and M. Feldman, 'Evolutionary Consequences of Niche Construction and Their Implications for Ecology', *Proceedings of the National Academy of Sciences of the United States of America*, 96.18 (1999): 10247.

BIBLIOGRAPHY

Agamben, Giorgio. *Homo Sacer: Sovereign Power and Bare Life*. Translated by Daniel Heller-Roazen. Stanford: Stanford University Press, 1998.

Anders, Günther. *Die Antiquiertheit des Menschen. Über die Seele im Zeitalter der zweitenindustriellen Revolution*. München: Beck, 1956.

Baudelaire, Charles. *Oeuvres complètes. Volume 1: Les Fleurs du Mal*. Paris: Gallimard, 1918.

Bellah, Robert N. and Hans Joas (Eds.). *The Axial Age and Its Consequences.* Cambridge, MA: Belknap Press, 2012.
Benjamin, Andrew. *Working with Walter Benjamin: Recovering a Political Philosophy.* Edinburgh: Edinburgh University Press, 2013.
Benjamin, Walter. *The Origin of German Tragic Drama.* Translated by John Osborne. London and New York: Verso, 1998.
———. *The Arcades Project.* Translated by Howard Eiland and Kevin McLaughlin. Cambridge, MA, and London: The Belknap Press of the Cambridge University Press, 1999.
———. *Selected Writings Volume 1: 1913–1926.* Edited by Marcus Bullock and Michael W. Jennings. Cambridge, MA, and London: The Belknap Press of the Cambridge University Press, 2004.
———. *Selected Writings Volume 4: 1938–1940.* Edited by Howard Eiland and Michael W. Jennings. Cambridge, MA, and London: The Belknap Press of the Harvard University Press, 2006.
Buck-Morss, Susan. *The Dialectics of Seeing: Walter Benjamin and the Arcades Project.* Cambridge, MA: MIT Press, 1989.
Chelazzi, Guido. *L'impronta originale. Storia naturale della colpa ecologica.* Torino: Einaudi, 2013.
De Cauter, Lieven. *Entropic Empire: On the City of Man in the Age of Disaster.* Rotterdam: NAI, 2013.
Fenves, Peter. *Arresting Language: From Leibniz to Benjamin.* Stanford: Stanford University Press, 2001.
Freud, Sigmund. *Beyond the Pleasure Principle.* Translated by C.J.M. Hubback. London and Vienna: The International Psycho-Analytical Press, 1992.
Friedlander, Eli. *Walter Benjamin: A Philosophical Portrait.* Cambridge, MA, and London: Harvard University Press, 2012.
Gilloch, Graeme. *Myth & Metropolis: Walter Benjamin and the City.* Cambridge: Polity Press, 1997.
Hamacher, Werner. 'Afformative, Strike. Benjamin's "Critique of Violence"'. In *Walter Benjamin's Philosophy: Destruction and Experience.* Edited by Andrew Benjamin and Peter Osborne, 110–138. Routledge: New York, 1994.
Heidegger, Martin. *Being and Time.* Translated by Joan Stambaugh. Albany: State University of New York Press, 1996.
Koselleck, Reinhart. *Futures Past: On the Semantics of Historical Time.* Translated by Keith Tribe. New York: Columbia University Press, 2004.
Laland, K.N., J. Odling-Smee and M. Feldman. 'Evolutionary Consequences of Niche Construction and Their Implications for Ecology'. *Proceedings of the National Academy of Sciences of the United States of America,* 96.18 (1998): 10242–10247.
———. 'Cultural Niche Construction and Human Evolution'. *Journal of Evolutionary Biology,* 14.1 (2001): 22–33.
Löwith, Karl. *Meaning in History: The Theological Implications of the Philosophy of History.* Chicago: University of Chicago Press, 1949.
———. *Nietzsche's Philosophy of the Eternal Recurrence of the Same.* Translated by J. Harvey Lomax. Berkeley and Los Angeles: University of California Press, 1997.

Marcuse, Herbert. *Eros and Civilization*. Boston: Beacon Press, 1966.
Marx, Karl and Friedrich Engels. *A Critique of the German Ideology*. Marx-Engels Internet Archive, 2000. Accessed 19 February 2015. http://www.marxist.org/archive/marx/works/download/Marx_The_German_Ideology.pdf.
Menke, Bettine. *Das Trauerspiel-Buch. Der Souverän – das Trauerspiel – Konstellationen – Ruinen*. Bielefeld: Transcript, 2010.
Morton, Timothy. *Ecology without Nature: Rethinking Environmental Aesthetics*. Cambridge, MA: Cambridge University Press, 2009.
———. *Hyperobjects: Philosophy and Ecology after the End of the World*. Minneapolis: University of Minnesota Press, 2013.
Odling-Smee J., K.N. Laland and M. Feldman. *Niche Construction: The Neglected Process in Evolution*. Princeton: Princeton University Press, 2003.
Randers, Jorgen. 2052: *A Global Forecast for the Next Forty Years*. White River Junction, VT: Chelsea Green, 2012.
Salzani, Carlo. 'Experience and Play: Walter Benjamin and the Prelapsarian Child'. In *Walter Benjamin and the Architecture of Modernity*. Edited by Andrew Benjamin and Charles Rice, 175–198. Melbourne: re.press, 2009.
Sloterdijk, Peter. *Im Weltinnenraum des Kapitals*. Frankfurt am Main: Suhrkamp, 2005.
Smith, Barry. 'Toward a Realistic Science of Environments'. *Ecological Psychology*, 21.2 (2009): 121–130.
Smith, Barry and Achille Varzi. 'The Niche'. *Noûs*, 33.2 (1999): 214–238.
———. 'Surrounding Space. The Ontology of the Organism-Environment Relations'. *Theory in Biosciences*, 121.2 (2002): 139–162.
Steiner, Uwe. 'The True Politician: Walter Benjamin's Concept of the Political'. *New German Critique*, 83 (2001): 43–88.
Vico, Giambattista. *The New Science of Giambattista Vico*. Translated by T. Goddard Bergin and M.H. Fisch. Ithaca, NY: Cornell University Press, 1948.
Wackernagel, Mathis and William Rees. *Our Ecological Footprint: Reducing Human Impact on the Planet*. Gabriola Island: New Society, 1998.
Weber, Samuel. *Benjamin's Abilities*. Cambridge, MA: Harvard University Press, 2010.
Wohlfarth, Irving. 'On Some Jewish Motives in Benjamin'. In *The Problems of Modernity: Adorno and Benjamin*. Edited by Andrew Benjamin, 157–215. London and New York: Routledge, 1989.

Chapter Ten

Nature, Technology and Conscious Evolution

A Post-human Constructive Philosophy

Debashish Banerji

COSMOGENESIS AND INDIVIDUATION

The turn of the nineteenth century into the twentieth saw the implementation of what has been called the Second Industrial Revolution marked by universal electrification, mass production and the birth of the world market. This brought the post-Enlightenment episteme into the properly modern phase of its actualization, the practical horizon of a global humanity. For the first time in human history, the assumption of a species identity for all humans and the yoking of all humanity in a common global life made itself a ubiquitous anthropological possibility. The ontological consequences of such an epistemic change were dimly grasped by the leading thinkers of the time, in their varied ramifications. These included ideas which projected a global expansion of human subjectivity, read retrospectively back to cosmogenetic processes. It should be noted that Enlightenment philosophies had already arrived at a formalization of an evolutionary ideology in Hegel's philosophy of history, which saw an involved rationality in Matter and a cosmic Time Spirit (*Zeitgeist*) working out its experiments in synthesizing opposites towards the emergence of the Logos as free thought in social and political life.[1] In this lineage of thought, a deterministic principle of evolution is assumed, whose intelligence motives cosmogenesis. It is important to note that creature agency is undervalued in this process, the progressive experiments of the *Zeitgeist* leave their results culturally fossilized moving on to other 'races' (an east-to-west drift) and human subjectivity remains bounded within predetermined limits. Nietzsche's refusal of ideological truths on the grounds of their being historically contingent and politically established and his exaltation of human agency as the instrument of a cosmogenetic will to power was largely a reaction to Hegel's deterministic evolutionism. The new evolutionary philosophies which arose through the last decades of the nineteenth century and over the first half of the twentieth century were closer, in this regard, to Nietzsche in positing immanent forms of evolution in which creature/human agency played a key part and human subjectivity underwent radical change/expansion. It should also be noted that such philosophies arose in the wake of Darwinian evolution, but whereas the latter was restricted to morphological change based on accidental functional adaptations in which agency or consciousness played no part, the new philosophies recognized changes in consciousness underlying evolutionary processes and resulting from immanent ideas actualized through acts of will.

Three such thinkers of this period are the two Frenchmen Henri Bergson (1859–1941) and Pierre Teilhard de Chardin (1881–1955) and the Indian, Sri Aurobindo (1872–1950). In looking for a common key to describe the works of these thinkers, one can isolate a convergent identification of cosmogenesis and individuation in their works. 'Cosmogenesis' is a term used by Teilhard to refer to a process of increasing complexity, self-organization and self-awareness of the cosmos.[2] 'Individuation' seems more common in its usage but is deceptive due to its varied connotations and inflections. Presently, this term is more usually associated with C.G. Jung (1875–1961), a psychological emergence of singular personhood out of the amorphous Unconscious and its movement towards universalization.[3] Though such a process could have practical similarities with individuation as theorized by more recent philosophers like Gilbert Simondon (1924–1989)[4] and Gilles Deleuze (1925–1995),[5] these latter include an ontological foundation to individuation which is absent in Jung. Closer in sense to these later thinkers, Henri Bergson (1859–1941) uses the term to refer to creative differentiation of instances,[6] and Teilhard and Sri Aurobindo, though they don't explicitly use the term, refer to ontogenetic processes akin to individuation. Teilhard, for example, writes of hominization, personalization, anthropogenesis and christogenesis as roughly synonymous terms to a becoming-individual of the cosmos[7] (which is simultaneously a becoming-cosmos of the individual), while a similar evolution towards universalization of the person-element (purusha) in the cosmos is envisaged by Sri Aurobindo in what he calls psychisization.[8]

METAPHYSICS OF CONSCIOUS EVOLUTION

In Teilhard[9] and Sri Aurobindo[10] a panentheistic consciousness is immanent in all entities in the cosmos and seeks to individuate itself through them. In the case of Bergson,[11] a creative immanent consciousness in the cosmos and all its creatures, the *élan vital*, multiplies diversity and pushes towards an increasing complexity that can be intuited and be the source of knowledge and action in each of its creatures according to their orientation and capacity. Such an ontogenetic foundation evades the hubris of anthropocentrism but empowers the individual, variously locating the evolutionary will as entity agency. This is where these thinkers differ from philosophers of deterministic history, such as Hegel, for whom cosmogenetic agency, even when immanent, can be said to be located in a transcendence within the immanence. In these thinkers, one finds both these dimensions of transcendence and immanence assuming active potency in beings/entities, along a gradient in which Teilhard can be seen as slanted closer to the transcendence and Bergson towards the immanence. Of the three, Sri Aurobindo, while acknowledging an immune transcendence, yet posits two other forms of self-perception of this transcendence, an objectified self-perception (Matter as cosmic immanence of the Subject) and a self-multiplied prospection as every individual possibility within this immanence, or in other words, the complete immanence of conscious Being (Brahman) in every particle of the material cosmos, thus representing a coeval individual agency in conjunction with cosmic agency.[12] While individual agency has been instinctually active and secondary to cosmic agency ('Nature') prior to the appearance of the human, individualized consciousness in the human represents a new level of conscious independence from cosmic agency and thus able to determine its own destiny, superseding Nature's conditioning and capable of transforming it.[13]

Sri Aurobindo's theological metaphysics has profound correspondences with Teilhard's Christology, founded on an exile and redemption mythos. In Teilhard's mystical Christology, the 'redemption' is not 'completed' by the historical personage of Christ, but this historical event becomes a symbolic promise for its multiplied realization in human individuals leading to a cosmic 'return' through christogenesis in the individualized collective realization of the 'Omega Point'.[14] The separation from Origin implied in a mythos of exile is also present in Sri Aurobindo; though, founded in the Vedic theme of sacrifice as expressed in the Purusha Sukta,[15] such a separation is not an 'act of Evil' burdened on the human and thus requiring redemption, but rather an 'act of God' on the body of God, and thus a self-sacrifice, leading to an ontology of separation in which, nevertheless, the One becomes self-multiplied as monadic immanence.[16] Similarly, instead of 'redemption', then, the evolutionary drift of such a cosmic condition would be a recovery of cosmic and transcendental Oneness through identification of each individual with the fullness of Purusha (Being as Person), reconstituting its sacrificed body in a collective manifestation which Sri Aurobindo referred to as a 'divine life' on earth.[17]

However, as mentioned in the previous paragraph, individual agency coexists with cosmic agency in Sri Aurobindo's metaphysics. This implies a theology in which the Vedic sacrifice of Purusha (Person, the 'Who') is accompanied (in fact, preceded) by the sacrifice of Prakriti (Cosmos, the 'What'), creating the substantial and operational cosmic condition of Inconscience in which the fragmented dismemberment of Purusha may seed itself.[18] This cosmic latency of Consciousness self-constrained as Inconscience becomes the basis for the evolution of Nature. According to Sri Aurobindo, all evolution is accomplished through the double process of memorial aspiration (ascent of consciousness) and responsive grace (descent of consciousness).[19] The stirrings of the memory of Consciousness within the Inconscient turn into an 'ascending aspiration'[20] which invokes the 'descent' of successive gradations of Consciousness, each with its characteristic properties marking its difference in kind. Such a successive gradation of Consciousness in Nature (Prakriti) based in the Inconscience of Matter affords increasing possibilities of freedom and self-manifestation (swayambhu) to the individualized immanence of Purusha in each of its dispersed units. Thus, the evolution of Prakriti affords the evolution of Purusha.[21]

EVOLUTION AND PSYCHOLOGICAL PRAXIS OF SRI AUROBINDO

In Sri Aurobindo's cosmology of consciousness, the Purusha (person-element) is present in the particulate appearance of Matter as physical or material purusha, a spiritual inherence; in discrete life forms as vital purusha (pantheist or animist soul) and with the appearance of Mind, as mental purusha (conscious observer or witness). These three qualitative differentiations of the soul–nature dyad are emergent phenomena of the evolution of cosmic nature. This immanence of Purusha acts as the cosmogenetic individuating property in each of its prakritic (matter, life, mind) manifestations. Hence, each of these successive forms of personhood is more 'awake' than its predecessor, better able to experience its freedom and sovereignty from its constraining bounds of nature and hence express greater agency. In the human, the coexistence of physical, vital and mental prakriti implies the triple presence of physical, vital and mental purushas or conscious centres/souls, a compound and heterogeneous existence in which the freedom of the intelligence (buddhi) from the rest of the human constitution enables a higher degree of potential freedom of the mental purusha, resulting in an alienation from Nature but also holding the possibility of its transcendence and conscious reidentification.[22] Such a possibility of purusha's freedom in one of the constituents of prakriti results in what may be called an anthropogenesis,[23] a new form of ontogenesis in the human. This anthropogenesis is a new birth of personhood, described by Sri Aurobindo in terms of the appearance of a more centralized dimension of immanent purusha in the human, capable of integrating the physical, vital and mental purushas. Sri Aurobindo refers to this central purusha as 'psychic being' or 'soul personality'.[24] At this point, Purusha's emergent evolution is capable of taking an independent turn, no longer dependent on the evolution of Prakriti (cosmic nature) but able to transcend, master and transform Prakriti.[25]

Being free of the burden of guilt, Sri Aurobindo's evolutionary monadology may be seen as an individualized 'adventure of consciousness and joy' and in this respect closer to Bergson's (and Nietzsche's) personal exercise of a cosmic creativity (élan vital/will-to-power). It is also in this respect that such an exercise of personal creative will has been theorized by Sri Aurobindo as a praxis discursively continuous with long traditions of Indian yoga,[26] though put to a life-affirming end of social and cosmic transformation. Thus, of these three thinkers, Sri Aurobindo provides the most developed methodology for a cosmic and transcendental expansion of (post-)human personhood, based in the capacities of the source of individuation – the psychic being – to integrate the personality, identify itself with cosmic being (Overmind) and finally transcend cosmic existence in an identity with a transcendental source, the Supermind.[27] Each of these developmental phases may be thought of as a phase of cosmogenetic individuation, yielding collective (social and cosmic) transformations. Sri Aurobindo refers to this process as 'the triple transformation'.[28] Yet, as one can see from the above, such a process is intensely psychological, a 'practical psychology'[29] as Sri Aurobindo terms it, which seems to minimize or invalidate any concern for social or cultural conditions.

Such an appearance, however, is misleading and arises due to the disciplinary specialization of discourse as an epistemic aspect of modernity. We have noted how Sri Aurobindo's metaphysics involves relationally the evolution of universal conditions (prakriti) and individuation of consciousness (purusha). This relationality does not disappear with the emergence of the human. If the practical psychology of the triple transformation is concerned primarily with ontic evolution of the Purusha as outlined in Sri Aurobindo's philosophical (*The Life Divine*, 2005) and 'yogic' (*The Synthesis of Yoga*, 1999) works, Sri Aurobindo's social and political texts delineate the continuing evolution of prakriti (nature) at the level of human society, moving towards global conditions of human unity, a trajectory fraught not merely with promise but danger, needing political and ethical negotiation through its relationship with human agency.[30] But the implications of such ethical and political agency are easily lost sight of, due to the above-mentioned separation of his social and psychological texts and the privileging of the latter over the former.

SOCIAL PRAXIS AND TECHNOLOGY

This continuing evolution of prakriti at the level of human society and civilization in its varied relations with human choices (evolution of purusha) can be elaborated into a critique of modernity, something Sri Aurobindo himself undertakes to some extent in his social and political texts.[31] He presages a phase of globalization led by capital and outlines the dangers of 'economic barbarism' and fascist politics.[32] He predicts the eventuality of a world government and analyses the struggles of individual and subcultural agency in the face of homogenizing or hegemonizing tendencies.[33] He stages the opposition of superpower politics and federalist participation.[34] He sees the importance of promoting the forces of individual freedom, fraternity and internationalism over the ideological investments of state-controlled planning or aggressive nativism or religious fundamentalism.[35] At the micro-social level of the individual and the community, he promotes increasing autonomy with direct individual participation in shaping the communitarian life moving in the direction of a spiritual anarchy. Yet, as I discuss in the next paragraph, the ubiquitous mediation of technology as the sign of contemporaneity, emerging after his time, is not independently addressed by Sri Aurobindo.

While a comparative study of these three thinkers would be very interesting (and has been attempted in part by several scholars), what concerns me here is the contemporary relevance of the paradigm or episteme that finds form in these thinkers. In this regard it is the unthought within the thought, the obvious medium of existence that often makes possible the perception of an idea but remains invisible or imperceptible and concretizes itself over time, demanding a new engagement. Such is the place of technology in the articulation of these thinkers. One may say that the question of human subjectivity and its transformation (the 'who') accompanies the thought of post-Enlightenment modernity from its inception as part of its anthropological project. But it is tied to the question of the transformation of the world (the 'what') as it arises from its knowledge (science). This project of world transformation is attributed to the application of science – that is, technology – and thus the appearance of new assessments of the relation of human subjectivity to the cosmos with the advent of new technologies is almost to be expected. Yet the possibilities opened up by the new technologies on human consciousness are elided in the new philosophies of conscious evolution and/or the evolution of consciousness. To be fair to these philosophers, it isn't as if they ignore the advances of science and technology. Along with other humanistic thinkers of this period, they hold an ambiguous view of technology, part critique of its alienating and destructive effects from/on nature and part admiration for its productive and world-uniting possibilities. But technology does not receive a systematic treatment in relation to the possibilities of human consciousness from any of these thinkers.

HEIDEGGER AND THE QUESTION CONCERNING TECHNOLOGY

Indeed, it is only after the passing of this generation of thinkers and more properly from about the 1960s that technology becomes increasingly addressed with reference to consciousness, due to its ontological ubiquity. Perhaps the first serious and systematic consideration of this kind was Martin Heidegger's essay 'The Question Concerning Technology' published in 1954.[36] In this essay, Heidegger seeks out the 'essence of technology' and finds it not in technology itself but in the kind of revealing it makes possible. Heidegger relates technology, in its essence, to fabrication, a 'making' which is 'indebted' to four kinds of 'causes' – the earth as a provider of raw materials, a form of self-disclosure and gifting in relation to the human (material cause); the history of cultural forms, related to the function it serves (formal cause); the use and larger contextual goal or terminal function within which the fabricated object serves its function, ultimately a sacralizing or sacrificing to a transcendent realm or order (final cause); and the human fashioner who addresses all these causes and shapes the functional object (efficient cause).[37] Attention to all these causes or 'obligations'/'debts' makes the work of technology (*techne*) equivalent to a work of art, or invoking Heidegger's Greek term, *poiesis*.[38] Modern technology, Heidegger avers, does not respect the material cause or final cause. It challenges and sets itself upon the earth and it ignores the sacralizing function of aspiring for the Transcendent, the openness to the messianic future.[39] Heidegger uses two terms, 'enframing' (*Gestell*) and 'standing reserve' (*Bestand*), to describe the alienating and violent form of disclosure involved in modern technology,[40] marked by information exploitation, ordering all subjects and objects in the cosmos as static resources always available to be put to one's bidding. This alienation from the temporality or seasonality of the earth and its power to disclose the self-manifestation of Being, as well as its rupture from the sacred sphere, is the chronic malaise of our times, the epistemic violence of modern technology. Enframing thus refers to an attempt at a spatial reduction of cosmic contents, a mode of existence in which all things are objectified as resource, shorn of the mystery of temporal disclosure or spatial openness. Standing reserve is another way of addressing the status of beings or subjects thus reduced, objectified, commodified and exploited. As a mode of existence, therefore, modern technology is seen by Heidegger as modernity's episteme, utilizing the methodology and the systemic objectifying descriptology of science to 'gather' reality into a single flattened frame so as to order its contents at will.[41] Such an ontological critique of technology puts us in view at once of both the globalization and alienation of our times. An abstract, absolute description of the world usurps the place of the world. Modern and contemporary continental philosophy leans heavily on this insight of Heidegger. It becomes the basis for Habermas's 'colonization of the lifeworld'[42] and of Jean Baudrillard's 'virtual reality'.[43] Looked at in terms closer to us, in the key of contemporary technology which Heidegger was not privy to, one could say that what Heidegger describes here is a mode of existence where reality is perceived as an omnidatabase with all entities classified and organized in terms of their relations and properties, waiting to be 'harvested', 'utilized' or 'exploited' by whoever had power to access this construct. Undoubtedly, such a view seems bleak, holding little comfort or positive potential for human subjectivity. In relation to the philosophers of conscious evolution I started with, if human subjects are brought without exception under a regime of objectification and potential exploitation, they have little wriggle room to expand subjectively, and the promise of an integration and cosmisization of the human subject would seem an impossibility. Of course, such an ontology would also be uneven, affording degrees of freedom and privilege in access and exploitation of the 'standing reserve'. But under a universal ontology, even such subject positions of privilege in power and capital would be constrained to the maintenance of the ontological order. Heidegger's appeal is a return to *poiesis*, respect for the four causes or debts that human beings find themselves embedded in all their fabrications (*homo faber*) or technological undertakings (*techne*). This would need a 'wresting' of agency from the established order of our times and the re-establishment of a more 'authentic' mode of existence in the individual and the collective, the creation of a new 'I' and 'we' that resists the automatic gravitation of slippage into the 'they'.[44, 45]

Apart from this foregrounding of technology as the epistemic ontology of our times, in situating beings existentially within a temporal horizon constituted by the self-disclosure of Being, Heidegger created a language that folded interiority in historicity, thus articulating simultaneously the realities of the individual and society. The wresting of *poiesis* from an objectified *techne* is a praxis historically embedded within the modern horizon of Being. Such a praxis can be related to the practical psychology of yoga, a revolutionary transformation of subjective consciousness making possible a new horizon of Being's self-disclosure. This overcoming of the disciplinary specialization and separation of psychological and sociological studies marked a departure from the considerations of an earlier generation, like that of the philosophers of creative evolution we have considered, such as Sri Aurobindo, whose works had been produced in disciplinary isolation, as mentioned above, much to their detriment. Continental philosophers, such as Michel Foucault, Jacques Derrida, Pierre Bourdieu and Gilles Deleuze, who have followed in the wake of Heidegger, have continued an articulation that undercuts such disciplinary boundaries.

Heidegger's originality and break with the past may also be seen in his rejection of metaphysical idealism in favour of an ontology grounded in phenomenology. This turn in Heidegger may more properly be credited to his teacher, Edmund Husserl, the father of modern phenomenology, who felt that the modern domination of epistemology by science could no longer be overlooked by philosophy, which needed, in response, to refuse metaphysical speculation but also to eschew science's privileged objectification. Heidegger goes one step further in overcoming the subject–object dualism through his ontology and thus inaugurates a trend in which the critique of and break with metaphysics is treated as final. Thinkers such as Foucault and Derrida, following in the wake of Heidegger and largely in continuation of his work, have shied away not only from metaphysics but also from ontology as a result, more concerned to situate ontology in historical and political determination. Among this generation of important late-twentieth-century continental thinkers, only Gilles Deleuze, influenced strongly by Bergson, has continued to address metaphysics and ontology, but from a vantage of empiricism and ontogenesis. As a result, Deleuze can be constellated in important ways with our philosophers of evolution. However, I am not including a consideration of his ideas here, except where relevant, because though he has commented on technology in our times, this is not one of his primary concerns. Nonetheless, he was profoundly influenced by his contemporary, Gilbert Simondon, who engaged deeply with the question of technology, and in this chapter I wish to relate the ideas of conscious evolution to Simondon's thinking on ontogenesis and technicity.

MCLUHAN: MEDIA TECHNOLOGY AND CONSCIOUSNESS

However, before that, in thinking of a later generation who have engaged the ideas of the philosophers of conscious evolution with the ubiquity and ontology of modern technology, one must consider the Canadian philosopher of media technology Marshall McLuhan (1911–1980). Both McLuhan and Simondon may be seen to have direct links to the philosophers of conscious evolution – McLuhan to Teilhard de Chardin and Simondon to Bergson.[46] Though McLuhan's references to Teilhard are few, the cultural critic Tom Wolfe has pointed to the pervasive influence and substructural presence of Teilhard's ideas in McLuhan's insights on media.[47] McLuhan is responsible for a large number of neologisms that have become current in contemporary popular culture, three of his most well-known phrases being 'global village', the distinction between 'hot and cool media'[48] and 'the medium is the message',[49] later further finessed in the eponymous book title *The Medium is the*

Message.[50] Regarding technology both as an exteriorization and amputation of human organs and capacities, such as the nervous system or the memory,[51] McLuhan articulated many of the ideas that have led to contemporary posthumanist thought. In seeing new technologies as amputations of human capacity, he was echoing Plato's concerns with 'writing' as a technology leading to the attenuation and eventual loss of human memory (*Phaedrus*), but this was counterbalanced, for McLuhan, by the global expansion of collective consciousness made possible by technologies of communication, transportation and exchange. Yet, though the gains of collective consciousness were promising, the natural attenuation of individual capacities and the subjection of the individual to mass determinants were problematic consequences of technology that McLuhan was much concerned about all his life.

He saw and wrote of the subject-altering powers of media arising from new equations and engagements of the human sensory system[52] and reinflected this idea more powerfully in terms of ontological subjection in the tweaked variant 'the medium is the message'. One can easily see the extended mileage of this idea in contemporary posthumanist thought, as in Katherine Hayles's books *How We Became Posthuman* (1999) or *My Mother Was a Computer* (2005). McLuhan was developing his ideas in a world dominated by television and died in 1980, prior to the emergence of the desktop computer and long before the appearance of the World Wide Web. Yet, his pronouncements predict a world characterized by these developments in the 1960s. He discussed the ontological changes related to transitions of dominant media from print through film and television to multimedia and interdependent computing, coining the phrase 'global village' to describe the last phase. In his 1962 text *The Gutenberg Galaxy: The Making of Typographic Man*, he describes the promises and dangers of such a society:

> Instead of tending towards a vast Alexandrian library the world has become a computer, an electronic brain, exactly as an infantile piece of science fiction. And as our senses have gone outside us, Big Brother goes inside. So, unless aware of this dynamic, we shall at once move into a phase of panic terrors, exactly befitting a small world of tribal drums, total interdependence, and superimposed co-existence. [...] Terror is the normal state of any oral society, for in it everything affects everything all the time. [...] In our long striving to recover for the Western world a unity of sensibility and of thought and feeling we have no more been prepared to accept the tribal consequences of such unity than we were ready for the fragmentation of the human psyche by print culture.[53, 54]

One can see here the recovery of a collective human unity, now extended to a global dimension, out of the fragmentation implied in the complexification of tribal culture with the ascendance of civilization, marked as per McLuhan by print media and its subjective correlate of individualism. But at the same time, it is a return of subjective inundation by mass behaviours and instincts (tribal drums), least common denominators of consciousness (terrors) and surveillance and control by corporate or ideological authority (Big Brother). Behind this global culture one may intuit the cosmogenesis of Teilhard, a materialization of a cosmic consciousness or noosphere mediated by technology. Yet, for Teilhard, such a collective dimension could only be a stage in anthropogenesis, a precursor to christogenesis, or the generation of a cosmic and transcendental individual in each person. McLuhan could perceive the dangers and difficulties towards this eventuation, its easy derailment under the powers of subjection conditioning individuals more ubiquitously than ever before.

In response, he sought ways to maximize creative expression under these circumstances, indicating conditions and practices enabling agency, engagement and the autonomy and expansion of subjectivity. It is in such a context that, in his text *Understanding Media*, he distinguished between 'hot and cool media', media which enabled consumption and disabled participation (hot) as against those that were intrinsically interactive (cool).[55] Interestingly, he classes movies as being hot and television as cool, due to the latter needing more mental and emotional interactive response than the former. Today, such a distinction seems odd in the context of television, to which we more commonly attribute the function of producing 'couch potatoes'. However, the distinction could be seen as valuable in general for our consideration. McLuhan was not blind to the relative scale of these terms and displays his prescience once again when he compares television and multimedia computing:

> The next medium, whatever it is—it may be the extension of consciousness—will include television as its content, not as its environment, and will transform television into an art form. A computer as a research and communication instrument could enhance retrieval, obsolesce mass library organization, retrieve the individual's encyclopedic function and flip into a private line to speedily tailored data of a saleable kind.[56]

When compared to Heidegger, we see that McLuhan does not subscribe to the former's unrelieved pessimism regarding modern technology, though he is not naive about the detrimental effects of conditioning and state or corporate control implied by it. Instead he opens the possibility of achieving a Teilhardian vision of collective noogenesis through new technologies. This promissory note extended by McLuhan has informed a number of contemporary techno-optimists, who feel that the World Wide Web, in conjunction with other global telecommunication technologies, has inaugurated a new utopian age for humankind. In Gilbert Simondon, we will see another late-twentieth-century contemporary of McLuhan who holds out similar horizons for the human future, albeit with greater nuance and further reach. The question of human subjectivity inaugurated by Heidegger in terms of modern ontology remains, however. To what extent are human beings available to realize such a promise, or are they all the better transformed into fodder bereft of agency within enormous global systems of surveillance, classification, control and use, conditioned to believe that they are happy and free through dynamic and ubiquitous technologies of memory, persuasion and invisibility, as predicted by Gilles Deleuze in his 'Postscript on the Societies of Control'?

SIMONDON'S PROCESS METAPHYSICS

Gilbert Simondon (1924–1989) is undoubtedly the most sophisticated of the late-twentieth-century philosophers of technology, who have continued in the wake of the early-twentieth-century philosophers of evolution. As mentioned before, he was influenced by Bergson, whose idea of creative evolution and inventive fertility of becoming receives an updated treatment contemporary with a constellation of more recent concepts associated with modern science such as emergence, systems theory, chaos theory, information theory, cybernetics and self-regulating systems.[57] This is not to say that Simondon drew from these concepts, rather he represents a milieu of thought in which such concepts were emerging and have since become current. As per my characterization at the beginning of this article, the central idea in Simondon's oeuvre could be delineated as 'cosmogenetic individuation', though as a form of becoming and not as a metaphysical principle. In keeping with the post-Husserlian dictum in philosophy to keep away from idealistic metaphysics, Simondon does not develop an elaborate theory grounding becoming in a transcendent principle or choice, as does Teilhard or Sri Aurobindo. Rather, he positions the structures of becoming within becoming itself, proceeding empirically to verify and describe his ontogenetic processes. In this, however, he is not too far from Sri Aurobindo, whose metaphysics (darshan) is based in a praxis of transformation (yoga) which has an empirical basis for participation in a 'cosmogenetic individuation'. Moreover, though Sri Aurobindo's panentheism involves a spiritual transcendence and material immanence, these do not exist as an ontological duality, or as a top-down/active-passive hylomorphism,[58] but rather as an 'effective' duality existing as forms of self-perception in perpetual relation. As such, it wouldn't be too far to see them as coexisting heterogeneous orders of becoming in disparation, using the model of Simondon.

Simondon's process metaphysics deals with a pure immanence of becoming. In his thought, a stable unitary Being would remain transcendent and be incapable of manifestation. However, a purely unstable being would lead to a chaotic manifestation. Instead, he posits a 'metastable' Being, 'more than a unity and an identity', in other words marked by a radical excess, which can double itself through a phase shift (referred to by Simondon as 'disparation') and thus generate gradients of exchange between two heterogeneous series, which are problematic fields of becoming.[59] Each solution to such a problem would be a singular individuation that would remain in metastable equilibrium with the larger field or problematic (the milieu) and the totality of the metastable being (pre-individual being). Though relatively stable at the point of individuation, each individuated being and its milieu would remain capable of further individuation due to its continued metastability in relation to pre-individual being. Such further individuations may push an individuated being into another order of solutions belonging to a different problematic gradient, expressing new properties and degrees of freedom and agency. The information exchange along each gradient of becoming would be modulated by the properties of the medium of exchange, thus determining commonalities, degrees of variance and boundaries of each order of individuation. Simondon referred to these information transfers between heterogeneous gradients and media and leading to resolution and individuation as 'transduction'. Thus, individuation remained an 'open' and ever-unfinished process, representing a negentropic tendency of Being generating ever-higher orders of cosmogenetic individual and collective becoming.

ORDERS OF INDIVIDUATION: SIMONDON AND SRI AUROBINDO

Simondon identifies three such orders of individuation, the physical, the vital and the psychic. Physical individuation pertains to entities of material nature, vital individuation refers to the order of living beings and psychic individuation is of mental subjects (human beings). As discussed, each of these individuations occurs at the levels of the individual and the milieu. One may bring to mind here the evolution of purusha (person) and prakriti (cosmic/psychological nature) along the modalities of physical, vital and mental consciousness in Sri Aurobindo. The evolution of prakriti along each of these levels can be related to the individuation of the milieu, while the evolution of purusha corresponds to the individuation of the individual. One may also note that Sri Aurobindo includes the evolution of the psychic being, which expands into the triple transformation and leads to the cosmogenesis of the individual and beyond.

In Simondon's case, psychic individuation is an order of mental evolution which extends vital individuation, just as the latter extends physical individuation into an order of living beings. The transition from physical individuation to vital individuation is accompanied with the formation of an interiority and exteriority (individual and milieu) with more elaborate relations between the two through the development of sensation (perception) and intensity (affect), marking the interior and leading to increasingly efficient phylogenetic lineages (evolutes) of internal structuration and external action conserving an autopoietic dynamic entity. In the further transition from vital to psychic individuation, mentality emerges as a new order of properties transforming the vital elements and structures of the interior and resulting in a new relation with the exterior milieu. Thus, perception and affect of vital individuation are mentalized into thought and emotion, along with other properties of their commingling, such as imagination, ethics, aesthesis and Eros. Mediating the transfer of information between interior and exterior, these properties tend to structure not only the interior but also the exterior of the individual through their ability to develop commonalities of signification. This sets up a collective individuation in synchrony with individual individuation. The leap in power of agency represented by this new order of psychic individuation is given distinction by Simondon by naming the interior (individual) individuation as individualization and the collective individuation as transindividuation. Thus, transindividuation is the process towards a universalized collective socius enabling an open-ended diverse individuation in individual and collective existence.

It is important to keep in mind that for Simondon, ontogenetic individuation is an ongoing and never-finished process. It expresses and conserves the ubiquitous drive for unity and eternity[60] across the differentiated though undetermined potentia of the radically infinite pre-individual. Thus, every order and instance of individuating entities preserves within itself the infinity of the pre-individual, expanding its structure of relationality across both interiority and exteriority through an evolution of its powers. At the level of psychic individuation, individual agency participates in elaborating individuation across the boundary separating inside and outside in terms of 'two seemingly opposite, though reciprocally codependent directions: ... interiorizing the exterior, while, exteriorizing the interior'.[61] Such an agency grants content to Simondon's revised idea of 'soul'.[62] Soul for Simondon, then, is an emergent property, the appearance of an individualized personality as a stage of cosmogenetic individuation, that of the transindividual.

As we saw earlier, Sri Aurobindo uses the term 'psychic being' to refer to the soul personality in human beings. Though in his case, the immanence of the principle of individuation or personhood in all entities, which he calls purusha or 'psychic entity', ensures their ongoing evolution, conscious agency towards the integration of interiority (inner being) within itself and with its social and natural milieus is also accomplished through the emergence of the psychic being at the level of the mentalized human. Thus, psychic being, for Sri Aurobindo, is not a static structure. Moreover, if we are to consider Sri

Aurobindo's psychic principle of individuation in terms of essential operational property rather than substance, this is given by him as 'aspiration', whether subconscious agent in non-human living beings (psychic entity) or conscious agent in humans (psychic being). Sri Aurobindo's description of 'aspiration' can be expressed in terms identical with Simondon's description of the essential 'soul' quality operational within the individuation of every individual – 'the desire for eternity'.[63] As mentioned earlier, in Sri Aurobindo, it is this immanent aspiration which receives a response from the Transcendent, opening new possibilities of becoming which allow for the creative expression of new powers of being in the individual, resulting in greater states of stabilized relational integration. At the human level, the emergence of conscious agency in the psychic being allows for this aspiration to be consciously formulated, focused and intensified, leading to the integration of the internal elements of the physical, vital and mental beings (the 'inner being') around the psychic aspiration, a process called 'psychisization'. This is further extended by the universalization of the individual (cosmisization) followed by the integration of the psychisized and cosmisized individual with a transcendental consciousness (supramentalization), affording a cosmic transformation so as to express states of being not yet manifest in Nature. This is the revised content Sri Aurobindo gives to the Sanskrit term 'yoga', traditionally used to refer to processes of psychophysical practice leading to an escape from the cosmic condition, either in an ineffable transcendental trance (samadhi) or an extra-cosmic 'heaven' (loka) of perfection. In Sri Aurobindo, yoga instead becomes a process for the transformation of life through a heightened power of integration achieved through an extension of consciousness. Translating to the Simondonian key, if psychisization can be thought of as the individuation of the individual, cosmisization may be related to states of collective integration tantamount to transindividuation.

In Sri Aurobindo's own texts however, he does not see cosmisization and supramentalization in terms of transindividuation but as the results of the freedom and extension of individual consciousness and personhood (psychic being) achieved through the exercise of consciousness. Rather, states of cosmic and supramental consciousness achieved by groups of individuals are seen by him as the prerequisites for a kind of transindividuation, which he calls the 'gnostic community'. Theorized by him more in terms of a universal philosophical anthropology and individual psychological praxis in his philosophical and psychological texts, in his social and political texts and in practice in the habitus of his ashram in Pondicherry, the relationship between the psychic and the collective developments include a cultural dimension pertaining to global or planetary unity. In 1968, after Sri Aurobindo's passing, his spiritual partner and collaborator, Mirra Alfassa aka The Mother, founded the city of Auroville as a 'planetary city' and a 'site of material and spiritual researches for a living embodiment of an actual human unity'. She also coined the term 'collective yoga' to refer to the relational extension of the individual yoga at the collective level, open to a planetary culture, and increasingly spoke of the processes of universalization or cosmisization in terms of 'collective yoga' using a language which, though inflected in terms of consciousness, is distinctly reminiscent of what Simondon would call transindividuation.

DYNAMICS OF (TRANS)INDIVIDUATION

To draw this comparison closer, we may consider the dynamics of individuation and transindividuation as described by Simondon and Sri Aurobindo/the Mother. In Simondon, there is no substantial principle of individuation in beings but a process which expresses it as a result of ontogenetic metastability. The process monism implied in this gives significance to the becoming of being and all beings of becoming for Simondon. Thus, time takes its meaning from evolutionary processes of individuation leading to transindividuation and beyond. Time here does not follow a pregiven telos but stabilizations of individuation increasing in complexity and efficiency towards the integration, power and relationality of transindividuation. Each such stabilization is effected through an integration of elements expressing their powers and properties in ways that maximize their efficiency of functional integration of interiority and formation of a stable relationship with the external milieu. This state of stabilization in an individual's individuation is termed 'concretization' by Simondon. Simondon speaks of the concretization phase of individuation in a being as a precipitation of 'the future', demonstrating the operation of a nascent transindividuation at all stages of individuation. In effect, this idea of the communication of information from the future, a reversal of time's arrow, is hardly different from the precipitation of transcendental conditions as a response to psychic aspiration in Sri Aurobindo.

Tracing back to the cosmogenesis of Teilhard, one can see here how Simondon revises the transcendental metaphysics of the former to affirm the simultaneity of a double process of cosmogenesis materializing itself through transindividuation – individuals becoming cosmos and cosmos becoming individual. Though the structuration of this double process becomes materially articulated at the level of psychic individuation, the process itself is primordial and originary.

Individuation at this level, as at all levels, is accomplished across heterogeneous orders of being through transduction. The process monism of Simondon makes for the emergence of analogical morphologies and potentia across the different orders of becoming. These form nodes of resonance within and across the emergent orders that can amplify through intensification and exchange information through transduction. Such information transfer between elements of a unit and between units in a collective, interacting under the immanent impulse of 'the desire for eternity', activates the relations of individuation and transindividuation within and between self-organizing individuals and across different orders of their becoming. This causes the internal and external structures and functions to differentiate and evolve in classes of beings along phylogenetic lineages. The concretization phase of individuation occurs at a stage when the autopoietic entity achieves a state of functional integration where its elements express their powers not merely as parts of the whole but as co-adapting superpositionalities of the whole.

In comparison, Sri Aurobindo's monism is both substantial and processual.[64] The immanence of the purusha as psychic entity, and in the human as psychic being, catalyses a similar information transfer within and across the different orders of being in the individual and between individuals in the form of physical aspiration, vital aspiration and mental aspiration, evolving in agency and power of integration around the psychic centre. At the human level, it is possible to intensify this action more consciously, leading to an accelerated tendency towards integration (psychisization) in the individual and the collective (transindividual).[65] As mentioned earlier, for the transindividuation of the human being, the Mother articulated this integration in terms that echo the condition of elemental superposition in the concretization phase of Simondon, though in terms appropriate to the expansion of individual consciousness:

> Sri Aurobindo tells us that a true community – what he calls a gnostic or supramental community – can exist only on the basis of the inner realisation of each of its members, each one realising his real, concrete unity and identity with all the other members of the community, that is, each one should feel not like just one member united in some way with all the others, but all as one, within himself. For each one the others must be himself as much as his own body, and not mentally and artificially, but by a fact of consciousness, by an inner realization.[66]

Again, in 1973, the year of her passing, the Mother gave a New Year message which tied the goal of psychic evolution to a collective yoga at the planetary level: 'When you are conscious of the whole world at the same time, then you can become conscious of the Divine'.[67]

TRANSINDIVIDUATION, TECHNOLOGY AND COLLECTIVE YOGA

What is meant by being conscious of the whole world at the same time? It seems to me the preparation of a psychic subjectivity identified with the subjective life of the world and its pre-individual excess. How can one prepare oneself to be conscious of the whole world at the same time? For the followers of Sri Aurobindo's yoga, who have privileged his yoga texts, this might mean the expansion of individual consciousness through meditation and union with a cosmic consciousness. But those who read his social texts or who have been privy to the Mother's texts on collective yoga or her words related to Auroville may say that it is through the intensification of aspiration, its extension in relations and its psychic engagement with the cultural history of the world. For Simondon, this would be the preparation for the planetary transindividual:

> All individual ensembles have thus a sort of non-structured ground from which a new individuation can be produced. The psycho-social is the transindividual: it is this reality that the individuated being transports with itself, this load of being for future individuations.[68]

Such a preparation would bring to light the history of technology for Simondon. If the major part of Simondon's doctoral thesis at the Sorbonne was titled 'Psychic and Collective Individuation', his minor paper, which was published first both in the French original and the English translation, and for which he is better known, is 'The Mode of Existence of Technical Objects'. Following the anthropologist Leroi-Gourhan, Simondon sees a technogenetic individuation co-evolving with psychic individuation in the human as an inevitable differentiation towards transindividuation. Machines intervene to bridge the rupture between humans and nature arising from the displacement of a primitive vital individuation to the order of a 'civilized' mental individuation; yet machines, which emerge to heal human alienation, eventuate in alienating humans even further. Yet, technical objects are neither fully determined nor contiguous with humans. As a mode of existence, though conceptually and functionally bound to human becoming, they represent an order of independent individuation. The evolution of lineages of technical objects, Simondon shows, follows like other forms of individuation, a transductive process leading to an efficient stabilization of elements that has its own life outside of individual inventors, manufacturers or commercial interests. Simondon sees the individuation of technical objects following three orders related to three historical phases of human individuation: the premodern agrarian phase marked by artisanal manual tools, the modern industrial phase marked by thermodynamic engine-driven machines and the postmodern and post-industrial phase marked by information processing.

If the human relationship with technology during the pre-industrial phase was one which involved physical skill and implied a harmonious relationship between human, technical object and nature, the modern industrial phase has been one of increasing alienation between these three. Modern industrial machines have an enormous footprint and consume huge quantities of natural resources, disturbing the earth's ecological balance and depleting her reserves; mass-produce enormous quantities of finished products, for which large industries of persuasion must be formed so as to manufacture desire for consumption; and excrete tremendous quantities of waste which must be disposed, poisoning the earth and the habitats of the underprivileged. To produce, operate and maintain these machines, human beings must subject their bodies to the movements, speeds, temperatures, pressures and other unnatural properties of large-scale thermodynamic machines and their ensembles. Simondon sees these conditions of human–machine interaction as an unpleasant phase in their mutual transduction, resulting in the alienation that humanists have attributed to the machine. However, even in the 1960s, Simondon foresaw the overpassing of this phase and its replacement by a new post-industrial phase of information processing, where the individuation of microprocessor-based, information-processing computational devices would tend towards networks of collective ensembles accessible through terminals and offer a ubiquitous medium and milieu for planetary transindividuation.[69] Indeed, like McLuhan, Simondon was seeing these visions of the future in the 1960s. Freed from subjection to industrial complexes, human beings would be able to interact creatively with nature and the world through a mostly invisible layer of the being of technology individuated collectively in relation with human transindividuation.

UTOPIA OR DYSTOPIA?

Is this the inexorable future utopia towards which global humanity is moving today with its P2P smart phones and other networked digital prosthetics and bionics? Is the experience of 'being conscious of the whole world at the same time', announced by the Mother as the distant goal of an arduous spiritual development, just a form of cheap purchase universally bestowed upon humanity through the transindividuation of technology? Was Heidegger's ontological subjection by the new mode of Being's disclosure through technology– seen as modernity's episteme – but a mistaken identification of a passing phase for the noons of the future?

Simondon's brilliance has been acknowledged by many major thinkers of his and our times. One of his greatest contemporaries, who reviewed his thesis with unreserved praise and borrowed heavily from him in his own work, was Gilles Deleuze, and one of the great philosophers of our times, who continues to be indebted to him and thinks using his concepts of psychic and collective individuation, is Bernard Stiegler. Writing in the 1980s, Deleuze, in his 'Postscript on the Societies of Control', warns about the mutations of capital from the industrial to the post-industrial age. If the ubiquitous presence of the machine extended an era of biopolitics related to the disciplining of human bodies in keeping with the needs of industry in the age of thermodynamic machines, our age of information processing sees a new kind of subjection. The miniaturization and invisibility of the machine hides its versatile and flexible control over human lives. The enhanced flexibility of work and movement, increased plethora of choices and extended reach over time and space present a commodified freedom and happiness, within which capital controls human lives, denying true creative engagement with pre-individual being, which would make new individuations possible. Similarly, in our own times, Bernard Stiegler has warned about real-time corporate and governmental profiling and targeting, fragmentation of subjectivity through chronic technologies of attention capture and the remaking of public memories through mnemotechnics.

What Simondon saw as the promise of a new utopian phase of human–machine transduction/transindividuation leading to an individual and collective cosmogenesis is not a given that will arise automatically through the press of new buttons. Simondon was not oblivious to these dangers. The transindividuation of humans and their co-individuation with machines could move, in his opinion, towards the fulfilment of its positive possibilities, only following the break from conditioning, the habitual structures of the 'inter-individual' and the emergence of individuating personal agency. In asserting this, Simondon aligns himself with Nietzsche, drawing on the latter's rendition of Zarathustra, the prophet who extricates himself from his entanglement with the crowd that has embraced mediocrity, devoid of aspiration, through a period of isolation and silence. This asceticism and the related parable of the funambulist lays the ground for the conditions of subjective agency towards transindividuation, a preparation not dissimilar from that enunciated by Sri Aurobindo and the Mother, drawing on the traditions of yoga for their own purposes of planetary unity. Moreover, as articulated by the prophet at the end of the parable, what is further required is the need for a milieu of like individuals available and ready for transindividuation, collective conditions requiring a wresting of the individual from the ubiquitous co-optation of global capital, analogous to the call given by Heidegger in his analysis of modern technology.

Looking at the yoga of Sri Aurobindo, the arduous subjective disciplines necessary for 'the triple transformation' also need a milieu dedicated to inner development for its habitus, something less and less possible in our present age globally networked for corporate interests of production, seduction and consumption. Yet, to speak about an expansion or integration of consciousness without recourse to an engagement with technology is a romanticism that wills its self-exile and eventual obsolescence in the face of a globalizing technical milieu. New experimental collective environments are required for the development of subjective technologies (technics) freed from conditioning and rendered creative to co-individuate alongside distributed ensembles of information processing. Simondon's techno-aesthetic milieu and Sri Aurobindo's expansion of consciousness through yoga need creative engagement with a world culture made available through new forms of McLuhan's 'global village' dedicated to perpetual cosmogenetic individuation. Enhanced subjective disciplines of psychisization and cosmisization as per Sri Aurobindo, or psychic and collective individuation as per Simondon, moving towards the self-making of new subjects 'conscious of the whole world at the same time', must arise as the subjective correlate of co-individuating technical ensembles under experimental conditions of the collective life. This is the promise of the future, but it needs relational post-human agency and a subjectivity that can measure itself against the objective materialization of the cosmos in the form of global technology.

NOTES

1. Georg Wilhelm Friedrich Hegel, *Lectures on the Philosophy of World History: Introduction, Reason in History.* Trans. H.B. Nisbet (New York, NY: Cambridge University Press, 1975).

2. Pierre Teilhard de Chardin, *The Phenomenon of Man.* Trans. Bernard Wall (New York, NY: HarperCollins, 1959).

3. Carl G. Jung, *Psychological Types* (Princeton, NJ: Princeton University Press, 1971).

4. Gilbert Simondon, *L'individuation à la lumière des notions de forme et d'information* (Paris: Editions Jerome Millon, 2005); David Scott, *Gilbert Simondon's Psychic and Collective Individuation: A Critical Introduction and Guide* (Edinburgh: Edinburgh University Press, 2014).

5. Gilles Deleuze, *Difference and Repetition.* Trans. Paul Patton (New York, NY: Columbia University Press, 1995).

6. Henri Bergson, *Matter and Memory.* Trans. N.M. Paul and W.S. Palmer (New York, NY: Zone Books, 1988).

7. Teilhard de Chardin, *The Phenomenon of Man.*

8. Sri Aurobindo, *The Life Divine. Complete Works of Sri Aurobindo, Vols. 21* and *22* (Pondicherry: Sri Aurobindo Ashram, 2005), 922–952.

9. Teilhard de Chardin, *The Phenomenon of Man.*

10. Sri Aurobindo, *The Life Divine.*

11. Bergson, *Matter and Memory.*

12. Sri Aurobindo, *The Life Divine*, 309–335.

13. Sri Aurobindo, *The Life Divine*, 856–879.

14. Teilhard de Chardin, *The Divine Milieu* (New York, NY: HarperCollins, 2001).

15. The Purusha Sukta is hymn 90 in Book X of the Rig Veda. It presents infinite conscious Being as a transcendental Person who presents himself as cosmos and 'sacrifices' himself (becomes immanent) as the creatures and humans of various castes.

16. Sri Aurobindo, *The Synthesis of Yoga. Complete Works of Sri Aurobindo, Vols. 23* and *24* (Pondicherry: Sri Aurobindo Ashram, 1999), 106; The Mother, *Questions and Answers 1956. Volume 8, Collected Works of the Mother* (Pondicherry: Sri Aurobindo Ashram, 2004 [1977]), 74.

17. Sri Aurobindo, *The Life Divine*, 1051–1108.

18. Sri Aurobindo, *The Mother with Letters on the Mother. Complete Works of Sri Aurobindo, Vol. 32* (Pondicherry: Sri Aurobindo Ashram, 2012), 17.

19. Sri Aurobindo, *The Mother with Letters on the Mother,* 3; *The Life Divine*, 730–753.

20. Aligning this thought to that of Teilhard's and Simondon's, this may be thought of as a 'cosmogenetic intensity'.

21. Sri Aurobindo, *The Life Divine*, 272–274.

22. Sri Aurobindo, *The Life Divine*, 856–879.

23. It should be noted that ontogenesis and anthropogenesis are terms more common to Teilhard than Sri Aurobindo; nevertheless, I have used these terms since I feel them to be appropriate.

24. Sri Aurobindo, *The Life Divine*, 856–879.

25. Sri Aurobindo, *The Life Divine*, 856–879.

26. Sri Aurobindo, *The Synthesis of Yoga,* 41–52.

27. Sri Aurobindo, *The Life Divine*, 922–952.

28. Sri Aurobindo, *The Life Divine*, 922–952.

29. Sri Aurobindo, *The Synthesis of Yoga,* 44.

30. Sri Aurobindo, *The Human Cycle, The Ideal of Human Unity, War and Self-Determination. Complete Works of Sri Aurobindo, Vol. 25* (Pondicherry: Sri Aurobindo Ashram, 1997).

31. Sri Aurobindo, *The Human Cycle, The Ideal of Human Unity, War and Self-Determination,* 15–221.

32. Sri Aurobindo, *The Human Cycle, The Ideal of Human Unity, War and Self-Determination,* 44–54; 73–81.

33. Sri Aurobindo, *The Human Cycle, The Ideal of Human Unity, War and Self-Determination,* 279–578.

34. Sri Aurobindo, *The Human Cycle, The Ideal of Human Unity, War and Self-Determination,* 505–547.

35. Sri Aurobindo, *The Human Cycle, The Ideal of Human Unity, War and Self-Determination,* 548–570.

36. Martin Heidegger, *The Question Concerning Technology and Other Essays.* Trans. William Lovitt (New York, NY: Harper Torchbooks, 1982).

37. Heidegger, *The Question Concerning Technology and Other Essays,* 6.

38. Heidegger, *The Question Concerning Technology and Other Essays*, 8, 34.
39. Heidegger, *The Question Concerning Technology and Other Essays*, 9–10.
40. Heidegger, *The Question Concerning Technology and Other Essays*, 11–13.
41. Heidegger, *The Question Concerning Technology and Other Essays*, 17.
42. Jürgen Habermas, *The Theory of Communicative Action*. Trans. Thomas McCarthy (New York, NY: Beacon Press, 1984).
43. Jean Baudrillard, *Simulacra and Simulation*. Trans. Sheila Faria Glaser (Ann Arbor, MI: University of Michigan Press, 1994).
44. Heidegger, *Being and Time*. Trans. John Macquarrie and Edward Robinson (New York, NY: Harper & Row, 1962), 415.
45. It would be interesting to bring this viewpoint to bear on Michel Bauwens's essay on P2P systems, which may be called a subject-oriented database model as opposed to top-down algorithmic or horizontal object-oriented models implied in the 'enframing' of 'standing reserve'.
46. Simondon is also known to have quoted Teilhard de Chardin favourably, and an important commentator on Simondon, Jean-Hugues Barthélémy, has drawn attention to Simondon's debt to Bergson and Teilhard de Chardin, especially to Chardin's cosmogenetic individuation: https://fractalontology.wordpress.com/2007/10/22/translation-jean-hugues-barthelemy-on-simondon-bergson-and-teilhard-de-chardin/, accessed 4 October 2016.
47. Tom Wolfe, *Introduction to 'Marshall McLuhan Speaks: Centennial 2011'*, accessed 12 January 2014, 2011. http://marshallmcluhanspeaks.com/introduction/.
48. Marshall McLuhan, *Understanding Media: The Extensions of Man* (New York, NY: Mentor, 1964), 22.
49. McLuhan, *Understanding Media*, chapter 1.
50. McLuhan and Quentin Fiore, *The Medium is the Message: An Inventory of Effects* (New York, NY: Random House, 1967).
51. McLuhan, *Understanding Media*, 11.
52. McLuhan, *The Gutenberg Galaxy: The Making of Typographic Man* (Toronto: University of Toronto Press, 1962), 41.
53. McLuhan, *The Gutenberg Galaxy*, 32.
54. This passage is closely connected to McLuhan's discussion of a passage by Teilhard de Chardin in his work *The Phenomenon of Man*.
55. McLuhan, *Understanding Media*, 22.
56. McLuhan, *The Gutenberg Galaxy*, 158.
57. Jean-Hugues Barthélémy, *Penser l'individuation. Simondon et la philosophie de la nature* (Paris: L'Harmattan, 2005).
58. Simondon is concerned to reject the hylomorphic model which subordinates one principle to another in a dualistic master-slave or original-copy relation. Metaphysics, since Plato, has generally been conceived in this key as, for example, spirit/matter, soul/body, mind/body and culture/nature. Sri Aurobindo's panentheism also eschews this form of hylomorphic relationship, extending agency relationally along all heterogeneous orders, as may be viewed from the following quote: 'In a sense, the whole of creation may be said to be a movement between two involutions, Spirit in which all is involved and out of which all evolves downward to the other pole of Matter, Matter in which also all is involved

and out of which all evolves upward to the other pole of Spirit' (Aurobindo, *The Life Divine,* 137).

59. Simondon, *L'individuation psychique et collective* (Paris: Aubier, 2007 [1989]).

60. Scott, *Gilbert Simondon's Psychic and Collective Individuation*, 103; Simondon, *L'individuation psychique et collective*, 127.

61. Scott, *Gilbert Simondon's Psychic and Collective Individuation*, 103.

62. Scott, *Gilbert Simondon's Psychic and Collective Individuation*, 103, 104; Simondon, *L'individuation psychique et collective*, 157–158.

63. Simondon, *L'individuation psychique et collective*, 157–158.

64. In this sense, it is closer to the monism of Spinoza, and following him, Deleuze. This is what allows Deleuze to theorize extraordinary states of consciousness based on experimentation. Simondon, who is also deeply influenced by Spinoza, nevertheless, eschews the latter's substantialism.

65. Echoing Vivekananda, Sri Aurobindo defines yoga in a number of places as 'accelerated evolution'.

66. The Mother, *Questions and Answers*, 141–142.

67. The Mother, 'New Year Message, 1973', 1973, accessed 12 February 2014, http://sriaurobindoashram.com/Content.aspx?ContentURL=/_staticcontent/sriaurobindoashram/-07%20Messages/New%20year%20Messages/1973.htm.

68. Simondon, *L'individuation psychique et collective*, 193.

69. 'Today,' Simondon writes, 'the technical tends to reside in ensembles; it can now become a basis of culture which will bring a power of unity and stability, making it adequate to the reality it expresses and rules' (1989, p. 15).

BIBLIOGRAPHY

Aurobindo, Sri. *The Human Cycle, The Ideal of Human Unity, War and Self-Determination. Complete Works of Sri Aurobindo, Vol. 25.* Pondicherry: Sri Aurobindo Ashram, 1997.

———. *The Synthesis of Yoga. Complete Works of Sri Aurobindo, Vols. 23 and 24.* Pondicherry: Sri Aurobindo Ashram, 1999.

———. *The Life Divine. Complete Works of Sri Aurobindo, Vols. 21 and 22.* Pondicherry: Sri Aurobindo Ashram, 2005.

———. *The Mother with Letters on the Mother. Complete Works of Sri Aurobindo, Vol. 32.* Pondicherry: Sri Aurobindo Ashram, 2012.

Barthélémy, Jean-Hugues. *Penser l'individuation. Simondon et la philosophie de lanature.* Paris: L'Harmattan, 2005.

Baudrillard, Jean. *Simulacra and Simulation.* Translated by Sheila Faria Glaser. Ann Arbor, MI: University of Michigan Press, 1994.

Bergson, Henri. *Matter and Memory.* Translated by N.M. Paul and W.S. Palmer. New York, NY: Zone Books, 1988.

Deleuze, Gilles. 'Postscript on the Societies of Control'. Translated by Martin Joughin. *October,* 59 (Winter 1992): 3–7.

———. *Difference and Repetition*. Translated by Paul Patton. New York, NY: Columbia University Press, 1995.
Habermas, Jürgen. *The Theory of Communicative Action*. Translated by Thomas McCarthy. New York, NY: Beacon Press, 1984.
Hayles, N. Katherine. *How We Became Posthuman: Virtual Bodies in Cybernetics, Literature and Informatics*. Chicago: University of Chicago Press, 1999.
———. *My Mother Was a Computer: Digital Subjects and Literary Texts*. Chicago: University of Chicago Press, 2005.
Hegel, Georg Wilhelm Friedrich. *Lectures on the Philosophy of World History: Introduction, Reason in History*. Translated by H.B. Nisbet. New York, NY: Cambridge University Press, 1975.
Heidegger, Martin. *Being and Time*. Translated by John Macquarrie and Edward Robinson. New York, NY: Harper & Row, 1962.
———. *The Question Concerning Technology and Other Essays*. Translated by William Lovitt. New York, NY: Harper Torchbooks, 1982.
Jung, Carl G. *Psychological Types*. Princeton, NJ: Princeton University Press, 1971.
McLuhan, Marshall. *The Gutenberg Galaxy: The Making of Typographic Man*. Toronto: University of Toronto Press, 1962.
———. *Understanding Media: The Extensions of Man*. New York, NY: Mentor, 1964.
McLuhan, Marshall and Quentin Fiore. *The Medium is the Massage: An Inventory of Effects*. New York, NY: Random House, 1967.
The Mother. *Questions and Answers 1956. Volume 8, Collected Works of the Mother*. Pondicherry: Sri Aurobindo Ashram, 2004 [1977].
———. 'New Year Message, 1973', 1973. Accessed 12 February 2014, http://sriaurobindoashram.com/Content.aspx?ContentURL=/_staticcontent/sriaurobindoashram/-07%20Messages/New%20year%20Messages/1973.htm.
Scott, David. *Gilbert Simondon's Psychic and Collective Individuation: A Critical Introduction and Guide*. Edinburgh: Edinburgh University Press, 2014.
Simondon, Gilbert. *Du mode d'existence des objets techniques*. Paris: Aubier, 1989.
———. 'The Genesis of the Individual'. Translated by Mark Cohen and Sanford Kwinter. In *Incorporations*. Edited by Jonathan Crary and Sanford Kwinter, 297–319. New York: Zone Books, 1992.
———. *L'individuation à la lumière des notions de forme et d'information*. Paris: Éditions Jerome Millon, 2005.
Simondon, Gilbert. *L'individuation psychique et collective*. Paris: Aubier, 2007 [1989].
Teilhard de Chardin, Pierre. *The Phenomenon of Man*. Translated by Bernard Wall. New York, NY: HarperCollins, 1959.
———. *The Divine Milieu*. New York, NY: HarperCollins, 2001.
Wolfe, Tom. *Introduction to 'Marshall McLuhan Speaks: Centennial 2011'*, 2011. Accessed 12 January 2014. http://marshallmcluhanspeaks.com/introduction/.

Part III

AFTER MAN

Chapter Eleven

Being without Life

On the Trace of Organic Chauvinism with Derrida and DeLanda

Richard Iveson

In the posthumously published *The Animal That Therefore I Am* (2006), philosopher Jacques Derrida argues that the long history of Western philosophy has been dominated by the 'recurrence of a schema that is in truth invariable'.[1] This schema, he continues, is one in which everything deemed the exclusive property of 'Man' derives from an originary *fault* or *lack*, 'and from the imperative necessity that finds in it its development and resilience'.[2] This schematic default, in other words, bestows upon the human animal its exceptional ontological status, ring-fencing everything from technology, language and time to society, politics and law for humanity alone. Hence, this dominant schema is also a schematic domination, continuing to ensure the human's 'subjugating superiority over the animal'.[3] While existing only insofar as it comes after death, this late work continues Derrida's projected deconstruction of the human–animal dichotomy, the beginnings of which can be found as far back as his first major work, *Of Grammatology* (1967), wherein he introduces the structure of the *trace* as the constitutive condition of *all* living beings.

This is itself reason enough for any rigorous thinking with animals to continually return to the 'quasi-concept' of the trace. However, it is just such a rigorous engagement with this 'quasi-concept' that compels us to ask a further question: Is it possible that *Derrida* himself remains blind to, and thus complicit with, an even more basic philosophical schema – that which philosopher Manuel DeLanda terms 'organic chauvinism'?[4] Such a schema, in other words, is that of a dominant *zoo*-centrism that bestows exceptional ontological status upon the *living*.

Our question, then, concerns Derrida's desire to place secure limits on 'the living' through the reiterated construction of an abyssal border separating 'living beings' from 'non-living things'. A question, then, that moves Derrida's thought beyond his own examples of amoeba and annelid to beings that are not quite things and things that are not quite beings – entities such as viruses, Martian microbes, quanta and silicate crystals – and, further, to every material existent, past, present and future. Perhaps, then, it is not by chance that, in his final seminar, Derrida finds himself haunted by the figure of the *zombie*, that fearful thing-being hesitating between life and death. More importantly, it is only by refusing to impose contingent limits upon 'life' that a materialist and posthumanist praxis becomes possible, one that affirms the potential of 'bodyings' that are truly radical.

TRACE, SPACE AND TIME

In its starkest formulation, for Derrida there is no being *as such* without a *living* being. From the first, Derrida installs an abyss between the living and the non-living when, in *Of Grammatology*, he posits the 'emergence' of the trace – as the '*new*' logical structure of non-presence that is the unity of the double movement of protention and retention – as synonymous with the emergence *of life*.[5] This, for Derrida, is the denaturalizing movement *of* life, *the originary technicity of living being*, its structural unity accounting for the 'originary synthesis' that is 'the becoming-time of space or the becoming-space of time'.[6] Put as simply as possible, these paired definitions describe the impossibility of an indivisible *presence*, that is, of an entity fully present in and of itself. Rather, Derrida argues, for some entity to appear on what is the *scene* of presence, it must necessarily both keep within itself 'the mark of the past element' and let itself 'be vitiated by the mark of its relation to the future element'.[7] In other words, in order for an entity to *be*, that is, to endure in time and thus appear as present, this very appearing necessarily recalls both the trace of the past element (retentions) and the trace of the future element (protentions). Given this, the constitution of the so-called present thus depends a priori upon its relation 'to what it absolutely is not', in that an interval or *spacing* 'must separate the present from what it is not in order for the present to be itself'.[8]

Furthermore, this unity of protention and retention accounts for the originary synthesis described by Derrida as the becoming-time of space or the becoming-space of time. Here, Martin Hägglund's analysis helps to clarify this complex relation. Insofar as the instant of the *now*, of the *present*, can only appear by disappearing (given its a priori relation to what it absolutely is not), it therefore must, writes Hägglund, be inscribed as a trace simply in order to 'be'.[9] This, he continues, is the becoming-space of time insofar as every trace is necessarily *spatial*, since 'spatiality is characterized by the ability to remain in spite of temporal succession'.[10] For an entity to *endure*, in other words, it must be spatial, that is, it must take *place*. Spatiality, however, can never be 'pure simultaneity', as simultaneity as such is 'unthinkable without a temporalization that relates one spatial juncture to another'.[11] Space is thus at once a becoming-time, without which there could be no trace in the first place.

While I have neither the space nor the time to further elucidate the structure of the trace, what is important for us here is that the trace, *by definition*, is the constitutive condition of everything temporal, that is, of anything and everything that endures upon the scene of presence. Indeed, with admirable brevity and clarity Hägglund makes just this point in a recent paper: 'Everything that is subjected to succession', he writes, 'is subjected to the trace, whether it is alive or not'.[12] *Why*, then, does Derrida equate the trace with 'life in general' while innumerable finite entities continue to endure without the 'genetic description' supposedly regulative of life? Why, in other words, does he set limits on the trace when, in so doing, he simultaneously imposes limits on the living? While apparently simple, to state that the trace is the structural condition of everything that endures, and thus *is*, nonetheless opens the door to a radical and far-reaching critique – an opening from which Derrida, and Hägglund after him, unfortunately turn away.

THE STICKY QUESTION OF CREATION

Returning to the schematic domination of Western philosophy, irrespective of whether they concern human hubris or organic chauvinism, the questions such schema are constructed to counter are basically the same. Today's humanist descendants of Darwin, for example, lacking the fallback position of a divine Creator, must nonetheless be able to account for the emergence of the human as both coming *from* the animal and yet no longer *being* animal. Perhaps surprisingly, Derrida's organic chauvinism is staged to counter this very same problem, albeit with an essentially superficial shifting of terms. It is, as is so often the case, a problem of delimitation, that is, it concerns the foundation, construction and maintenance of borders. Thus, Derrida, similarly lacking a divine fallback position, must also be able to account for the emergence of the living as both emerging *from* the inanimate and yet *no longer* being inanimate. He must, in other words, address the precise historical moment in which the living presumably 'emerges' from the non-living. This problem, for the secular humanist as for the organic chauvinist, is, in short, that of *creation ex nihilo*. Ultimately, such dominant – nearly but not quite invariable – historical schema are not constructed to *solve* but rather to *dissolve* such problems, that is, to obviate the question.

Derrida, as we have seen, refers to the movement of the trace as 'an emergence' – but an emergence from *what*, exactly? And so we find ourselves back to the question of fence-building and of creation ex nihilo. Presumably, the trace – as a 'new structure of non-presence' synonymous with 'life' – could only emerge from a world composed entirely of inorganic, inanimate objects. This, however, not only contradicts its own logic but also opens deconstruction to the pejorative charge of 'correlationism' as defined by philosopher Quentin Meillassoux in *After Finitude: An Essay on the Necessity of Contingency* (2006).

Let us take the issue of logical contradiction first. Given that the trace is, as Derrida maintains throughout, the constitutive condition of existence itself, then how can the double movement of the trace *emerge* from out of anything? Rather, only the *nothingness* of the endless void could possibly precede its 'emergence' insofar as its apparently 'new structure of non-presence' at the same time constitutes the condition for the appearing or enduring of any entity whatsoever. Hence, 'life' as synonymous with the trace ultimately results in a return to the theological, demanding as it does creation ex nihilo.

Turning now to correlationism, Meillassoux defines as correlationist any philosophical position that depends upon an a priori co-relation of world and consciousness in the form of 'givenness'.[13] As such, all correlationist philosophies – and for Meillassoux at least this means everything from Kant onwards – are incapable of accounting for the existence of the world prior to the existence of conscious life forms as a result.[14] It is because of this, he continues, that the problem of correlationism can be seen at its clearest when considering 'ancestral statements', that is, statements made about reality anterior to the emergence of 'life'. Such statements, writes Meillassoux, are impossible for the correlationist philosopher for whom *being* is co-extensive with *manifestation*, in that the past events to which ancestral statements refer could not, by definition, be manifest *to* anyone. As such, 'what *is* preceded *in time* the *manifestation* of what is',[15] meaning that manifestation is *not* the givenness of a world but is instead an intra-worldly occurrence that can in fact be dated. In other words, to make the emergence of life synonymous with the 'worlding' of world is to evoke the emergence of manifestation amidst a world that pre-existed it. Hence, *insofar as* Derrida makes the emergence of the trace synonymous with the emergence of living beings, deconstruction too has no answer to the challenge the ancestral poses to correlationism: namely, how to conceive of a time in which the given as such passes from non-being into being? This challenge concerns not the empirical problem of the birth of living organisms but the ontological problem of the coming into being of givenness as such. It is a problem, however, *only insofar as we accept the unacceptable limits Derrida imposes upon the trace* – limits that, as we know, presuppose an abyssal living/non-living distinction.

The trace structure, however, refers to neither the site of ontological division nor a property a priori reserved for an exclusive subsection of beings but rather describes a *general structure of being*. The structural logic of the trace, in other words, is *the condition of possibility of beings in general* and, as such, inscribes *chance* as a necessary component of *all* forms of being. As the condition of possibility of formal structure – of being-form and being-formed – *being* is no longer co-extensive with givenness, no longer always already having *been given to* someone irrespective of whether that 'one' is judged human, conscious, living or whatever.

LATE-STAGE VITALISM

Why, then, might Derrida have sought to put an end to all life, an end he named the trace? Returning once again to the key passage in *Of Grammatology*, we find Derrida pointing to the 'essential impossibility' of avoiding 'mechanist, technicist and teleological language at the very moment when it is precisely a question of retrieving the origin and the possibility of movement, of the machine, of the *technè*, of orientation in general'.[16] Remembering that this is his first major work, I think that, above all else, Derrida here signals his desire to avoid exactly those accusations: namely, that underneath it all, he is in fact positing a rigid, mechanistic universe. To this end, however, he only succeeds in offering a late form of *vitalism* in its place. This notion of a 'late-stage' vitalism comes from DeLanda's analysis of what he deems a 'troubling aspect' of Henri Bergson's philosophy, namely the fact that he 'embraced a late form of "vitalism" which rigidly separated the worlds of organic life and human consciousness, where innovation was possible, from the realm of the merely material, where repetition of the same was the rule'.[17] As should be clear, this same 'late form' of vitalism equally troubles *Derrida's* philosophy, and we too should manage to rid it 'of its troubling aspects'.

Furthermore, Derrida may well have imposed these restrictions upon the trace as a result of concerns related to any would-be 'retrieval of the origin' – not in this case the 'origin of *Man*', of course, but rather the 'origin of *life* itself' – concerns which may be reflected in the fact that Derrida here offers nothing whatsoever in regard to what is the utterly extraordinary but still presumably historical event of the trace's emergence. What is important to us, here, is the fact that the structure of the trace, in accordance with its own logic, could quite simply never have been '*new*'.[18] This obscure 'locating' of the origin of 'life in general' is both odd and paradoxical. While we do well to wonder at Derrida's lifelong refusal to engage with the more radical implications of his own theoretical position, the incongruity of such a refusal is intensified by the fact that these same implications are perfectly consistent with contemporary accounts from within fields as diverse as philosophical Darwinism and synthetic biology regarding the processes by which nonlife is thought to 'invent' life and the inorganic to 'create' the organic. Moreover, I will argue, what these same contemporary interpretations collectively *lack* is the requisite philosophical background provided by the discourse of deconstruction in general, and by the indissociable 'quasi-concepts' of iterability and trace in particular.

NON-LINEAR DARWINISM

Here, we begin to circle back, albeit indirectly, to Hägglund, who singles out the work of Daniel Dennett as providing an easily accessible account of current, post-Darwinian understandings of evolution. Along the way, Hägglund underscores an absolutely central point in this regard: 'Rather than vitalizing matter, philosophical Darwinism *devitalizes life*'.[19] In so doing, moreover, it burrows its way through every abyssal distinction aimed at separating life from non-life, sending across its caesura a vast, web-like network of contact that renders null and void every simplistic division of the organic from the inorganic.

Hence, taking Hägglund's advice, we find that Dennett's *Darwin's Dangerous Idea: Evolution and the Meanings of Life* (1995) does indeed offer a clear account of evolution that, as 'a system of replication with variation', adheres to the fundamental Darwinian principle.[20] Dennett also notes that, while Darwinism is without doubt a mechanistic materialism, it is nonetheless the only philosophical theory currently on offer that doesn't get bogged down with inevitable questions of purpose and design, and thus theology and teleology. Instead, the very mechanicity of its materialism serves to open up what for so long has been the secure boundary erected between the disciplines of physics and biology.

While I do not have the space to recount Dennett's exposition in full, it will nonetheless suffice for us here to note a few fundamental points along the way. First, long before the appearance of bacteria, there existed 'much simpler, *quasi-living things*, like viruses',[21] but also unlike viruses insofar as they as yet had no host upon which to exist parasitically. Viewed by a chemist rather than a biologist, however, these entities are instead simply large, complex *crystals*, albeit with the added bonus that they self-replicate. Moreover, these ancient crystalline 'viruses' depend for their very survival upon an ongoing *reiteration* of repetition with variation – a reiteration that, if successful, brings about accelerating feedback loops and, if not, results in the decomposition of the 'virus' in accordance with the second law of thermodynamics.

In order to understand this notion of accelerating feedback loops, it remains to briefly introduce Manuel DeLanda's notion of *non-linearity*.

While Derrida insists that without *life* there can be neither *affect* nor *event*,[22] DeLanda argues that affect and event are part of the space of the structure of possibilities of *every* entity. The being of a given entity, he argues, can never be separated from its future possibilities and thus must be considered in terms of its properties, capacities and tendencies. Taking 'knife' as an example, its properties – such as sharpness and solidity – exist independently of its relation with other entities. Capacities, meanwhile, consist of an entity's potential *affect*; the knife, for example, has the capacity *to cut*, a capacity that is always double insofar as it requires a *relation*, that is, requires other entities capable of being affected in their turn. Thus, a knife's capacity 'to cut' is always the mark of a relation: *to-cut–to-be-cut*. Moreover, capacities are potentially infinite insofar as they depend on affective combinations with other entities, combinations that are theoretically without limit. Finally, every entity possesses certain tendencies understood as possible states of *stability* towards which it tends. Hence, while our knife tends to be solid, given different conditions it could equally tend to be liquid or even gaseous, with every such transition being actualized as an *event*.

As such, potential affective combinations characterize the being of every entity – an affectivity that ensures the *non-linearity* of history understood in its broadest sense. For DeLanda, innovation, and thus non-linearity, occurs in any system 'in which there are strong mutual interactions (or feedback) between components'.[23] As such, what might be respectively termed 'pre-cellular' and 'post-cellular' evolution must therefore *both* be understood as *non-linear*, described by DeLanda as that 'in which there are strong mutual interactions (or feedback) between components'.[24] Moreover, writes DeLanda, when it comes to the non-linear, it is entirely irrelevant whether 'the system in question is composed of molecules or of living creatures' since both 'will exhibit endogenously generated stable states, as well as sharp transitions between states, as long as there is feedback and an intense flow of energy coursing through the system'.[25]

Such dynamic, non-linear phenomena irredeemably fracture Darwin's original conception of evolution as a strict linear teleology with only the one possible historical outcome, namely, the perfect manifestation of a single optimal design. Instead, non-linearity presupposes only what DeLanda in his later work *Philosophy and Simulation* terms '*gradients* of fitness', wherein a gradient functions only so long as *differences* of fitness remain so as to 'fuel a process of selection' that favours the replication (with variation) of one kind over another.[26] Here, DeLanda once again draws our attention to the crucial point that such gradients can be applied as much to 'molecular replicators and their different capacities to produce copies of themselves' as it can to 'the differential reproductive success of embodied organisms'.[27]

ITERABILITY, AGAIN

What should be noted here is the fact that both non-linearity and contemporary Darwinism *presuppose with every replication* the structural logic of what Derrida terms *iterability* and, as such, the double movement of the trace. For Derrida, we recall, iterability is the very *possibility* of repetition. Iterability, he writes, is the structural characteristic that permits any mark to function ritualistically as language. At the same time, however, iterability determines that every production of such a text is necessarily subject to variation or mutation – what Derrida calls dissemination or 'destinerrance' – insofar as repetition (replication or reproduction) inevitably divides the apparently indivisible presence of the text by way of the double movement of protention and retention, that is, by the structural logic of the trace. It is right here that deconstruction must shed its 'late-stage vitalism' in order to reconstitute itself as a fully materialist practice – indeed, as a mechanistic materialism, albeit one that refuses the linear notion of a fully deterministic universe, putting in its stead a structural modality of non-linear *in*determinism. To this end, it is far from incidental that we find Derrida in full agreement with DeLanda as to the central importance of *history* in just this regard, describing iterability as 'historical through and through' insofar as it allows both contextual elements of great stability *and* the possibility of transformation, 'which is to say history, for better or for worse'.[28]

Reconsidering iterability in light of our key thesis – that the trace continues to function irrespective of whether there is life or not – has, I would argue, the potential to radically transform the theoretical practice of deconstruction. Indeed, it is all too easy to perceive the enormous impact that, far beyond the work already done by Derrida, a rigorous deconstruction of living/non-living division would have upon such simplistic normative pairings as animal–human, instinct–intelligence and reaction–response.

CONCERN CONCERNING CONCERN

Such a claim, however, requires the following important proviso: simply to make this point regarding the functioning of the trace beyond the limits of life is, in and of itself, by no means a *guarantee* of any such productive mutation. Hence, in returning to Martin Hägglund, we soon discover that, irrespective of how important his 'radical atheist' critique of Derrida's equating of *différance* with life undoubtedly is, its radical potential is nonetheless quickly muffled insofar as he almost immediately re-employs that critique as the justification for reinstating what is arguably the most traditional and pervasively normative of all metaphysical binaries.

Hägglund begins this process by first making explicit 'a *continuity* between the living and the nonliving in terms of the structure of the trace'.[29] Here, he uses Meillassoux's example of the radioactive isotope, describing the latter as '*surviving* – since it remains and disintegrates over time – but it is not alive'.[30] This disintegration or decay of matter, continues Hägglund, answers to both the *becoming-time of space* insofar as its successive stages of decay can never be simultaneous and to the *becoming-space of time* insofar as such disintegration could not take place without a spatialized material support. Survival, then, characterizes every finite entity – *every* entity, in other words – who or which endures in time-space.

Survival is, in short, synonymous with being. All well and good, you might say, except that Hägglund immediately follows this demonstration with a rhetorical question: 'What difference is at stake, then, in the difference between the living and the non-living?'[31] This is, as we have seen, a profoundly important question, and the answers cannot simply serve to obviate the question. Hägglund, however, does just this. The difference, he writes (somewhat tautologically), is that a non-living being is 'indifferent to its own survival, since it is not alive', whereas 'only a living being cares about maintaining itself across an interval of time'.[32] For Hägglund, then, *to be alive is to be concerned with one's ongoing survival* – it is, in short, the constitutive condition of 'being-alive'. Here, however, such an ontologically definitive 'concern' inevitably implies some form of minimal consciousness or, at the very least, a degree of *intentionality*. As such, a host of beings must once again join the (very long) queue for judgment: Are ants, for example, concerned with survival? What of microbes? Of extremophiles like the Martian hyperthermophiles who, having crash-landed on this planet billions of years ago, still exist today? What of nanobots – are they concerned and thus alive? And antibodies? Artificial Intelligence? What of *viruses*? Indeed, what of *urine*? Its production certainly takes place within the bodies of a huge range of 'living' beings, all of whom, should this production cease, would very quickly become 'non-living'. Is urine a 'living' or a 'non-living' material? Is it, in other words, concerned or unconcerned about survival?[33]

Here, then, by once again redefining the living over and against the nonliving, Hägglund not only neutralizes his crucial point concerning the trace but also in fact reintroduces the well-worn metaphysical opposition between 'the living' as willing, intentional and conscious beings and the 'non-living' as mere reactive mechanisms. A distinction, in short, between the mindful (i.e. concerned with survival) and the mindless (and thus unconcerned about anything). The problem here centres largely on Hägglund's notion of the living as an open *and* closed (autopoietic) system, but with no explanation as to why entities deemed non-living do not *also* constitute an open–closed system that is *in some sense* concerned with survival understood as enduring, especially given that the latter accords far better with Hägglund's understanding of the trace structure, an understanding backed up by the findings of molecular biology. Indeed, in the context of a discussion concerning stable states and their critical phase transitions, Derrida himself says that both the trace and iterability ensure that *nothing* can remain absolutely stable. No system, he writes, can be absolutely closed, as this would imply full presence, that is to say, 'sub-stance, stasis, stance'.[34] Ultimately, Hägglund ends up turning full circle, ultimately reducing innumerable unspecified entities to both the state and status of mindless Cartesian machines. It is somewhat ironic, therefore, that the most radical deconstruction of the limits imposed upon life by Derrida should itself end up reiterating the very opposition between response and reaction that Derrida himself spent a lifetime breaking down.

ISLAND LIVING (AND DYING)

At this point, one might well object that Derrida has in fact dealt with the living/non-living binary on any number of occasions – finitude, and thus death and dying, being of central concern. This is indeed the case. However, Derrida only ever considers the living/*dead* binary, that is, the division between the living and the *no-longer* living. What he does *not* consider, by contrast, is the division between the living and the *not-yet* or *never* living. This is not to say, however, that Derrida's deconstruction of the living/dead binary has no relevance here. Taking death as the subject of his very last seminar, Derrida begins by declaring that, even today, neither science nor philosophy is in fact capable of ascertaining with any certainty the difference between a living body and a corpse. Later, he engages with the trace directly, arguing that any 'presentation' of the trace in general necessarily 'leaves in the world an artifact that speaks all alone … without the author himself needing to do anything else, not even be alive'.[35] In other words, the trace – which for Derrida, as we know, is only ever the trace of a *living* being, this despite the previously stated impossibility of ascertaining any rigorous distinction between life and death – is already a dead-but-living artefact. Such, he writes, is finitude, is *survivance*: the trace entrusted 'to the sur-vival in which the opposition of the living and the dead loses and must lose all pertinence'.[36] Every artefactual trace, he continues, is rather a dead body buried in material institutions and yet resuscitated each time anew by 'a breath of living reading'.[37] For Derrida, then, finitude – as the archive as survivance at work – is the active, radical dissemination that constitutes the originary forcing of 'life in general'.

Given, however, that the trace functions whether there is life or not, and given the acknowledged impossibility of distinguishing absolutely between the living and the dead – an impossibility that is in fact a *consequence* of the continued functioning of the trace, that is, of the material enduring of the corpse – it thus becomes necessary to rewrite this notion of finitude upon a much broader scale. Finitude, as the archive as survivance at work, thus becomes *the active, radical dissemination that constitutes the originary forcing of everything that exists and thus endures*, however, whenever and wherever this may be.

Until we recognize as fully as possible that all beings in the world are finite and thus subject to the logical structure of the trace, we inevitably find ourselves marooned not on *Crusoe's* island, but on *Derrida's*.[38] Access to the latter, as is well known, has been decreed by Derrida to depend solely upon a single, apparently simple and seemingly uncontentious criterion: that of the capacity to *suffer* (or, put another way, to share in common the suffering of an *in*capacity). Following Jeremy Bentham, then, 'to-suffer or not-to-suffer?' becomes for Derrida the question and the foundation upon which an inclusive and posthumanist ethics should stand. Such a foundation and others like them, however, can never stand up against everything that remains to come. To limit the world to the *human*, Derrida argues, is to forever remain with Robinson Crusoe upon his island, helpless but to interpret everything 'in proportion to the insularity of his interest or his need'.[39] Such limits placed upon the world, he continues, are 'the very thing that one must try to cross in order to *think*'.[40] If, then, we are to *follow* Derrida in a way that remains faithful to his thought, we are obliged first and foremost to cross those very limits that *Derrida* himself imposes upon the world, insofar as such limits inevitably make over the world as an island once again. In this case, Derrida populates his island solely with such entities as are securely classified as organic living beings and, as such, deemed proper members of the set of those whose capacity for suffering can be readily identified in accordance with an institutional context.[41] Our question, then, is *whose* island is this exactly, that is, what interests and needs might support its interpretive schema?

Derrida's island is an exclusive place, and poor in world indeed, based upon a qualifying criterion that is both utilitarian and anthropocentric insofar as the very notion of 'capacity to suffer' relies upon the extrapolation of *human* experience and, as such, thus seems to make any claim for ethical citizenship dependent upon the possession or otherwise of a central nervous system comparable to that of the human. At this point, it is highly instructive to return briefly to the first volume of *The Beast and the Sovereign* (2009) and, in particular, to what Derrida has to say about what he describes as the 'principle of ethics or more radically of justice'. Any such principle, he writes, 'is perhaps the obligation that engages my responsibility with respect to the most dissimilar, the entirely other, precisely, the monstrously other, the unrecognizable other'.[42] Indeed, he continues, while it is a fact that we feel more obligations towards those who are closest to us, '*this fact will never have founded a right, an ethics, or a politics*'.[43]

At issue here is not the living and the non-living, however, but rather the necessary consequences of the trace as the unity of protention and retention – one such consequence being that the living/non-living *opposition* must be broken down and a differential *relation* installed in its place. As such, once arbitrary criteria are abolished, tables as much as tigers become living/non-living entities insofar as the coherence and persistence of both depend upon energy and differential gradients. In other words, if 'life' consists of varying combinations of forces, then a table is alive: stable yet finite and subject to abrupt phase transitions as a *result of its being subject to the structural logic of the trace*. Similarly, if a single RNA microbe is not qualified as 'living', then neither is a tiger, whose finite existence too is composed of stable combinations of forces whilst remaining subject to critical phase transitions.

NEITHER VITAL NOR MECHANICAL: SPECTRAL

None of this, however, implies some variant of vitalism. As we have seen, the post-Darwinian universe is nothing if not mechanistic and material. Nonetheless, our final step must necessarily engage with the issue of vitalism and mechanism in relation to an expanded notion of the trace, as only then will it become possible to conceive of a mechanistic materialism that in no way presupposes a reductionist view of 'life'. And, once again, it is Derrida who provides the necessary theoretical tool: in this case, the important notion of *spectrality*.

According to Derrida, the originary technicity that is the iterability of the trace ensures that *every* being – that is, every *living* being for Derrida – is 'a dead body buried in material institutions', one that awaits resuscitation, we recall, by way of the '*breath* of a living reading'.[44] Once again, and despite the somewhat anachronistic resuscitation of the notion of breath, of *pneuma*, we are compelled to ask whether, prior to its pneumatic reincarnation, this 'dead body' is living or non-living, neither or both, or in-between. Derrida's only response is to note that the 'gestural, verbal, written, or other trace' is entrusted 'to the sur-vival in which the opposition of the living and the dead loses and must lose all pertinence'.[45] The domain in which this opposition loses pertinence is, unsurprisingly, that of the *spectre*, and of *spectrality* in general. Furthermore, it is just this figure of the spectre – this being for whom life or death is neither here nor there, for whom the question of living or non-living is without relevance – who/which ensures that deconstruction can never be reduced to a reductionist view of 'life'. Spectrality, then, not only annuls the opposition between life and non-life, but it also renders the issue a non-issue. '"I don't know"', writes Derrida, is 'the very modality of the experience of the spectral, and moreover of the surviving trace in general'.[46]

Following our argument here, then, the fact that *the spectral is the modality of the trace in general* also means that the 'redemptive' possibility of the *spectre* or the *phantasm* – which Derrida describes as the braiding of the intolerable, the unthinkable, and the 'as if' – must therefore be extended to *all* beings. As a consequence of the logical structure of the trace, in other words, the spectral modality of 'I don't know' presupposes a position between the two extremes of complete mechanistic determinism on one side and on the other, complete indeterminism in which causality and historical contingency play no role whatsoever – what DeLanda calls an 'intermediate determinism'.[47] Furthermore, *this spectral modality of 'I don't know' is thus the modality of existence itself*, that is, of everything that endures – from the Martian hyperthermophile to the image it evokes, and from the compression of volcanic rock over the eons of geological time to the blinding flash of sunlight off chrome.

Here, then, is a mechanistic materialism that nevertheless has 'I don't know' as its modality – a modality that, instead of reducing life to the clockwork of complete determinism, rather ensures the emergence of a *non-linear history* insofar as *every* existence is subject to abrupt phase transitions at critical points, yet without ever requiring a transcendent factor. At last, then, we take our place within a fully populated world, a world in which the living/non-living *opposition* has neither purchase nor relevance.

NOTES

1. Jacques Derrida. *The Animal That Therefore I Am.* Trans. David Wills (New York: Fordham University Press, 2008), 45.
2. Derrida, *The Animal That Therefore I Am*, 45.
3. Derrida, *The Animal That Therefore I Am*, 45.
4. Manuel DeLanda. 'The Machinic Phylum', *TechnoMorphica* 1998, no pagination, http://www.egs.edu/faculty/manuel-de-landa/articles/the-machinic-phylum/.
5. Jacques Derrida, *Of Grammatology, revised edition.* Trans. Gayatri Chakravorty Spivak (Baltimore and London: The Johns Hopkins University Press, 1997), 84.
6. Jacques Derrida 'Différance', in *Margins of Philosophy.* Trans. Alan Bass (Chicago: University of Chicago Press, 1984), 13.
7. Derrida, 'Différance', 13.
8. Derrida, 'Différance', 13.
9. Martin Hägglund, *Radical Atheism: Derrida and the Time of Life* (Stanford: Stanford University Press, 2008), 18.
10. Hägglund, *Radical Atheism*, 18.
11. Hägglund, *Radical Atheism*, 18.
12. Martin Hägglund 'Radical Atheist Materialism: A Critique of Meillassoux', in *The Speculative Turn: Continental Materialism and Realism,* Eds. Levi Bryant, Nick Srnicek and Graham Harman (Melbourne: re.press, 2011), 119.

13. See Quentin Meillassoux, *After Finitude: An Essay on the Necessity of Contingency.* Trans. Ray Brassier (London and New York: Continuum, 2006), 1–27.

14. Of course, the attribute of 'consciousness' has long served as constitutive of the ontological distinction between 'Man' and 'Animal', with the result that 'life' here nearly always refers exclusively to '*human* life'.

15. Meillassoux, *After Finitude*, 14.

16. Derrida, *Of Grammatology*, 84–85.

17. DeLanda, 'The Machinic Phylum', n.p.

18. Derrida, *Of Grammatology*, 84.

19. Hägglund, 'Radical Atheist Materialism', 121.

20. Daniel C. Dennett, *Darwin's Dangerous Idea: Evolution and the Meanings of Life* (London: Penguin, 1995), 152.

21. Dennett, *Darwin's Dangerous Idea*, 156.

22. Jacques Derrida, *The Beast and the Sovereign Volume II.* Trans. Geoffrey Bennington, Eds. Michel Lisse, Marie-Louise Mallet and Ginette Michaud (Chicago and London: The University of Chicago Press, 2011), 149.

23. Manuel DeLanda, *A Thousand Years of Nonlinear History* (New York: Swerve Editions, 1997), 14.

24. DeLanda, *A Thousand Years of Nonlinear History*, 14.

25. DeLanda, *A Thousand Years of Nonlinear History*, 14.

26. Manuel DeLanda, *Philosophy and Simulation: The Emergence of Synthetic Reason* (London: Bloomsbury Academic, 2011), 48.

27. DeLanda, *Philosophy and Simulation*, 48.

28. Jacques Derrida, '"This Strange Institution Called Literature": An Interview with Jacques Derrida'. Trans. Geoffrey Bennington and Rachel Bowlby, in *Acts of Literature*, Ed. Derek Attridge (New York and London: Routledge, 1992), 63–64.

29. Hägglund, 'Radical Atheist Materialism', 123: emphasis added.

30. Hägglund, 'Radical Atheist Materialism', 123: emphasis in original.

31. Hägglund, 'Radical Atheist Materialism', 123.

32. Hägglund, 'Radical Atheist Materialism', 123.

33. In *Regenesis: How Synthetic Biology Will Reinvent Nature and Ourselves* (New York: Basic Books, 2012), George Church and Ed Regis note that work done in four areas – 'the synthesis of urea, the investigation of mirror molecules, the investigation of polymers ... and the self-reproduction of molecules' – renders impossible any distinction between living and non-living *matter* (19). While this again is beyond the scope of this chapter, what is important is their insistence on the impossibility of secure distinctions both between living and non-living and between organic and inorganic. Staying with this last example of urine, urea was in fact the first 'organic' compound to be synthesized from an 'inorganic' substance (ammonium cyanate), way back in 1828.

34. Jacques Derrida, '"Eating Well", or the Calculation of the Subject'. Trans. Peter Connor and Avital Ronell, in *Points ... Interviews 1974–1994* (Stanford: Stanford University Press, 1995), 270.

35. Derrida, *The Beast and the Sovereign, Volume II*, 86–87.

36. Derrida, *The Beast and the Sovereign, Volume II*, 130.

37. Derrida, *The Beast and the Sovereign, Volume II*, 131.
38. For Derrida's discussion of *Robinson Crusoe*, in which Crusoe's island isolation serves as a particularly fertile figure of human exceptionalism, see *The Beast and the Sovereign, Volume II*.
39. Derrida, *The Beast and the Sovereign, Volume II*, 199.
40. Derrida, *The Beast and the Sovereign, Volume II*, 198; emphasis in original.
41. Whilst the setting of the scene of the possible is, as Derrida writes, the 'always necessary context of the performative operation', such a context is, like every convention, always already 'an institutional context' ('The University without Condition', in *Without Alibi*. Trans. and Ed. Peggy Kamuf (Stanford: Stanford University Press, 2002), 235–236.
42. Jacques Derrida, *The Beast and the Sovereign, Volume I*. Trans. Geoffrey Bennington, Eds. Michel Lisse, Marie-Louise Mallet and Ginette Michaud (Chicago and London: The University of Chicago Press, 2009), 108.
43. Derrida, *The Beast and the Sovereign, Volume I*, 109.
44. Derrida, *The Beast and the Sovereign, Volume II*, 131: emphasis added.
45. Derrida, *The Beast and the Sovereign, Volume II*, 130.
46. Derrida, *The Beast and the Sovereign, Volume II*, 137.
47. DeLanda, 'The Machinic Phylum', n.p.

BIBLIOGRAPHY

Church, George and Ed Regis. *Regenesis: How Synthetic Biology Will Reinvent Nature and Ourselves*. New York: Basic Books, 2012.

DeLanda, Manuel. 'The Machinic Phylum'. *TechnoMorphica*, 1998, http://www.egs.edu/faculty/manuel-de-landa/articles/the-machinic-phylum/.

———. *A Thousand Years of Nonlinear History*. New York: Swerve Editions, 1997.

———. *Philosophy and Simulation: The Emergence of Synthetic Reason*. London: Bloomsbury Academic, 2011.

Dennett, Daniel C. *Darwin's Dangerous Idea: Evolution and the Meanings of Life*. London: Penguin, 1995.

Derrida, Jacques. 'Différance'. In *Margins of Philosophy*. Translated by Alan Bass, 1–28. Chicago: University of Chicago Press, 1984.

———. '"This Strange Institution Called Literature": An Interview with Jacques Derrida'. In *Acts of Literature*. Translated by Geoffrey Bennington and Rachel Bowlby, edited by Derek Attridge, 33–75. New York and London: Routledge, 1992.

———. 'Eating Well, or the Calculation of the Subject'. In *Points ... Interviews 1974–1999*. Translated by Peter Connor and Avital Ronell, edited by Elisabeth Weber, 255–287. Stanford: Stanford University, 1995.

———. *Of Grammatology*. Revised edition. Translated by Gayatri Chakravorty Spivak. Baltimore and London: The Johns Hopkins University Press, 1997.

———. 'The University without Condition'. In *Without Alibi*. Translated and edited by Peggy Kamuf, 202–237. Stanford: Stanford University Press, 2002.

———. *The Animal That Therefore I Am.* Translated by David Wills. New York: Fordham University Press, 2008.
———. *The Beast and the Sovereign, Volume I.* Translated by Geoffrey Bennington, edited by Michel Lisse, Marie-Louise Mallet and Ginette Michaud. Chicago and London: University of Chicago Press, 2009.
———. *The Beast and the Sovereign, Volume II.* Translated by Geoffrey Bennington, edited by Michel Lisse, Marie-Louise Mallet and Ginette Michaud. Chicago and London: University of Chicago Press, 2011.
Hägglund, Martin. *Radical Atheism: Derrida and the Time of Life.* Stanford: Stanford University Press, 2008.
———. 'Radical Atheist Materialism: A Critique of Meillasoux'. In *The Speculative Turn: Continental Materialism and Realism.* Edited by Levi Bryant, Nick Srnicek and Graham Harman, 114–129. Melbourne: re.press, 2011.
Meillasoux, Quentin. *After Finitude: An Essay on the Necessity of Contingency.* Translated by Ray Brassier. London and New York: Continuum, 2006.

Chapter Twelve

Returning to Text
Deconstructive Paradigms and Posthumanism
Danielle Sands

> *Deconstruction was a textualism and it is only textualism with its accompanying scandalous horror of idealism that might allow us to retrieve thought from the myopias of posthumanism.*[1]

That Claire Colebrook's deliciously unfashionable endorsement of a textual deconstruction sounds vaguely shocking testifies to quite how *démodé* this particular philosophical paradigm has become. From pre-millennial crosspollination between theory, literary studies and 'continental' philosophy, we have witnessed as philosophy has dissolved these links, favouring instead a politicized philosophy (Alain Badiou, Slavoj Žižek), a 'turn toward reality itself' (Speculative Realism)[2] or a focus on life, affect and the body (Rosi Braidotti, Donna Haraway). Whilst Žižek was perhaps overhasty to conclude that 'the Derridean fashion is fading away',[3] a blunted version of Derrida's work has proved a convenient counter against which new schools of thought cut their teeth. In turn, keen to render Derrida's work relevant and radical – and battling on another front against Derrida's religious defenders – Derrida scholars have repackaged Derrida as a 'radical atheist' (Martin Hägglund) or a posthumanist (Cary Wolfe) or, like Catherine Malabou, exchanged writing for alternative paradigms such as 'plasticity', thus consigning textual Derrida to the forgotten past. There are multiple issues at stake here: the question – noisily debated in the 1970s and 1980s and now largely forgotten – of the meaning and status of 'text' for deconstruction, the political value of Derrida's work and the current pressing demand for a philosophically literate response to the looming environmental crises we face. In this chapter I shall revisit the notion of text within the context of twenty-first-century concerns, using the notions of inhuman and post-human to assess the claims of posthumanism, the ongoing value of a textual deconstruction and the compatibility between the two.

DECONSTRUCTION, MATERIALISM, 'TEXT'

For its current critics, deconstruction is often perceived as being complicit with the 'linguistic turn'. Rosi Braidotti regards Derrida as peripheral to the 'new materialist' project, due to his 'linguistic frame of reference'.[4] Quentin Meillassoux's Badiou-endorsed critique of 'correlationism'[5] is aimed squarely at popular notions of Derrida and has contributed to the widely held belief that deconstruction is surplus to twenty-first-century thought. In *Religion, Politics, and the Earth: The New Materialism*, an initial scepticism towards this position soon gives way to general acceptance, as Clayton Crockett and Jeffrey W. Robbins write: 'We do not want to diminish or wish away the question of language and the difficult issue concerning its relationship to reality. At the same time, we need tools to think beyond the implicit opposition between human language and reality'.[6] Accordingly, in their book, Derrida and deconstruction go virtually unmentioned.

The conflation of deconstruction with the 'linguistic turn' conveniently enables thinkers such as Badiou to claim that we have moved beyond deconstructive navel-gazing to philosophies with more political (and even philosophical) traction. If explained at all, this conflation tends to hinge on a face-value reading of Derrida's infamous claim that *'There is nothing outside of the text* [there is no outside-text; il n'y a pas de hors-*texte*]'.[7] Such a reading takes Derrida as asserting that we are trapped within language, separated from matter, and therefore doomed to an ineffectual politics which speaks a language inescapably disconnected from our material conditions. Our frame of reference is singularly human – Cartesian, even – and thus condemns us to anthropocentrism. This reading, which places Derrida firmly within the 'linguistic turn', is unambiguously resisted by Derrida, who, in an interview with Richard Kearney, observes:

> I never ceased to be surprised by critics who see my work as a declaration that there is nothing beyond language, that we are imprisoned in language; it is, in fact, saying the exact opposite. The critique of logocentrism is above else the search for the 'other' and 'the other of language'.[8]

In the sense Derrida uses it here, 'language' becomes a shorthand for the closure and systematicity associated with the linguistic system and 'text', a counter-force of disruption or dispersion. It is helpful to think of 'language' and what Derrida calls the book on one hand, linked to recuperation, sameness and totality, and the de-constituting effects of 'text' or 'writing' on the other. As Derrida notes in *Of Grammatology*,

The idea of the book, which always refers to a natural totality, is profoundly alien to the sense of writing. It is the encyclopedic protection of theology and of logocentrism against the disruption of writing, against its aphoristic energy, and, as I shall specify later, against difference in general.[9]

Crucially, Derrida's use of the term 'text' is not limited to 'language' in the popular sense. Rather, if we think of 'language' as shorthand for a certain sense of systematicity, then 'text' is, in Colebrook's terms: '[A]n "untamed genesis", an anarchic dispersal, a *mal d'archive* or an evil that works against logic, works against "gathering", and against any notion of life as *oikos*'.[10] 'Text' speaks of a difference, of *différance*, which is not classifiable or recuperable in the system yet renders the system possible. It is, Derrida tells us, 'limited neither to the graphic, nor to the book, nor even to discourse, and even less to the semantic, representational, symbolic, ideal, or ideological sphere'.[11] Thus 'text' is neither singularly human nor linguistic, hence Derrida's emphasis on marking and tracing, and Colebrook's link to an inhuman thinking of life.

Colebrook is not the only thinker who notes that 'text' exceeds the linguistic frame usually ascribed to Derrida's thought. Identifying the similarities between systems theory and deconstruction, and the former's need for the latter, Cary Wolfe observes that in the work of systems theorist Niklas Luhmann, 'writing takes center stage as a paradigm of communication, but only because it exemplifies a deeper "trace" structure [...] of meaning'.[12] That this trace structure is not unique to the human is maintained by Derrrida from *Of Grammatology* right through to *The Animal That Therefore I Am*, in which he insists that 'Mark, gramma, trace and *difference* refer differentially to all living things, all the relations between living and non-living'.[13] Speaking directly to the materialist dismissals of deconstruction, Colebrook, alongside critics such as Pheng Cheah and Vicki Kirby, emphasizes both the value of thinking deconstruction materially and the challenge that deconstruction poses to the very materialisms which critique it.

For these thinkers, 'text' is framed as a way of thinking materiality without succumbing to a metaphysical materialism. 'Text', Cheah notes, provides the opportunity '[t]o think of matter outside the oppositions that have imprisoned it'.[14] One issue here, as Vicki Kirby observes in her challenge to John Protevi's critique of deconstruction, is the sense in which terms such as 'text', 'language' and 'matter' are employed. That such terms are, for Derrida, 'sites of excavation and discovery',[15] rather than terms whose meaning is pre-given, often leads to misunderstanding. See, for example, Derrida's discussion, via de Man in 'Typewriter Ribbon: Limited Ink (2)', of 'materiality' as 'a very useful generic name for all that resists appropriation'.[16] In this sense, as Colebrook remarks, 'matter' cannot, as for the materialists, 'be retrieved as some prior originating ground', but rather it has 'a strategic force'[17] as that which is inappropriable. 'Matter', she writes, 'is differential rather than substantial'.[18]

In her rereading of 'il n'y a pas de hors-*texte*' along similar lines, Vicki Kirby contends that Derrida's work demands that we open the notion of 'text' to the non-human, in particular by viewing 'language' – in its broadest sense – as the 'playful affirmation'[19] of nature and evidence of 'an inseparability between representation and substance'[20] rather than a marker of the division between nature and culture. She asks, 'Could the generalized origin of re-presentation, the hiccough of this subject/object shimmering as the "always already not yet", be thought as the Earth's own scientific investigations of itself?'[21] There is an apparent inconsistency, however, between Kirby's conflicting aims to demonstrate the ways in which textuality precedes the nature/culture divide and 'to *naturalize* language'.[22] Identifying a recent trend to naturalize deconstruction – as a rebuttal to the charge that it is narcissistically and anthropocentrically linguistic – Claire Colebrook argues that it undermines the real force of deconstruction. She insists, '[t]o posit textuality as first is to erase nature'.[23] Kirby, nonetheless, reiterates the deconstructive challenge to the assumption of the secondariness or belatedness of textuality; if language is 'a maze of in-finite differentiation whose fundamental dimensions are still being drawn',[24] which precedes rather than derives from culture, we no longer regard it 'as forfeit and substitution',[25] as a poor second to presence.

If Colebrook, Cheah and Kirby all to some extent advocate a textualist deconstruction as the only effective challenge to a materialism which takes the nature of matter as a given, Colebrook is unique in anchoring this in a recuperation of a specific notion of 'theory'. She pinpoints two types of theory. The first theory is informed by the kind of textual deconstruction I have been discussing, which recognizes an inhuman and irrecuperable force within structures perceived as singularly human. She writes, 'Theory is an acceptance of a distinction between a strong sense of the inhuman (that which exists beyond, beyond all givenness and imaging, and beyond all relations) and an unfounded imperative that we must therefore give ourselves a law'.[26]

This kind of theory is defined by distance, interruption and estrangement, by 'a world that is not ourselves and a force that cannot be returned to the human'.[27] It is this estrangement that has been tempered by a domestication of theory and of deconstruction in particular. The counter to this type of theory is, for Colebrook, associated with strains of neo-vitalism and posthumanism, whose aims are often primarily recuperative, looking to salvage a set of lost relations, to re-embed the human in an environment from which she/he has become detached. This latter type of theory focuses more on recognition than difference and overlooks the theoretical distancing of a textual deconstruction in favour of a turn to practice. One might be forgiven in thinking that the latter, in its apparent flight from theory to practice, is more useful, given the environmental crises which we face – indeed, that it is more radical. However, Colebrook challenges the vitalist turn both on the grounds of its apparent absurdity – that it appears right when the separation of man as a species with devastating effects becomes clear and 'when life, bodies and vitality have reached their endpoint and face extinction'[28] – and on the grounds of its uncritical approach to 'life' itself, its naivety in assuming that thought's Cartesian history is contingent and escapable. Accordingly, she asks,

> What if all the current counter-Cartesian, post-Cartesian or anti-Cartesian figures of living systems (along with a living order that is one interconnected and complex mesh) were a way of avoiding the extent to which man is a theoretical animal, a myopically and malevolently self-enclosed machine whose world he will always view as present for his own edification. What if, as Derrida suggested in his essay on Foucault, the attempts to step outside Cartesian man and break with the history of dominating reason were the most Cartesian of gestures.[29]

This leaves us with two different notions of life: the first in which man's self-enclosure and 'self-englobing reason'[30] are errors which might be overcome in order to liberate a post-human future with man resituated in his environment and the second 'textualist' notion in which life is an errant force, which does not call us to reverence for 'the earth' or 'life' or 'Gaia' – a call which is itself made possible by theoretical man – but reminds us that 'there is no pure earth that might be reclaimed'.[31] Whereas the posthumanism that Colebrook critiques reproduces the same ethical and political horizons which have brought us here, a textual deconstruction – perceived as politically impotent or anthropocentric – challenges us to look beyond the 'ethos of the present'.[32]

DECONSTRUCTION AND THE
POST-HUMAN: WOLFE AND MORTON

It's probably clear by now that I welcome Colebrook's appeal to a textual deconstruction and the challenges she poses not only to the more short-sighted elements of posthumanism but to the knee-jerk rejections of the textual paradigm from those for whom 'politics', 'life' or the body seem more fresh or radical. It is however possible that just as some of the posthumanists move too quickly over the insights of deconstruction, Colebrook moves too quickly over posthumanism, rendering it an uncritical parody of itself, as she asserts, for example, that posthumanism 'is perhaps the only humanism that thought has ever known' because '[o]nly today, with the notion of man as a seamless emergence from life, or man as aspect of the cosmos, do we have a humanism that does not problematize and destroy itself'.[33]

With this in mind, I want to turn to Cary Wolfe's – avowedly deconstructive – account of posthumanism. Claire Colebrook is not unique in challenging the idea of a deconstructive posthumanism. There's an interesting parallel between Colebrook's recent work and Timothy Morton's 2007 book *Ecology without Nature*, as both thinkers search for appropriately critical, post-deconstructive approaches to current environmental crises. Morton outlines his position as a counter to the posthumanism of Cary Wolfe, arguing that Wolfe takes refuge in an alternative vocabulary instead of facing up to the problems of the 'human'. In his later book, *The Ecological Thought*, Morton argues, 'Post-humanism seems suspiciously keen to delete the paradigm of humanness like a bad draft ... What if being human is the encounter with the strange stranger or in other words, at a certain limit, an encounter with the inhuman?'[34] The stress on the importance of the inhuman in constituting the human, and on the non-self-identity of the human, is shared both by Morton and Colebrook and by Cary Wolfe, who notes, ' "[W]e" are not "we"; we are not that "auto-" of the "autobiography" that "humanism gives to itself". Rather, "we" are always radically other, already in- or a-human in our very being [...]'.[35] Here there is apparently little to choose between the three thinkers, so why the strikingly different positions they take on posthumanism? What is at stake here? Why does Wolfe endorse such a seemingly problematic term?

The answer to this is not immediately clear. In fact, Wolfe devotes considerable time to distinguishing his work from numerous other strands of posthumanism and transhumanism and in rejecting the conflation between humanism and Enlightenment which such posthumanisms sometimes make. Furthermore, he corrects any simplistic reading of the 'post' of posthumanism as meaning *after* the human or humanism. At most, the 'post' of posthumanism names a dislocation from the fantasies of humanism and the difficulty of finding a position from which to critique constructions of either the human or humanism. There are two points at which Wolfe seems to diverge from Colebrook, however: the first is his claim that posthumanism witnesses a unique historical moment 'in which the decentering of the human by its imbrication in technical, medical, informatic and economic networks is increasingly impossible to ignore'[36] – a point where the technological embedding of the human recalls us to its biological embedding. The second point is Wolfe's perception of posthumanism both as a 'mode of thought' and as a mode of direct engagement with anthropocentrism.[37] From this, it becomes clear that Wolfe is interested in the practical possibilities or operational value of posthumanism, not just its theoretical significance. He is looking to ground an ethic of posthumanism in the parasitic logic of deconstruction. What is the problem with this?

As you may recall, Claire Colebrook defined 'theory' as 'an acceptance of a distinction between a strong sense of the inhuman (that which exists beyond, beyond all givenness and imaging, and beyond all relations) and an unfounded imperative that we must therefore give ourselves a law'.[38] Wolfe draws upon Derrida to emphasize that the inhuman, 'the estranging prostheticity and exteriority of communication – is shared by humans and nonhumans the moment they begin to respond to each other by means of any semiotic system in the most rudimentary sense'.[39] This forms the basis of the posthumanist critique of the self-sufficient humanist subject, which cannot account for or correct its own 'constitutive blindness'[40] and, for Wolfe, reopens the question of human and non-human animal ethical relations. What is interesting is that Wolfe's posthumanism seems oblivious to the tension which is created here – the tension which Colebrook calls 'theory', but it might just as well be called deconstruction – that is, between the dislocation and dispersion of the inhuman and the human desire to 'give ourselves a law'. Indeed, for Wolfe, the inhuman grounds an ethical law via the notion of the 'other'. He further reifies the inhuman by arguing that we should regard 'animal studies' as a paradigm of posthumanist disciplinarity because in its very approach it critiques the humanist subject and reveals the shared finitude of human and non-human animals.

It is here that Wolfe's post-humanism comes adrift from his deconstruction, as he lets go of the deconstructive tension between inhuman dislocation and human law, viewing one term, the inhuman, as a route to the other, the ethico-political ends of posthumanism. Of particular note is Wolfe's failure to critique this tendency to reterritorialize the inhuman by 'giving ourselves a law'. By beginning with the ethico-political outlook of posthumanism, Wolfe can do nothing more radical than reinforce what Colebrook calls 'the ethos of the present'. Yet Wolfe's divergence from deconstruction to forge a more practical, political posthumanism is neither novel nor surprising, rather it is the latest iteration of a familiar critical frustration with deconstruction's apparent lack of functional political value.

DECONSTRUCTION, 'TEXT', POSTHUMANISM

Despite its swerve to recuperate a familiar ethico-political horizon, in its double aspect, Wolfe's account of posthumanism strongly echoes the doubling of deconstruction. See, for example, Wolfe's claim that

> [p]osthumanism can be defined quite specifically as the necessity for any discourse or critical procedure to take account of the constitutive (*and*

constitutively paradoxical) nature of its own distinctions, forms, and procedures – and take account of them in ways that may be distinguished from the reflection and introspection associated with the critical subject of humanism. The 'post-' of posthumanism thus marks the space in which the one using those distinctions and forms is not the one who can reflect on their latencies and blind spots while at the same time deploying them.[41]

If we accept Wolfe's explanation of the 'post', then this position is compatible with Colebrook's endorsement of a return to 'theory' – it is a post- not pre-deconstructive posthumanism. But where does the combination of Wolfe's posthumanism and Colebrook's textual deconstruction leave us? Certainly the value of Colebrook's textual deconstruction lies in its potential for challenging the social and political imaginaries. The problem, however, is how we construct ethics *at all* after this, given that the resultant ethics could only be a counter-ethics, or anti-ethics, an ethics without *ethos*, divested of a fully rooted human identity. More realistically, a genuine commitment to 'life' would require us to put aside ethics, *ethos* and polity, instead imagining 'texts as lines drawn without any preceding or ideal community'.[42] Colebrook does not fully pursue the scepticism of her vision here; the tension which she perceives between inhuman dislocation and human law is a lived tension and precludes definitive escape from 'self-englobing reason'. But how does this play out? I want to try to answer this by coming back to the question of 'text'.

Attempts to recuperate the deconstructive notion of 'text' from the 'linguistic turn' have often entailed distinguishing Derrida from literary proponents of deconstruction, particularly those of the Yale School, such as Paul de Man, Geoffrey Hartman and J. Hillis Miller. In an early response, which looked to outline a more explicitly political deconstruction, Michael Ryan described 'textuality' as simply 'the name for radical heterogeneity' which 'has little if anything to do with an idealist concept like "the literary"'.[43] More recently, in *Telling Flesh*, Vicki Kirby also looks to separate 'writing' from the literary in order to liberate the former from its attachment to the human. She explains,

> Concepts such as 'writing in the general sense', *écriture*, 'trace', text', and so on, are commonly interpreted within the conventional literary context that would normally define them. As a consequence, the radical purchase in these neologisms is often lost in the ease of this recuperation.[44]

Kirby's description of this process as a 'recuperation' is telling and fits with her assertion that '"writing" is no longer just a literary notion'.[45] At stake in her 'just' is a host of assumptions about the literary, first and foremost – and chiming with the belief in the secondariness of writing – that 'writing in the narrow sense articulates its status as representation'.[46] Not only is the ease with which Ryan separates Derrida's 'text' from 'literature' or the 'literary' misplaced, but so is Kirby's confidence in her definition of literature as conservative, recuperative and representational. The logic behind both is clear: For Ryan, it is an insistence on materialism in the face of idealist appropriations of Derrida; for Kirby, it is the relocation of 'text' into an extra-linguistic and less anthropocentric framework. However, Derrida's work does not endorse either position. On the one hand, reading *Of Grammatology*, for example, it is clear that the terms 'text' and 'writing' might not be confined to a linguistic framework. On the other, Derrida's preoccupation with language, particularly literary language and literary genres, evident, for example, in the interview 'This Strange Institution Called Literature', appears to return 'text' to the literary. See, for example, Derrida's claim that 'my [his] most constant interest, coming even before my philosophical interest I should say, if that is possible, has been directed towards literature, towards that writing which is called literary'.[47]

That 'literature' or the 'literary' comes to stand for something else – 'radical heterogeneity', in Ryan's terms, or 'the experience of a singularity that cannot be assimilated into any overarching explanatory schema',[48] according to Simon Critchley – is not in dispute here. Where Ryan is mistaken, however, is in his attempt to dissociate this 'heterogeneity' from 'literature' or the 'literary' as we traditionally understand them, to claim, not that they are 'sites of excavation', in Kirby's terms, but that Derrida's choice of these terms is arbitrary. Rather, I argue, first, that we should regard literature – reflexive about 'language' in the broadest sense of the word – as an instantiation of Derrida's 'text', a kind of counter-language which deconstructs or deconstitutes the closed systematicity of language (in Derrida's sense). And, secondly, I argue that literature is allied with Derrida's deconstruction of phonocentrism. Rather than thinking of literature as uniquely and definitively 'human', we might think of literature as an example of what Derrida calls 'the animality of the letter',[49] as an anti-systemic force which draws out the 'other' or inhuman within language and demonstrates the way that the technical and non-living materiality of writing invades the supposedly living and self-present speaking subject. Colebrook reiterates the insistence of the inhuman within 'textuality' as she writes: 'To consider textual worlds materially and to consider materiality textually is to admit that processes of language and meaning operate in the absence of human command, understanding and imagination'.[50] This is actually very close to Kirby's claim in her – confusingly titled – 'naturalization of language'. If we can demonstrate that there is a fundamentally inhuman force in our most human of endeavours, then the oppositions we have constructed between nature and culture, and the human and non-human, are no longer functional.

When Derrida speaks of the power and value of 'literature' or the 'literary', he often, counter-intuitively, frames it in political terms. In its affinity with the particular and the idiomatic, and its potential to challenge or transgress current conceptual structures, literature is connected to 'an authorization to say everything', which, he argues, is 'inseparable from what calls forth a democracy'.[51] If we are to take seriously the inhuman force of 'text' and the 'ethics without *ethos*' which it entails, then we may have to jettison – or at least examine – Derrida's language here, as it appears to remain committed to our current ethico-political horizon. Literature generates a kind of excess whose meaning cannot be foreclosed, but the existence of this excess is dependent on its initial adherence to a set of familiar conceptual categories. In this sense, it, too, enacts the tension, which Colebrook identifies in 'theory', between the dislocation and dispersion of the inhuman and the desire 'to give ourselves a law'. Colebrook's critique of posthumanism is rooted in her claim that it fails to acknowledge and respond to this tension as a tension, but, as Cary Wolfe's account of posthumanism suggests but does not fully realize, there remains the possibility of another posthumanism, one which both enacts this tension and frames it in terms of our most pressing contemporary questions.

NOTES

1. Claire Colebrook, 'Not Symbiosis, Not Now: Why Anthropogenic Change is Not Really Human', *The Oxford Literary Review,* 34.2 (2012), 201.

2. Levi Bryant, Nick Srnicek and Graham Harman, 'Towards a Speculative Philosophy', in *The Speculative Turn,* Eds. Levi Bryant, Nick Srnicek and Graham Harman (Melbourne: re.press, 2011), 3.

3. Slavoj Žižek, *The Parallax View* (Cambridge, MA: The MIT Press, 2006), 11.

4. Rosi Braidotti, *The Posthuman* (Cambridge: Polity, 2013), 30.

5. Quentin Meillassoux, *After Finitude: An Essay on the Necessity of Contingency.* Trans. Ray Brassier (London and New York: Bloomsbury, 2008), 5.

6. Clayton Crockett and Jeffrey W. Robbins, *Religion, Politics, and the Earth: The New Materialism* (New York: Palgrave Macmillan, 2012), 113.

7. Jacques Derrida, *Of Grammatology,* revised edition. Trans. Gayatri Chakravorty Spivak. (Baltimore: The Johns Hopkins University Press, 1997), 158.

8. Jacques Derrida, 'Deconstruction and the Other', in *States of Mind: Dialogues with Contemporary Thinkers on the European Mind,* Ed. Richard Kearney (Manchester: Manchester University Press, 1995), 123.

9. Derrida, *Of Grammatology*, 18.

10. Colebrook, 'Not Symbiosis', 196.

11. Jacques Derrida, *Limited Inc.* Trans. Samuel Weber and Jeffrey Mehlman, Ed. Gerald Graff (Evanston, IL: Northwestern University Press, 1988), 148.

12. Cary Wolfe, *What is Posthumanism?* (Minneapolis and London: University of Minnesota Press, 2010), 23.

13. Derrida, *The Animal That Therefore I Am.* Trans. David Wills, Ed. Marie-Louise Mallet (New York: Fordham University Press, 2008), 104.
14. Pheng Cheah, 'Nondialectical Materialism', *Diacritics,* 38.1–2 (2008), 145.
15. Vicki Kirby, *Quantum Anthropologies: Life at Large* (Durham and London: Duke University Press, 2011), x.
16. Derrida, 'Typewriter Ribbon: Limited Ink (2)', in *Without Alibi.* Trans. and Ed. Peggy Kamuf (Stanford, CA: Stanford University Press, 2002), 154.
17. Claire Colebrook, 'Matter without Bodies', *Derrida Today,* 4.1 (2011), 3.
18. Colebrook, 'Matter Without Bodies', 7.
19. Kirby, *Quantum Anthropologies,* 19.
20. Kirby, *Telling Flesh: The Substance of the Corporeal* (London and New York: Routledge, 1997), 61.
21. Kirby, *Quantum Anthropologies,* 34.
22. Kirby, *Quantum Anthropologies,* 83.
23. Colebrook, 'Matter Without Bodies', 6.
24. Kirby, *Quantum Anthropologies,* 34.
25. Kirby, *Quantum Anthropologies,* 18.
26. Colebrook, *Death of the PostHuman: Essays on Extinction, Vol. 1* (Open Humanities Press, 2014), 31.
27. Colebrook, *Death of the PostHuman,* 37.
28. Colebrook, 'Not Symbiosis', 194.
29. Colebrook, 'Not Symbiosis', 193.
30. Colebrook, 'Not Symbiosis', 187.
31. Colebrook, 'Not Symbiosis', 199.
32. Colebrook, *Death of the PostHuman,* 43.
33. Colebrook, 'Not Symbiosis', 201.
34. Timothy Morton, *The Ecological Thought* (Cambridge, MA and London: Harvard University Press, 2010), 3.
35. Wolfe, 'Humanist and Posthumanist Speciesism', in *The Death of the Animal: A Dialogue,* Ed. Paola Cavalieri (New York: Columbia University Press, 2009), 57.
36. Wolfe, *What is Posthumanism?* xv.
37. Wolfe, *What is Posthumanism?* xix.
38. Colebrook, *Death of the PostHuman,* 31.
39. Wolfe, *What is Posthumanism?* 119.
40. Wolfe, *What is Posthumanism?* 122.
41. Wolfe, *What is Posthumanism?* 122.
42. Colebrook, *Death of the PostHuman,* 44–5.
43. Michael Ryan, *Marxism and Deconstruction: A Critical Articulation* (Baltimore: The Johns Hopkins University Press, 1982), 103–104.
44. Kirby, *Telling Flesh,* 60.
45. Kirby, *Telling Flesh,* 60.
46. Kirby, *Telling Flesh,* 62.
47. Derrida, '"This Strange Institution Called Literature": An Interview with Jacques Derrida', in *Acts of Literature.* Trans. Geoffrey Bennington and Rachel Bowlby, Ed. Derek Attridge. (London: Routledge, 1992), 33.

48. Simon Critchley, 'Derrida: The Reader', in *Derrida's Legacies: Literature and Philosophy,* Eds. Simon Glendinning and Robert Eaglestone (London: Routledge, 2008), 2.
49. Derrida, *Writing and Difference.* Trans. Alan Bass (London and New York: Routledge, 2005), 89.
50. Colebrook, 'Matter without Bodies', 50.
51. Derrida, 'This Strange Institution Called Literature', 37.

BIBLIOGRAPHY

Braidotti, Rosi. *The Posthuman.* Cambridge: Polity, 2013.
Bryant, Levi, Nick Srnicek and Graham Harman. 'Towards a Speculative Philosophy'. In *The Speculative Turn.* Edited by Levi Bryant, Nick Srnicek and Graham Harman, 1–18. Melbourne: re.press, 2011.
Cheah, Pheng. 'Nondialectical Materialism'. *Diacritics,* 38.1–2 (2008): 143–157.
Colebrook, Claire. *Death of the PostHuman: Essays on Extinction, Vol. 1.* Open Humanities Press, 2014.
———. 'Not Symbiosis, Not Now: Why Anthropogenic Change is Not Really Human'. *The Oxford Literary Review,* 34.2 (2012): 185–209.
———. 'Matter Without Bodies'. *Derrida Today,* 4.1 (2011): 1–20.
Critchley, Simon. 'Derrida: The Reader'. In *Derrida's Legacies: Literature and Philosophy.* Edited by Simon Glendinning and Robert Eaglestone, 1–11. London: Routledge, 2008.
Derrida, Jacques. *The Animal That Therefore I Am.* Translated by David Wills, edited by Marie-Louise Mallet. New York: Fordham University Press, 2008.
———. *Writing and Difference.* Translated by Alan Bass. London and New York: Routledge, 2005.
———. 'Typewriter Ribbon: Limited Ink (2)'. In *Without Alibi.* Translated and edited by Peggy Kamuf, 71–160. Stanford, CA: Stanford University Press, 2002.
———. *Of Grammatology.* Revised edition. Translated by Gayatri Chakravorty Spivak, Baltimore: The Johns Hopkins University Press, 1997.
———. 'Deconstruction and the Other'. In *States of Mind: Dialogues with Contemporary Thinkers on the European Mind.* Edited by Richard Kearney, 156–176. Manchester: Manchester University Press, 1995.
———. '"This Strange Institution Called Literature": An Interview with Jacques Derrida'. In *Acts of Literature.* Translated by Geoffrey Bennington and Rachel Bowlby, edited by Derek Attridge, 33–75. London: Routledge, 1992.
———. *Limited Inc.* Translated by Samuel Weber and Jeffrey Mehlman, edited by Gerald Graff. Evanston, IL: Northwestern University Press, 1988.
Kirby, Vicki. *Quantum Anthropologies: Life at Large.* Durham and London: Duke University Press, 2011.
———. *Telling Flesh: The Substance of the Corporeal.* London and New York: Routledge, 1997.

Meillassoux, Quentin. *After Finitude: An Essay on the Necessity of Contingency*. Translated by Ray Brassier. London and New York: Bloomsbury, 2008.

Morton, Timothy. *The Ecological Thought*. Cambridge, MA and London: Harvard University Press, 2010.

Ryan, Michael. *Marxism and Deconstruction: A Critical Articulation*. Baltimore: The Johns Hopkins University Press, 1982.

Wolfe, Cary. *What is Posthumanism?* Minneapolis, MN: University of Minnesota Press, 2010.

———. 'Humanist and Posthumanist Antispeciesism'. In *The Death of the Animal: A Dialogue*. Edited by Paola Cavalieri, 45–58. New York: Columbia University Press, 2009.

Žižek, Slavoj. *The Parallax View*. Cambridge, MA: The MIT Press, 2006.

Chapter Thirteen

Primary and Secondary Nature

The Role of Indeterminacy in Spinoza and Bartleby

Christopher Thomas

Martial Gueroult's commentary on Spinoza's *Ethics* is a well-founded text in the interpretation of Spinoza, the reverberations of which can be seen in much French Spinozism of the latter half of the twentieth century.[1] And so when Gueroult states, regarding Spinoza's concept of the infinite, that to affirm Number in effect shatters Nature and affirms everywhere the discrete,[2] we must take his words without metaphor and in all their literalness. In its first instance, Gueroult's claim is an appeal to Spinoza's radically monist doctrine and the problem of the determination of things therein. But its point of contention reaches further than Spinoza scholarship alone, touching equally upon aspects of the social, economic, ecological and aesthetic crises that pervade our present epoch. Gueroult's statement is an appeal to a reconceptualization of dominant philosophical pretexts; it is a call for a reorientation of human and non-human bodies both to one another *and* to the whole in which they partake.

This problem is eminently philosophical, but its object can equally be seen in the themes of certain literary figures, none less than in Herman Melville's novella *Bartleby*. When Bartleby states that he is *not particular* and continues to utter his now infamous refrain, he, like Spinoza, is appealing to the necessity of the indeterminate, to the processual and continuous nature of Nature as theorized in Spinoza's metaphysical system. In a society whose habit is the Spinozian 'imagination', various difficulties arise when thinking the 'natural' through a logic of indeterminacy. These difficulties occur in the discontinuity between the determinate structures of the imagination and an adequate conception of the indeterminate. The juncture of this problem is a central theme in Melville's fable and is conceived in this chapter alongside Spinoza's concept of the infinite and its apprehension by the imagination and understanding respectively. More specifically, it is Bartleby's resistive act that gives reason to consider the ways in which the Spinozian individual both apprehends the world and conceives its place in the world and hence to think the problem of the 'subject' and 'aesthetics' in Spinoza's philosophy. The task for this chapter, then, is to conceive of certain life practices that disrupt the seriality of Number and the discreteness of things in favour of a knowledge of the essence and continuity of Nature. This chapter will develop along three sections. In the first, various specifics of Bartleby's formula will be put forth and thought alongside its theorization by Gilles Deleuze. Secondly, we will turn to Spinoza and, from a reading of select sections of the *Ethics* and *Letters*, put forward the ways in which the finite mode apprehends the world, the issue of Number and the problem of autonomy raised by human beings' 'natural tendency' to imagination. Finally, Bartleby's act will be considered alongside Spinoza, both in itself and through its creation by Melville. In this final respect, Bartleby and Spinoza will be thought together at once ethically and aesthetically, thus affording a literary-philosophical model through which to think the natural outside of Enlightenment models of division and classification.

BARTLEBY'S INDETERMINATE PROVOCATION

The five words *I would prefer not to* form the much-repeated refrain of Melville's narrative. Bartleby, we are told, is a figure without history, a scrivener that takes up his craft, as if from nowhere, at the office of an eminently 'safe' attorney in Wall Street. Like his character, the attorney's job is unambitious and concerned only with deeds, mortgages and bonds. He is Melville's narrator and his object, the subject of his narration, is his copyist, the figure of Bartleby, whose refrain *I would prefer not to* causes consternation and confusion among all who come across it. The linguistic power of Melville's invention and of Bartleby's refrain rests in its passive-resistive character and, more specifically, in its ability to resist determination. Bartleby's phrase, or as Deleuze will call it, Bartleby's 'formula', does not determine one thing any more than it determines everything; *I would prefer not to* leaves undetermined what it would prefer not to do. Indeed, Bartleby's repetition functions to exclude all alternatives and make any action other than its own utterance impossible. Within its rejection of proper nouns and its appeal to the infinitive, which is to say, through its rejection of an expressed subject, Bartleby's formula fails to determine the actions or references that allow *things* to be brought forth from the *totality of things*. Furthermore, Bartleby's formula and its perpetual iteration emerges as machinic or automatic appearing in the most part unchanging, without teleology and as if guided, blindly so, by mere necessity. In this respect we can say of Bartleby's formula that it is *radically indeterminate* for it contains no reference to determinate things, actions or goals with which to ascertain anything definite, including Bartleby's own volitions.

But insofar as Bartleby's formula stymies any attribution of particularities onto himself as an enunciating subject, the same cannot be said of his colleagues who are subjected to and ordered via their identifiable specifics. Indeed, the office that Bartleby works within is carefully ordered so as to repeat its particularities as regularly as Bartleby repeats his own refrain. This arrangement of particulars is composed by the attorney as a superior and a curator and deemed by him as a good 'natural arrangement' under the circumstances.[3] It is precisely this antagonistic duality of choreographed particulars on the one hand, and the indeterminacy of Bartleby on the other, that provides such ethical and philosophical richness. In this way the task of this present section is an inquiry after the relation of the attorney's *good natural arrangement* and Bartleby's rupture of this preconceived arrangement through the very structure that seemingly grounds the 'natural'.

This is, as Deleuze notes, the problem Bartleby poses in a society that is both carefully choreographed and whose language is based on an unspoken doctrine of linguistic presuppositions wherein an employer *expects* to be obeyed. Bartleby's formula, Deleuze tells us, undermines these presuppositions of language, inspiring fear in those such as the attorney who employ such governing structures.[4] To this extent, Deleuze's reading sets forth a linguistic agenda that is inextricable from the world. His is a reading that regards Bartleby's formula as an apparatus of subversion, a linguistic weapon that disrupts the dominant signifiers of language from within while simultaneously reinforcing the primacy of language in the material. To be more specific, Deleuze holds that the language employed in everyday discourse rests on a 'logic of presuppositions' where it is supposed that the words we use either contain references to specific things or objects or emit speech acts that are self-referential.[5] According to this, language – and the structure of language is always given at once – presupposes that we understand the references that words carry with them or that we follow the speech acts that convey a certain relation between interlocutor and receiver. With Bartleby's formula, however, we find a resistance to both of these linguistic conditions, its utterance functioning only to disassociate words from things referred to such that it serves merely to reference that which is without a referent, that is, the indeterminacy of its orator. Through its rejection of a subject and its indifference in affirming or negating this or that *thing* or *action*, all that remains after its diction is the reverberation of an absence. This absence is such that it references nothing other than its own indeterminate action, remaining ungraspable and unfathomable through conventional linguistic operations while simultaneously referencing everything that remains to be determined.

212   *Chapter Thirteen*

It is, as Deleuze suggests, the *agrammaticality* of Bartleby's five-word formula that is its 'logic of preference', and it is through this unique logic that Bartleby creates a vacuum within language that renders him in a position outside society.[6] For Deleuze, Bartleby becomes an *outsider* whose refrain resists a subject, *resists determination* and as such resists the references with which he may be attributed any such social position. He appears in Deleuze's reading, therefore, as *beyond* subjection.[7]

But what does it mean to attribute the position of outsider – the position without a determinable position – to that of Bartleby? In different words we might ask, in Deleuze's understanding, what is it that the figure of Bartleby is premised against as that which he is outside of?

> [Figures such as Bartleby] are beings of Primary Nature, but they are inseparable from the world or from secondary nature, where they exert their effect: they reveal its emptiness, the imperfection of its laws, the mediocrity of particular creatures.[8]

In respect to Bartleby's theorization as an outsider, Deleuze sets up a differentiation between two kinds of Nature, the former inextricable from the latter. We hear Deleuze state that creatures of 'secondary nature' are mediocre by reason of them being particular, by them having particularities in reference to a 'primary nature' *who they are at once inseparable from and yet distinct*. Bartleby, as an outsider, *is not particular*. His is a presence that absorbs the determinable positions offered him (bartender, bill collector, clerk, etc.),[9] internalizing all particulars at once with his formula. The vacuum that Bartleby opens up within secondary nature is affective not because of its negative refusal of things but because of its refusal to determine any *one* thing, which is equally to say, its inclusion of every particular and universal alike. If the act of determining singular things is that which simultaneously determines the choosing thing, then Bartleby prefers not to determine and in this respect confuses the dominant processes of subjectification. His radically indeterminate formula does not declare in any specificity the affirmation or negation of a thing or action but rather functions as a cyclical iteration of an ungraspable and indeterminate potency. This is a potency devoid of any particulars or identifiable centre with which to determine Bartleby as this or that *thing*, as having this or that *goal*. Bartleby would prefer not to be a bartender, but the possibility of him being one is perpetuated.

We can observe, then, that Bartleby's presence in a world where things are named, determined, classified and ordered is inherently problematic. Following this, we might ask, 'Where can Bartleby be situated if he carries no determinate references to speak of?' Indeed, we might equally ask, '*Where is the indeterminate to be situated among the determinate?*' This final question, with its metaphysical and theological implications, is the question that Bartleby and his refrain pose. This is the problem that Melville, through the figure of Bartleby, affords the reader.

SPINOZA AND THE NATURAL TENDENCY TO DIVISION

Like Bartleby, Spinoza's philosophy refuses the numerical and determinate structures that posit the discrete everywhere and govern, for the most part, our everyday lives. Spinoza too provides us with the same problem that Bartleby's radical indeterminacy presents the attorney. It is through Spinoza's critique of anthropocentricism in the appendix to part one of the *Ethics* that we can most clearly recognize his philosophy as a call for a conception of things as inherently continuous and without a central feature, be that feature anthropomorphic or otherwise. Indeed, the *Ethics* is an ethics that appeals to an apprehension of the universe that does not begin from a conception of the human individual as an isolated site among a distinct external world – as a *dominion within a dominion*, as Spinoza notes in the preface to part three of the *Ethics*.[10] Rather, the human individual is reconceived by Spinoza as a complex of affective, economic and intellectual relations between both human and non-human bodies. The individual is posited here as a site of potency and causal power, but this site of power does not emanate from an individual that pre-exists the effects it produces and undergoes; rather, these fluctuations of causal power are constitutive of the individual, and the individual cannot be said to exist in abstraction from them.

Because the individual is constituted in its individuality by its capacity to act and be acted upon by external bodies, this means that in the Spinozist universe no one individual can be said to be really distinct from any other individual. In theorizing the order of things as such, Spinoza undermines models of autonomy that are premised on a militant individualism – an autonomy that always begin with an 'I' and an act of internalized self-determination – instead affirming a recognition of the implication of 'external' individuals in the constitution of the individual's autonomy. Through the conception of *common notions* and their apprehension through reason, things are known truly through their agreement with one another and in their necessary involvement in one another's constitution and perseverance (IIP38, IIpostulateIV). In this respect, individual things are never understood in isolation and are not perceived through an imaginative order that posits the discrete and premises wholes against wholes as things that remain always extrinsic. Rather, things are acknowledged through the inextricability of one from all, thus conceiving a model of autonomy that retheorizes the dualities of internal and external, self and other (*Ep*32, IIP13L7Scol).

This thought on the relational structure of Spinoza's ontology and the reading of the individual that it permits, although not new,[11] is most evident, I believe, in his writings on the Infinite and the corresponding issue of imagination and understanding that this area of his philosophy raises. Within *Ep*12 and IP15 the indeterminate is defined and the problem of its relation to the determinate is worked out. It is from this area of Spinoza's thought, then, that we will approach the problem of the human 'subject' thinking its processual and relational nature in light of a rejection of symbolic thought and the subsequent possibilities for a Spinozian aesthetics that this reading engenders.

To begin we must note at the outset an epistemological problem of an ontology of the absolute. Spinoza states in part one of the *Ethics* and *Ep*12 that there are two principal ways of apprehending the infinite that correspond to discrete individual things on the one hand and the continuous order of Nature on the other. Regarding the former, Spinoza maintains that to consider corporeal substance to be composed of distinct, determinate things, each with an autonomy that renders them free from the next distinct thing, is to apprehend the absolutely infinite, Nature, by *imagination* (IP15ScholIV–V). On the other hand, to apprehend extended substance such that there is no vacuum and hence where no one thing can be said to be really distinct from the next thing is to conceive of substance really and through the *understanding* or intellect (IP15ScholIV–V). Put differently, Spinoza is claiming that perceiving things as discrete and causally isolated is to know things confusedly in the manner of individual substances, whereas things conceived through the understanding alone are known truly as modifications of the one substance. In the former way of conceiving things, the modes of substance are seen as ontologically distinct from substance, while in the latter, their inextricable relation to one another and to substance is conceived and upheld. Following this, Spinoza notes that the first or easiest way that we conceive substance is abstractly or superficially, both of which are conceptions of the infinite through imagination. This way of conceiving of substance is to apprehend it from *a* position, from the position of the finite. The second and more difficult way is to conceive of the infinite as substance alone, which is an apprehension of substance by the intellect with no interference from the imagination (IP15ScholV). Furthermore, because of Spinoza's naturalism and his claim of equivalence between God and the extended world, he also includes in his theory of extended substance the condition of *indivisibility*. Therefore, and as Spinoza states in both IP15 and *Ep*12, the former way of conceiving the infinite through imagination is the most common order of knowledge that we mostly subsist within, and this kind of knowledge compels us to think of substance as finite, divisible and composed of parts. While the latter way of conceiving substance through the intellect is a kind of knowledge that allows the true order of things as infinite, unique, and indivisible to be known. Indeed, on the primacy of the kinds of knowledge Spinoza goes so far as to say that we, as human beings, have a *natural tendency* to apprehend the world through imagination (*Ep*12). This 'natural tendency' of the human to division is an important point and one to which we will return.

Insofar as the above is correct, it is imperative that we not read Spinoza as setting up an appearance–reality dualism. Which is to say, the twofold conception of the same one thing – *Nature* – through either the imagination or the intellect does not offer, on the one hand, an inaccessible world of absolute reality conceived by the understanding and, on the other, a world of the imaginative unreal understood as its negation. Indeed, we might turn to Spinoza directly in order to reinforce the reality of the world of the individual that perceives through the imagination. To quote,

> This [the indivisibility of extension] will be sufficiently plain to everyone who knows how to distinguish between the intellect and the imagination – particularly if it is also noted that matter is everywhere the same, and that parts are distinguished in it only insofar as we conceive matter to be affected in different ways, *so that its parts are distinguished only modally, but not really.* (IP15SchoIV, emphasis added)

In the above, Spinoza states that 'parts', or what we might loosely describe as individuated modes, are distinguished from substance qua matter *modally* but not *really*. Furthermore, we may note that to conceive extended substance *really* one must conceive it through the intellect alone, and as such one will understand reality as continuous and without break. Equally, this is to say that one will conceive no *real distinction* between things but only a *modal distinction*, the latter not admitting the autonomy of things in the same sense as the former. The idea that there is no *real* distinction between things in Spinoza's universe is crucial. Indeed, because of Spinoza's substance monism, it is impossible that there exists a real or ontological distinction between things, as is the case with Cartesian substances (*Principles* 1, 60). Hence when Spinoza notes that things are never distinguished *really*, he is imploring the reader to conceive of a kind of differentiation that affirms modal individuation via proportions of motion and rest, consequently recasting the principles of Cartesian ideas by denying substantial difference or real distinction. It is within this conception of modal distinction that Spinoza denies the idea of material boundaries, instead affirming an exchange of power that forms a relational account of autonomy premised *against* any real distinction between things that the imagination might instil in the world. However, it must be made clear that what Spinoza is *not* saying is that the way we perceive reality most readily is false and that therefore we live in a world of appearance. Rather, he is stating that to observe things in the sense of a real distinction is to perceive nature confusedly, a conception of things that is, nevertheless, *actual*, but of a less adequate understanding of nature and one that only arises through modes of the imagination. We might also put it so and state that it is a *less perfect* way of conceiving the world where perfection is equivalent to reality and any difference between *this* and *that* is only a matter of degree (IID6). Furthermore, in turning to IIP49SchollII we read that the imaginations of the mind involve no error or deceit and, moreover, by IIP36 that the imaginings of man follow from God *with the same necessity* as do clear and distinct ideas.

If things perceived through the imagination are not 'non-actual' but rather a mere confused understanding of the real, we might now comment upon Spinoza's insistence that to conceive the world through imagination is a human being's *natural tendency*. In IP15ScholV Spinoza comments that man *by nature* is inclined to divide quantity. Likewise in *Ep*12 he comments that it is the *natural tendency* of man to divide substance. To the extent that the dominant disposition of human persons is given as the imagination, it is possible to suggest that its action appears as a kind of 'human nature' that instils the discrete into that which is fundamentally continuous. If to divide the indivisible is to apprehend through the imagination, then it follows that the *natural tendency* of man must be to a state of imagination (see also IIP16Cor1, IVP4Cor). According to Spinoza, then, to see things confusedly as discrete and abstracted from substance is not just *the most common way* that we, as human beings, perceive the world, but it is *by nature* that we conceive things in this way.

But why, we might ask, is man's natural tendency to imagine? As Spinoza notes in *Ep*12, the action of imagination removes modes from their relation to substance so that we may *more easily* form images of things in an otherwise imageless universe. Furthermore, from the division of substance via imagination there arise such things as Number and its derivatives Time and Measure. Insofar as the human individual perceives through modes of imagination, she is able to form images of things so that she can limit, order, classify and explain the things that she has sensible relations with. Man's natural tendency to construct modes of the imagination, then, is purely pragmatic. It allows the finite individual to orientate and situate its specific body among an otherwise limitless and ungraspable sensible world.

This orientation in the world through the action of the imagination has, however, the consequence of forming in the individual an image of a fixed and determinate position from which she is able to self-reflect in relation to what she is not. It is, we might say, an affirmation of the self founded on an act of negation. This conception of the individual is always the result of an inadequate knowledge of causes (the mistaking of first causes for final causes, as Spinoza puts it in the preface to part four) which leads only to the individual perceiving itself as discrete, removed from the order of nature and, finally, observing disagreement in that which truly agrees (*Ep*32). To conceive in this way is to know existences and finite things rather than 'essences' and their relation to the absolutely infinite. As Gueroult comments, to know things through the imagination is the expression of the finite while to conceive things through the understanding is the expression of the infinite.[12] For Spinoza, therefore, the true nature of reality is not to be found in the quantitative measurements of everyday life, for these are merely modes of the imagination and expressions of the finite. Indeed, such aids of the imagination only arise as a consequence of human beings' natural tendency to imagine. As such, Number is put forward by Spinoza as a primary limit to an adequate understanding of Nature. Ultimately, then, it is by observing the world through imagination that things appear discrete, and it is through the inadequate conception of a real distinction between things that Number begins to classify and project a fictional order onto our sensible world. This imaginary order, however, is nothing but individual beings that appear, confusedly so, as distinct individual substances abstracted both from one another and the single substance of Spinoza's monism. For Spinoza, therefore, to posit Number, to order that which when known truly is without order, is to limit Nature and extract man from its necessity.

INDETERMINACY AND RESISTANCE

To return to Gueroult's contention that Nature is shattered when the discrete is announced, we can suggest that he is referring to an apprehension of Nature that limits substance through a confused understanding of the universe as a composite of discrete, determinate things. In this respect, Bartleby appears as a manifestation of the rejection of this relation to the world in the extreme. When Bartleby denies the discrete, when, through his indeterminate refrain, he neither appeals to particular subjects nor determinate actions, he is instead appealing to the continuous nature of things through a practice of radical indeterminacy. Spinoza's contention for an active life is also of this kind. It is a kind of ethical knowledge that conceives things through the understanding, infinitely and in agreement, and not through the serial constructions of Number, Time and Measure, for these are merely modes of imagination, kinds of symbolic thought that only serve to obstruct a life more free (IVP66Schol). In this way we can say of the conceiving individual that as her knowledge of things becomes more adequate, her act of thinking comes to mirror Bartleby's refrain in the sense that it is increasingly an affirmation *that* something, but not *which*.

As an approach, therefore, Bartleby's refrain offers a strategy that seeks to realize the essence of a continuous Nature through a subversion of the imaginative structures of everyday life. Bartleby's formula emerges as an attempt to conceive Nature as a complex of interrelations and not to divide what is indivisible, affirming everywhere the discrete and in so doing shattering the Spinozian Nature. The determination of entirely autonomous things – the determination of the Cartesian 'I' against an external world of warring wholes – instils in Nature an order that it does not contain. We might suggest that it determines in Nature, following Deleuze in his essay on Bartleby, a *secondary nature*: a nature that pertains to generalities and particulars that only serve to break up primary nature and divide that which is truly indivisible. The world as apprehended by imagination is a world of Deleuze's secondary nature whereby things appear differentiated from one another by particularities that are inadequately assumed to constitute the individuation of finite modes. To appeal to the indeterminate, then, is to apprehend via the Spinozian intellect; it is to have a relation with the world that does not begin from an internal, preordained self but is rather the activity by which we produce an increasingly decentred and active being.

It is from such an understanding that we might begin to think how to produce and mobilize technologies of the indeterminate. Perhaps such things may consist of, among others, practices of art, literature and philosophy that aim both to reveal and to disrupt the fictional structures instilled in the world by the imagination, those structures which, as Spinoza remarks, lead man to search for intention and order in Nature (IAppendix). It is through such technologies that the Spinozian individual will become more perfect, more aligned with the totality of Nature and out of her natural tendency to see discontinuity in the continuous. Here we might recall that on the practice of writing, Virginia Woolf notes that if the writer were a free man and not a slave, his work would not include plot, comedy, tragedy, love interest or catastrophe in the accepted style but would rather be an incessant shower of innumerable atoms upon which accents perpetually fall differently.[13] No structure or singular meaning, no canon, would exist in literature if one were free, if one could write *sub specie aeternitatis*. The imaginative-self and any singular history that it may inscribe into Nature would be dissolved into an infinitely complex network of causal relations that is, always and necessarily so, incomplete and indeterminate. With this, the universal structures of the collective images of history would no longer obstruct the practice of writing. Rather, the author – the artist, the musician, the philosopher, the mathematician, etc. – would write *without place*, impersonally, and in an indeterminate practice of becoming free.

Far from lacking an aesthetics because of a misconstrued understanding of reason coupled with a critique of such fictitious universals as beauty and ugliness (IAppendix, *Ep*32), Spinoza's advocacy of reason and his rejection of symbolic thought must be understood to include such practices that aim to disrupt the imaginative order of things and return to Nature its fundamental continuousness and lack of teleology. In this respect, it is Bartleby's paradoxical vagrancy, '… he a vagrant, a wanderer, who refuses to budge?'[14] that resonates most keenly with Spinoza's ethical concern. Bartleby appears as the *immobile wanderer* whose autonomy is to be found in his openness to the world, in his double-movement of the refusal of one and the assimilation of all that renders him *immanent to the world*. For Spinoza, a mode of thought, either imaginative or reasoned, always carries within it an affirmation (IIP49SchollII). But a thought becomes increasingly adequate, and the mind that has it increasingly free, when its affirmation is not of a singular thing (an image implicated in *a* body) but when its object is *common to all things*. To see agreement in Nature (and nothing can agree in an autonomy founded on the imagination)[15] is to affirm neither self nor other as opposing wholes but rather to affirm their indistinctness and necessary implication in one another as parts of a greater whole.

This chapter has suggested that Melville's fable is a meditation on the place of the indeterminate within the determinate, giving rise to an ethics that can be used to outline a theory of aesthetics in Spinoza. From this Melville–Spinoza encounter, the 'subject' has emerged as the active juncture between the potency of 'primary nature' and the binaries of 'secondary nature' whereby, in view of a life more free, the latter is subjugated through methods of indeterminacy founded on the former. The stasis of Bartleby, therefore, his indifference to the 'application of the doctrine of assumptions',[16] is that which disrupts the dominant images of the social imagination through practices of the indeterminate. It is these practices that are at once reasoned and aesthetic. They are *ethical* and as such take as their purpose the aligning of part to whole, determinate to indeterminate.

ABBREVIATIONS

In the text I use the standard reference for the *Ethics*, whereby 'IP12Dem' denotes the Demonstration to Proposition 12 of Book One. All references to Spinoza's *Ethics* are from Edwin Curley's translation, and references to the *Letters* are from Samuel Shirley's translation and are referenced by their respective numbers, that is, Letter 12 becomes '*Ep*12'.

NOTES

1. Knox Peden, *Spinoza Contra Phenomenology: French Rationalism from Cavaillès to Deleuze* (Stanford: Stanford University Press, 2014), 65.
2. Martial Gueroult, *Spinoza's Letter on the Infinite (Letter XII, to Louis Meyer), in Spinoza: A Collection of Critical Essays,* ed. Marjorie Green, 200.
3. Herman Melville, *Bartleby and Benito Cereno* (New York: Dover, 1990), 8.
4. Gilles Deleuze, *Essays Critical and Clinical*. Trans. Daniel W. Smith and Michael A. Greco (Minneapolis: University of Chicago Press, 1997), 73.
5. Deleuze, *Essays Critical and Clinical*, 73.
6. Deleuze, *Essays Critical and Clinical*, 73.
7. Deleuze, *Essays Critical and Clinical*, 83.
8. Deleuze, *Essays Critical and Clinical*, 83.
9. Melville, *Bartleby and Benito Cereno*, 29–30.
10. III, Preface (Spinoza 1996: 152)
11. See Étienne Balibar, *Spinoza and Politics*. Trans. Peter Snowdon (London and New York: Verso, 1998); Aurelia Armstrong, *Autonomy and the Relational Individual, in Feminist Interpretations of Benedict Spinoza,* ed. Moira Gatens (Pennsylvania: Pennsylvania University Press, 2009), 43–63; Caroline Williams, '"Subjectivity Without the Subject": Thinking Beyond the Subject With/Through Spinoza', in *Spinoza Beyond Philosophy,* ed. Beth Lord (Edinburgh: Edinburgh University Press, 2012).
12. Gueroult, *Spinoza's Letter on the Infinite (Letter XII, to Louis Meyer)*, 209–210.
13. Virginia Woolf, 'Modern Fiction', in *Selected Essays* (Oxford: Oxford University Press, 2008), 9.
14. Melville, *Bartleby and Benito Cereno*, 27.
15. See William Sacksteder, 'Spinoza on Part and Whole: The Worm's Eye View', in *Spinoza: New Perspectives,* eds. Robert W. Shahan and J.I. Biro (Oklahoma: University of Oklahoma Press, 1978), 144–156.
16. Melville, *Bartleby and Benito Cereno*, 24.

BIBLIOGRAPHY

Armstrong, Aurelia. 'Autonomy and the Relational Individual'. In *Feminist Interpretations of Benedict Spinoza.* Edited by Moira Gatens, 43–63. Pennsylvania: Pennsylvania University Press, 2009.

Balibar, Étienne. *Spinoza and Politics.* Translated by Peter Snowdon. London and New York: Verso, 1998.

Curley, Edwin. *Behind the Geometrical Method: A Reading of Spinoza's Ethics.* New Jersey: Princeton University Press, 1988.

Deleuze, Gilles. *Essays Critical and Clinical.* Translated by Daniel W. Smith and Michael A. Greco. Minneapolis: University of Minnesota Press, 1997.

Deleuze, Gilles and Félix Guattari. *Kafka: Toward a Minor Literature.* Translated by Dana Polan, Minneapolis: University of Minnesota Press, 1986.

Descartes, René. *The Philosophical Writings of Descartes,* Vol. 1. Translated by John Cottingham, Robert Stoothoff and Dugald Murdoch. Cambridge: Cambridge University Press, 1985.

Gueroult, Martial. 'Spinoza's Letter on the Infinite (Letter XII, to Louis Meyer)'. In *Spinoza: A Collection of Critical Essays.* Edited by Marjorie Green, 182–212. New York: Anchor Books, 1973.

———. *Spinoza,* Vol. 1. Paris: George Olms, 1968.

Laerke, Mogens. 'Spinoza and the Cosmological Argument According to Letter 12', *British Journal for the History of Philosophy,* 21.1 (2013): 57–77.

Lloyd, Genevieve. *Part of Nature: Self-Knowledge in Spinoza's Ethics.* New York: Cornell University Press, 1994.

Melville, Herman. *Bartleby and Benito Cereno.* New York: Dover, 1990.

Peden, Knox. *Spinoza Contra Phenomenology: French Rationalism from Cavaillès to Deleuze.* Stanford: Stanford University Press, 2014.

Rancière, Jacques. *The Flesh of Words: The Politics of Writing.* Translated by Charlotte Mandell. Stanford: Stanford University Press, 2004.

Sacksteder, William. 'Spinoza on Part and Whole: The Worm's Eye View'. In *Spinoza: New Perspectives.* Edited by Robert W. Shahan and J.I. Biro, 139–159. Oklahoma: University of Oklahoma Press, 1978.

Spinoza, Benedict de. *Ethics.* Translated by Edwin Curley. London: Penguin, 1996.

———. *Ethics, Treatise on the Emendation of the Intellect, and Selected Letters.* Translated by Samuel Shirley. Indianapolis: Hackett, 1992.

Williams, Caroline. '"Subjectivity without the Subject": Thinking Beyond the Subject With/Through Spinoza'. In *Spinoza Beyond Philosophy.* Edited by Beth Lord, 11–27. Edinburgh: Edinburgh University Press, 2012.

Woolf, Virginia. "Modern Fiction." In *Selected Essays.* Edited by D. Bradshaw, 6–12. Oxford: Oxford University Press, 2008.

Index

ABP. *See* Anthropologically bounded posthumanism (ABP)
Aesthetic vitalism, 61
After Finitude: An Essay on the Necessity of Contingency (Meillassoux, Quentin), 182
Algorithmic cultures, 8
Ancient networks, 15
Animal architecture, 56
The Animal That Therefore I Am (Derrida, Jacques), 179
Anthropocene, 1
Anthropogenesis, 154
Anthropologically bounded posthumanism (ABP), 100
Anthropologically unbounded posthumanism (AUP), 100
Autonomy, 39, 99, 108, 161, 210, 213–215

Bohm's realism, 82
Book of Nature (Galilean), 23
Bounded posthumanism, 99–101
Brain, 55–58
Brownian motion, 36

Call transindividuation, 166
Capitalism, 4
  analysis of, 138
  Guattari's pertinent analyses of, 2
  history and nature within, 137
  unquestionable axiom of, 2
Capitalist machineries, 6–8
Capitalocene, 2
Cave streamed with light, 16–17
Classical mechanics, 26
Climate simulation, 89–94
Climate simulations, 89, 91–93
Code
  digital, 37
  manipulable, 48
  pre-existent, 2
  social, 2
Code systems, 44–46
Collective individuation, 127, 164, 168, 170–171, 174–175
Collective yoga, 167–169
Communion, 22
Computer simulations, 47, 89–92
Conscious evolution, 151–153, 155–157, 159, 161, 163, 165, 167, 169, 171, 173, 175
Conscious evolution, metaphysics of, 152–154
Consciousness
  cosmic, 161, 168
  creative immanent, 152
  extension of, 161, 165

imaginable, 75
individualized, 153
mental, 163
minimal, 187
panentheistic, 152
postulated rational, 3
supramental, 165
transcendental, 165
Consumer capitalism, 127
Contemporary genomics, 8
Contraction, 57
Correlationism, 59
Cosmic condition, 153, 165
Cosmogenesis, 151–152, 163
Cosmogenesis and individuation, 151–152
Critical posthumanism (CP), 100
Culturalism, 3

Dark precursors, 39
De Componendis Cifris, 45
Decomposition, 17, 184
Deconstruction, 196–199
    long questioned, 201
    political, 202
    and post-human, 199–201
    projected, 179
    radical, 188
    'text,' posthumanism, 201–204
    textualist, 198
Deontic attitudes, 107–110
Deontic statuses, 107–110
Dominant code, 3
Dualism, 4–7
Dystopia, 169–171

Ecological fault, 142
Ecological niche
    capitalism, 138–140
    history, 141–143
    roots and problems, 140–141
The Ecological Thought (Morton), 200
Ecology, 7, 49, 60, 62, 80, 95, 98, 122–123, 131–132, 134–135, 143, 147–149

Ecology without Nature, 138, 144
Ecosophy, 4
Eindeutigkeit principle, 28
Einstein, 26–28
Electromagnetic domain, 35
Energy flow, 128
Energy principle, 27
Entropy, 124–126
Equational technics, 45–47
Equivalence, 28
Evolutionary capacity, 2

First-class agents, 101–105
Functional technics, 45–47

Generic mediality
    channels, 44–45
    ciphers, 44–45
    electric circuitry, 36–38
    genuinely simulacral, 41–42
    Horla, 31–33
    keys, 44–45
    massive conductivity, 33–36
    potentiality, 38–41
    speculative (spectral) phenomenology, 42–44
Global warming, 39, 47, 81, 82, 89, 91, 92, 93, 94
Gothic ornamentation, 61
Gothic stone, 62–65
Grand narrative, 14
Great Universal Law of Equilibrium, 123

How We Became Posthuman (Hayles, Katherine), 160
Humanism, 86, 200, 202
Humanity, 5, 59–62, 112
Human life and nature, 3
Human relationality, 2
Hunting, 22
Hyperobjects, 79–83
Hyperobjects: Philosophy and Ecology after the End of the World (Morton), 80

Index

Indeterminacy and resistance, 217–219
Indeterminate provocation, 210–212
Individuation
  and cosmogenesis, 151–152
  orders of, 163–166
Information, 14
  matter and, 15–16
Intentional system (IS), 102, 108
Interpretationist defence, 110–111
Island living, 188–190

Knowledge equals administration, 5

Late-stage vitalism, 183–184
Le Parasite (Serres), 49
Literary, 203
Logic of Worlds (Badiou), 77

Materialism, 196–199
Materiality, 50
Mathematical concepts, 24
Matter and mirrors, 18–19
Matter-realism, 57
Measuring media, 43
Media entangled phenomenology
  climate simulation, 89–94
  hyperobfuscation, 79–83
  hyperobjects, 79–83
  measuring media, 73–74
  media time-criticality, 75–79
  medium, 74–75
  originary phenomenon, 84–89
  time-critical media measurement, 79
Media–nature–culture continuum, 8
Medianatures, 8
Media technology and consciousness (McLuhan), 159–162
Media time-criticality, 75–79
Medium, 74–75
Meeting the Universe Halfway (Barad, Karen), 86
Metaphysical principle, 27
Metaphysics, conscious evolution, 152–154

Metastability, 128–131
Modernist humanism, 5
Modernity, 5, 6
Monistic system, 7
My Mother Was a Computer (Hayles, Katherine), 160

Natural sciences, 21
Natural tendency, 213–217
Nature
  conception of, 122
  concept of, 23
  investigation of, 26
Nature–culture continuum, 2, 5
Naturecultures, 8
Negentropy, 14, 127–128
Neo-naturalistic turn, 8
Night, 17–18
Non-linear Darwinism, 184–185
Norm-grounding problem, 105–107
Noumenon, 85

Object-Oriented Ontology (OOO), 80–83
Of Grammatology (Derrida), 196
Ontological radicality, 84
OOO. *See* Object-Oriented Ontology (OOO)
Organic chauvinism, 181
Originality, 36
Originary phenomena, 47

Paradoxical transparent lucidity, 33
Philosophy After Nature, 21
Plantationocene, 2
Psychizisation, 165
Psychological praxis, 154–155

Quantum domain, 26
Quantum level, 83
Quantum phenomena, 47, 48
Quantum-theoretical concept, 88
Quasi-physical domain, 36
The Question Concerning Technology (Heidegger), 157

Reliable differential responsive dispositions (RDRDs), 104
Rotating revolutions, 18

Second-class agents, 101–105
Second Industrial Revolution, 151
Secular humanist, 181
Self-organizing capacity, 8
Simondon's process metaphysics, 162–163
Social constructivist method, 8
Social praxis and technology, 155–156
Space, 180–181
Speculative phenomenology, 32, 47
Speculative posthumanism (SP), 100
Sphere, 55
Spinoza's philosophy, 213
Sri Aurobindo's cosmology, 154–155, 163–166
Stones, 62–65
Subject–object relationship, 13
System-equilibrium model, 123
Systems, 122–124

Technical telecommunication media, 45
Technology, 167–169
Textual deconstruction, 199
Three Ecologies (Guattari, Félix), 4
Time, 180–181
Time-based media, 75
Time-critical event, 43
Time-critical media measurement, 79
Time-invariant event, 73
Trace, 180–181
Transindividuation, 167–169
(Trans)individuation, dynamics of, 166–167

Unbestimmtheitrelationen, 26
Unbounded posthumanism, 111–113
Univocal functions, 23
Utopia, 169–171

Vitalism, 190

Western modernity, 6
Western philosophy, 181

About the Authors

EDITORS

Rosi Braidotti (BA Hons. Australian National University, 1978; PhD, Université de Paris, Panthéon-Sorbonne, 1981; Honorary Degrees Helsinki, 2007 and Linkoping, 2013; Fellow of the Australian Academy of the Humanities [*FAHA*], 2009; Member of the Academia Europaea [*MAE*], 2014; Knighthood in the order of the Netherlands Lion, 2005) is Distinguished University Professor and the founding director of the Centre for the Humanities at Utrecht University. Her latest books are *The Posthuman*, 2013; *Nomadic Subjects*, 2011a and *Nomadic Theory: The Portable Rosi Braidotti*, 2011b. www.rosibraidotti.com

Rick Dolphijn is an assistant professor in media theory/cultural theory. His two books are *Foodscapes: Towards a Deleuzian Ethics of Consumption* (2004) and (with Iris van der Tuin) *New Materialism: Interviews and Cartographies* (2012). Besides that, he has written on new materialism, ecology/ecosophy and art and has great interest in the developments in continental philosophy and speculative thought. His academic work has appeared in journals like *Angelaki*, *Continental Philosophy Review* (with Iris van der Tuin), *Collapse* and *Deleuze Studies*. He edited (with Rosi Braidotti) *This Deleuzian Century: Art, Activism, Life* (2015), which is currently being translated into Turkish.

CONTRIBUTORS

Françoise Balibar is a historian of science and a professor emerita of physics at the Université Denis Diderot, Paris VII. She has published numerous works on Albert Einstein, the theory of relativity and on the history and epistemology of physics. She is a co-author (with Jean-Marc Lévy-Leblond) of a textbook on quantum physics, translated into English under the title Quantics (1990), and has translated several of Einstein's works into French (six volumes including scientific, philosophical and political writings).

Debashish Banerji is a professor of Indian philosophy and serves as Dean of Academic Affairs at the University of Philosophical Research, Los Angeles. He is also an adjunct faculty in art history at the Pasadena City College and a research fellow in Asian and Comparative Studies at the California Institute of Integral Studies (CIIS), San Francisco. Banerji has curated a number of exhibitions of Indian and Japanese art and is the author of two books: *The Alternate Nation of Abanindranath Tagore* (2010) and *Seven Quartets of Becoming: A Transformational Yoga Psychology Based on the Diaries of Sri Aurobindo* (2012).

Vera Bühlmann holds a PhD (summa cum laude) in media philosophy from the Institute for Media Sciences i/f/m, University of Basel. Her thesis, entitled 'Inhabiting media. Annäherungen an Herkünfte und Topoi medialer Architektonik', was part of the SNF Pro*Doc 'Aesthetics of Intermediality. Play—Ritual—Performance'. She originally studied English language and literature, philosophy and media sciences at the University of Zürich, where she completed her MA in 2002. Between 2005 and 2016, she worked as a lecturer and diploma coach at different academies of art and design in Switzerland (e.g. HGK Lucerne, HdK Berne, HyperWerk FHNW). In September 2016, Bühlmann was appointed as a professor for architectural theory at the University of Technology, Vienna.

Mark B. N. Hansen is a professor of literature and professor and director of Undergraduate Studies at Duke University. Recent publications include *Feed Forward: On the Future of 21st Century Media* (2014), (with Erich Hoerl) 'Medienaesthetik: Einleitung in den Schwerpunkt', *Zeitschrift fuer Medienwissenschaft*, vol. 8, pp. 10–17 (2013), *Bodies in Code: Interfaces with New Media* (2006), (with Taylor Carman) *The Cambridge Companion to Merleau-Ponty* (2005) and *New Philosophy for New Media* (2004).

Richard Iveson is a postdoctoral research fellow in the Institute for Advanced Study of the Humanities (IASH) at the University of Queensland. His first book, *Zoogenesis: Thinking Encounter with Animals*, was published in 2014 and his second, *Being and Not Being: On Posthuman Temporality*, is due for release in late 2017.

David Roden has worked for the Open University as a lecturer and associate lecturer. His published work has addressed the relationship between deconstruction and analytic philosophy, philosophical naturalism, the metaphysics of sound and posthumanism. He has written a chapter for the forthcoming volume *The Singularity Hypothesis: A Scientific and Philosophical Assessment*. His latest book *Posthuman Life: Philosophy at the Edge of the Human* was published in 2014.

Damiano Roberi recently earned his PhD in philosophy at the University of Turin. His main research topics are Walter Benjamin, the relationship between history and nature in twentieth-century philosophy (Bloch, Adorno, Löwith), Nicolaus Cusanus (particularly regarding the concept of Time within this author's works) and Giambattista Vico. He is co-editor (with A. Dall'Igna) of the book *Cusano e Leibniz. Prospettive filosofiche* (2012). Selected publications include 'The Problem of Historical Experience in the Works of Walter Benjamin' (in *The Truth of Experience – The Experience of Truth: Between Phenomenology and Hermeneutics*, edited by S. Tinning, D. Jørgensen and G. Chiurazzi, 2015), *Language and Nature in Benjamin: The Price of Messianism* ('Rivista italiana di filosofia del linguaggio', 2014) and 'The Janus-faced Foundation: Cusanus, Valla, Alberti' (in *Singularität und Universalität im Denken des Cusanus*, hrsg. von C. Ströbele, Regensburg, Roderer, 2015).

Danielle Sands is a lecturer in comparative literature and culture at Royal Holloway, University of London and a fellow at the Forum for European Philosophy, London School of Economics. She has interests across philosophy and literary studies and is currently completing her first monograph, *Writing Religion and Politics after Derrida.*

Michel Serres is a philosopher specialized in epistemology, a professor as well as a writer. Serres is not only an elected member of the prestigious French Academy (29 March 1990), but he has also received France's highest decoration, the National Order of the Legion of Honour. He taught at Vincennes, Paris I (from 1969 onwards) and Stanford University (from 1984 onwards) as a professor of the history of science. Recent publications include *Musique* (2011); *Petite Poucette* (2012); *Biogée* (2010) and *The Five Senses: A Philosophy of Mingled Bodies* (2008).

Christopher Thomas is an AHRC-funded doctoral candidate at the University of Aberdeen. His research is concerned with early modern philosophy, aesthetics and art theory, and his thesis explores Spinoza's unique understanding of art via his theory of 'complex bodies' and dynamic processes of individuation.

Ashley Woodward is a lecturer in philosophy at the University of Dundee. He is a founding member of the Melbourne School of Continental Philosophy and an editor of *Parrhesia: A Journal of Critical Philosophy*. His most recent book, *Lyotard and the Inhuman Condition: Reflections on Nihilism, Information, and Art*, was published in 2016.

www.ingramcontent.com/pod-product-compliance
Ingram Content Group UK Ltd.
Pitfield, Milton Keynes, MK11 3LW, UK
UKHW041404020525
1947IPUK00008B/18